Sport Histories

Sport Histories draws on figurational sociology to provide a fresh approach to analysing the development of modern sport. The book brings together ten case studies from a wide range of sports, including mainstream sports such as soccer, rugby, baseball, boxing and cricket, to other sports that until now have been largely neglected by sports historians, such as shooting, motor racing, tennis, gymnastics and martial arts. This groundbreaking work highlights key debates in the analysis of modern sport, such as:

- The relative influence of intra-national class conflict and international conflict
- The relative prominence of commercially led processes in different contexts
- The centrality of concerns over violence
- Differences between elite and mass-led sports developments

Above all, *Sport Histories* illustrates the distinctiveness of the figurational sociological approach and its usefulness in the study of the development of modern sport.

Eric Dunning is Emeritus Professor of Sociology at the University of Leicester and Visiting Professor of Sociology at University College Dublin and the University of Ulster at Jordanstown.

Dominic Malcolm is Director of Masters Programmes in the Centre for the Sociology of Sport at the University of Leicester.

Ivan Waddington is Visiting Professor at University College Chester, Centre for Sports Studies at University College Dublin, and the Norwegian University of Sport and Physical Education, Oslo.

Sport Histories

Figurational studies of the
development of modern sports

Edited by

**Eric Dunning, Dominic Malcolm
and Ivan Waddington**

Routledge
Taylor & Francis Group

LONDON AND NEW YORK

First published 2004
by Routledge
2 Park Square, Milton Park, Abingdon, Oxon, OX14 4RN

Simultaneously published in the USA and Canada
by Routledge
270 Madison Avenue, New York, NY 10016

Routledge is an imprint of the Taylor & Francis Group

Transferred to Digital Printing 2005

© 2004 Eric Dunning, Dominic Malcolm and Ivan Waddington

Typeset in Goudy by
Keystroke, Jacaranda Lodge, Wolverhampton
Printed and bound in Great Britain by
Antony Rowe Ltd, Chippenham, Wiltshire

British Library Cataloguing in Publication Data
A catalogue record for this book is available from the British Library

Library of Congress Cataloging in Publication Data
A catalog record for this book has been requested

ISBN 0–415–28665–4

Contents

Illustrations

Figure

Tables

Contributors

Barry Benn is Lecturer in Sport and Physical Education at the School of Education, Birmingham University, Lecturer on Gymnastics in Education and a former International Coach and International Breveted Judge for Men's Artistic Gymnastics.

Tansin Benn is Deputy Head of the School of Education and Director of Learning and Teaching at the University of Birmingham. She is a former Coach and Breveted Judge for Women's Artistic Gymnastics.

Daniel Bloyce is Lecturer in the Sociology of Sport, University College Chester.

Ian Cooper completed an MA in the Sociology of Sport at the University of Leicester and currently works as the Manager of a Leisure Centre in East Sussex.

Graham Curry recently gained his PhD from the University of Leicester and teaches PE at Tuxford School, Newark, Notts.

Eric Dunning is an Emeritus Professor of Sociology at the University of Leicester and Visiting Professor of Sociology at University College Dublin and the University of Ulster at Jordanstown.

Koichi Kiku is a Professor in the Institute of Health and Sports Sciences, University of Tsukuba, Japan.

Dominic Malcolm is Director of Masters Programmes in the Centre for the Sociology of Sport at the University of Leicester.

Ken Sheard is now retired but until 2002 was Lecturer in the Centre for Research into Sport and Society at the University of Leicester.

Stuart Smith is Lecturer in the Centre for the Sociology of Sport, University of Leicester.

Alex Twitchen is Senior Lecturer in the School of Sports Studies, University College Chichester, West Sussex.

Ivan Waddington is Visiting Professor at University College Dublin, the Norwegian University of Sport and Physical Education, Oslo, and University College Chester.

Andrew White is Senior Lecturer in Strategic Management and Sports Management at Farnborough College of Technology, Hampshire.

1 Introduction

History, sociology and the sociology of sport: the work of Norbert Elias

Eric Dunning, Dominic Malcolm and Ivan Waddington

The chapters in this volume were written by teachers, students or visiting scholars at the University of Leicester's now former Centre for Research into Sport and Society.[1] A guiding thread that runs through each of them is an understanding of the 'figurational' or 'process-sociological' approach developed by Norbert Elias (1897–1990), a pioneering figure in sociology generally as well as in the sociology of sport. Elias taught at or was otherwise associated with the Leicester Department of Sociology from 1954 to 1978. In this Introduction, we outline and comment on some of his key contributions, starting with a discussion of his view of time, the relations between history and sociology, and why sociology ought to be a process-orientated subject.

Processes in space–time: Norbert Elias on the relations between sociology and history

In 1991, sports historian, Dennis Brailsford, published a book entitled *Sport, Time and Society: The British at Play*. It is a well written book, solidly researched and packed with interesting information. However, it is only about 'time' in a taken-for-granted, unreflexive and conventional sense. Consider how Brailsford wrote about time in his preface. 'It is', he said, 'the collapse of the barriers of time that has made the present sporting world a possibility. Sport has conquered the calendar that confined it in the past, and can now invade every hour of every day of the year' (Brailsford 1991: xi). Brailsford may want to argue that he was being metaphorical in this passage but, in our view, he was closer to being metaphysical. That is, the literal implication of what he wrote is that it is not humans with their discoveries and inventions who have made the modern sporting world with, for example, its possibility of watching sport from all over the world for 24 hours a day on television, but an impersonal, non-human process involving 'the collapse of the barriers of time'. Towards the end of his book, Brailsford wrote in similar vein that:

> . . . there can be no final reflections on this theme of sport and time. There is no bottom line to be drawn. The pace of the years and the centuries will

continue to wreak its changes as long as humans continue to play. The splitting of seconds will become finer and finer. Time will continue to conquer distance. Sport will more and more create its own environments.

(Brailsford 1991: 161)

Contrary to a common misjudgement, this is a very un-Eliasian argument. That is because implicit here is a view of history as inevitable progress which makes Brailsford think he can predict the future. For present purposes, however, that is less important than the fact that his argument is based on a reified concept of time which serves as a blockage to understanding. That is, Brailsford's mode of conceptualization makes time itself and time concepts such as 'year' and 'century' into 'things' or 'forces' which act.[2] In other words, to use a term of Auguste Comte's (Andreski 1974), he is personifying abstractions much as the Ancients did when, for example, 'just actions became the goddess Justitia' (Elias 1992: 42) or as the alchemists in the European Middle Ages did when they said that 'nature abhors a vacuum'. Thus Brailsford has time 'conquering distance', and years and centuries 'wreaking change'. However, 'time', 'year', 'century' and so on are concepts, and concepts cannot act. They cannot conquer distance or wreak change. In the sense implied by Brailsford, only humans can. 'Time', 'year' and 'century' are symbols constructed by humans, means of orientation developed to aid their understanding and to control and coordinate their activities in the socio-physical universe in which they live. This fact is on one level relatively simple but it tends not to be grasped by scholars trained in a largely unreflexive, non-theory orientated tradition of history-writing in which concepts, including concepts such as 'time', are understood in a taken-for-granted sense.

It is not only historians who face difficulties on this score. Philosophers and philosophically orientated sociologists encounter them as well. British sociologist, Anthony Giddens, is an example. He conceptualizes modern developments in transport and communication as having facilitated what he calls 'time–space stretching' or 'time–space distanciation' (Giddens 1984: 34–5, 227ff.), rather than simply saying that modern science and technology enable people to travel and communicate faster over space; that is, over greater distances in a more limited time, than used to be the case. Giddens's confusion on this score becomes, in our view, more readily understandable when his dependency on the metaphysics of German philosopher, Martin Heidegger, is grasped. Giddens writes of time:

As the finitude of *Dasein*[3] and as 'the infinity of the emergence of being from nothingness', time is perhaps the most enigmatic feature of human experience. Not for nothing [sic] was that philosopher who has attempted to grapple in the most fundamental way with the problem, Heidegger, compelled to use terminology of the most daunting obscurity. But time, or the constitution of experience in time–space, is also a banal and evident feature of human day-to-day life. It is in some part the lack of 'fit' between our unproblematic coping with the continuity of conduct across time–space, and its ineffable character when confronted philosophically, that is the very essence of the puzzling nature of time.

(Giddens 1984: 34–5)

Both sides of this equation are problematic. Time, or to use Giddens's unnecessarily complex jargon, 'the constitution of experience in time–space', may be a 'banal and evident feature of human day-to-day life' in the modern world where we have inherited a reasonably workable calendar and highly efficient devices for measuring what we call 'time'. However, this has not always been the case as Elias showed when he wrote that: 'One forgets that for thousands of years the calendars people used ran into trouble again and again; they had to be reformed and improved repeatedly until one of them reached the near perfection the European calendar has attained since the last calendar reform' (Elias 1992: 193). Indeed, so far from being 'banal and evident' is this daily feature of human life, that there have been occasions – for example, in 1578 when Pope Gregory abolished the days 5 October to 14 October inclusive – when people were frightened by and opposed to calendar reform because they believed it would shorten their lives!

The other side of what Giddens wrote is problematic because he does not appear to have considered the possibility that the 'daunting obscurity' of Heidegger's terminology may be connected, not so much with the properties of time *per se* as with the fact that Heidegger approached the problem philosophically. That seems to us to be the case because, while the problems associated with 'time' remain *complex* if treated sociologically – and, from an 'Eliasian' or 'process-sociological' standpoint that means historically or, better, 'developmentally' – they are not 'obscure' and are accordingly less 'daunting' when viewed from a sociological perspective. On the contrary, from a sociological standpoint, though complex, they are perfectly straightforward. Sociologically, that is, time is a symbolic means of orientation, a human construct by means of which we use observable recurrent natural sequences such as the succession of night and day, the seasons or the uncoiling of a spring to control our relations with each other and with events and processes in the socio-physical universe in which we live; for example, planting the corn, starting the university year, beginning the football, cricket or baseball season. The only reality of time is as a social symbol in a universe where only events and processes, including human events and processes, demonstrably exist – are, if you like, demonstrably 'real'. That, at least, was the view of Norbert Elias. Here is how he expressed it:

> Linguistic habits . . . constantly reinforce the myth of time as something which in some sense exists and as such can be determined or measured even if it cannot be perceived by the senses. On this peculiar mode of existence of time one can philosophise tirelessly, as has indeed been done over the centuries. One can entertain oneself and others with speculation on the secret of time as a master of mystery, although actually there is no mystery.
>
> It was Einstein who finally set the seal on the discovery that time was a form of relationship and not, as Newton believed, an objective flow, a part of

creation like rivers and mountains which, although invisible, was like them independent of the people who do the timing. But even Einstein did not probe deeply enough. He too did not entirely escape the pressure of word-fetishism and in his own way gave new sustenance to the myth of reified time, for example by maintaining that under certain circumstances time could contract or expand.

(Elias 1992: 43–3)

So, processes and events, not symbols, are the only substantives, and 'time' is a relational symbol, not a process or event. 'Every change in "space" is a change in "time"; (and) every change in "time" is a change in "space"' (Elias 1992: 99–100). The people of today are the inheritors, not only of a social fund of more reality-congruent time symbols and more efficient time meters than were available to our ancestors, but also of a social fund of more reality-congruent knowledge about 'space', especially of the 'local space' that we inhabit; that is, the earth and the solar system of which it forms part. For example, we have at our disposal more reliable maps and devices such as compasses and radar for measuring relative positions in 'space–time'. These are crucial in many ways for the constitution and character of modern sport.

The principal relevance for sociology and history of the complex issues we have been discussing so far is the implication that these subjects have to be concerned with the study of events and processes in space and time. Some sociologists and perhaps even some historians might balk at this sort of idea but such an 'Eliasian' standpoint is, we think, less likely to arouse the ire of historians than of sociologists. Despite the growth in the popularity of historical sociology since the 1960s, many sociologists remain committed to present-centred or what Goudsblom (1977) called 'hodiecentric' approaches. Elias himself wrote in 1987 in this connection of 'the retreat of sociologists into the present' (Elias 1987a).

One of the most implacable opponents of the 'historicization' of sociology is John H. Goldthorpe of Nuffield College, Oxford. He was initially trained as a historian and, like Anthony Giddens, held his first academic post at the University of Leicester. Like Giddens, Goldthorpe resisted the influence of Elias and, in what we think is his most recent contribution to the history–sociology debate, he wrote: 'historians have for the most part to rely on evidence that they can discover in the relics of the past, while sociologists have the considerable privilege of being able to generate evidence in the present' (Goldthorpe 1991: 211). There is, of course, an element of truth in this statement. But we are less concerned with Goldthorpe's implicit view of sociology as an essentially method-driven subject than we are with the commonsense, non-processual distinction that he makes between 'past' and 'present'. Human societies exist in space–time, and time, as the old personifying adage has it, 'never stands still'. To express it more precisely, this means that what we call 'the present' is a constantly shifting reference point in the ceaseless flow of processes and events. For example, what was 'the present' when we started writing this sentence had already become part of the past when we completed it. In a word, 'the present' is an ambiguous concept but, dynamically understood, it has historical connotations. It follows that if one were to accept the contention that sociology is the study of 'the present', some more or less arbitrary judgement about the relatively recent past would need to be made. In other words, one would have to decide whether 'the present' refers to, say, the 1990s and 2000s, the years since the 1960s or the Second World War, or, perhaps, on a grander scale, the so-called era of 'modernity'. Whatever decision was made in this regard, any such study would necessarily involve an attempt to come to grips with aspects of 'the past'. In short, it would inevitably lead to involvement in some kind of 'historical' study. So committed are sociologists such as Goldthorpe to an archaic Popperian philosophy of science (Dunning 1977/2003) that they seem unable to appreciate the fact that sociological concepts, theories and methods ought to be attuned to the processual and relational character of the human social world. Let us briefly explore some of Elias's more concrete ideas on the relations between history and sociology.

History, sociology and the process-sociological approach of Norbert Elias

Of all the major sociologists of the twentieth century, Norbert Elias was probably the one who argued most consistently and strongly in favour of a 'historical' or developmental approach. The reasons why we have put the word 'historical' in inverted commas will become clearer as our exposition of Elias unfolds. One of his lengthiest statements on the relationships between history and sociology is contained in the Introduction to his book *The Court Society* (1983). He begins with a critical examination of the popular belief, expounded most systematically by the philosopher K.R. Popper in his book *The Poverty of Historicism* (1957), that history and historical sociology cannot possibly be 'scientific' because of the uniqueness and unrepeatability of historical events. In a word, 'science' is only possible with recurring phenomena and events because only then do you have the possibility of testing hypotheses and formulating 'laws'. Elias takes issue with this widely held view, suggesting on the contrary that uniqueness and unrepeatability are not inherent in history either as an 'object' or independently of the values and interests of people like Popper who make claims of this kind. According to Elias, such claims reflect the values of people in highly differentiated modern societies in which individual uniqueness is highly prized. Elias's case against Popper and others who propound similar views is complex. He begins to unravel the complexity by suggesting that:

> unrepeatable and unique phenomena are by no means confined to the sequences of events that historians take as the object of their studies. Such phenomena exist everywhere. Not only is each human being, each human feeling, each action and each experience of a person unique, but each bat and bacillus. Every extinct animal species is unique. The Saurians will not return.

In the same sense, Homo sapiens, the human species as a whole, is unique. And the same can be said of each speck of dust, of our sun, the Milky Way and every other formation: they come, they go and when they have gone they do not return.

(Elias 1983: 10)

These observations suggest to Elias that 'uniqueness' and 'unrepeatability' are questions of levels. 'What is unique and unrepeatable on one level can be seen on another as a repetition, a return of the never changing.' Take, for example, the uniqueness of individual humans, often touted as a major reason why sociology cannot be a 'science'. According to Elias, this provides a good example of a phenomenon which involves uniqueness on one level and unrepeatability on another. That is the case, Elias says, because 'individual human beings are themselves repetitions of an unchanging form'. That is, each of us is a unique variation on the form of a general category, the species Homo sapiens.

This observation allows Elias to question the degree of 'reality congruence' of the argument that human history consists of a unique sequence of unrepeatable events; that is, the degree to which such an argument 'fits the facts'. Is it, he asks, a product of unprejudiced critical analysis or the result of an ideological manipulation in which historians and philosophers from highly differentiated and individualized societies project their specific social conditioning and short-lived values onto their 'object of study, the historical process itself'? This question, says Elias, cannot be answered in simple 'yes-or-no', 'either-or' terms. It cannot be reduced to a simple formula. That is not the case, however, regarding the 'societies' of non-human animals and insects. According to Elias:

How and why unique, individual aspects play a special part in the history of human societies can be seen by even a cursory comparison with the history of animal societies. If we are to see the problem in the correct light, such a comparison is almost indispensable. The relationship, the interdependence between ants, bees, termites and other social insects, the structure of their societies can, as long as the species stays the same, be repeated over many thousands of years without any change. This is so because the social forms, the relationships and mutual dependencies, are largely anchored in the biological structure of the organisms. Leaving aside minimal variations, the social structures of social insects and, with slight differences of degree, of all other animals that form specific social figurations, change only when their biological organization changes. It is one of the specific peculiarities of the societies formed by human beings that their structure, the form of individual inter-dependencies, can change without a change in the biological organization of human beings. The individual representatives of the species Homo sapiens can form societies of the most diverse kinds without the species itself changing. In other words, the biological constitution of the species makes it possible for the nature of its social life to develop without the species developing. The transition from the *ancient régime* to the early industrial régime of the nineteenth century, the change from a primarily agrarian village society to a more urbanized one, was the expression of a social, not a biological development.

(Elias 1983: 13)[4]

This deceptively simple observation leads Elias to stress the need to define clearly both the differences and the relationships between three concepts, namely 'biological evolution', 'social development' and 'history'.[5] The failure to do this up to now, says Elias, has acted as a blockage to knowledge. He wrote:

> The whole discussion of the relationship between sociology and history is impeded by the fact that up to now even scholarly studies have neglected to define clearly both the difference and the relationship between biological evolution, social development and history. There were no doubt biological, evolutionary changes in the social relationships and structures of our forebears. We know little about this side of the evolution of hominids, possibly because bio-sociological problems of this kind receive little attention from specialists in human pre-history. But the changes in human social life that come within the view of historians and sociologists take place within the framework of one and the same biological species. Whether we are concerned with the social and historical relationships of the ancient Sumerians and Egyptians, of the Chinese and Indians, the Yoruba and Ashanti, or of the Americans, Russians and French, we are always dealing with people of the nature of *Homo sapiens*. The fact that in this case changes in the social life of individual organisms take place without changes in the biological, innate and hereditary constitution of the organism itself, is explained finally by the fact that the behaviour of these human beings is governed to a far greater extent than that of any other organism known to us by the experience of the individual organism, by individual learning and, indeed, must be so governed. The innate and hereditary biological peculiarity of the human constitution, the dependence of behaviour on the experience of the individual from childhood on, is therefore the reason why human societies, unlike ant societies have what we call 'history' or, with a different emphasis, 'social development'.

(Elias 1983: 12)

In sum, it is Elias's contention that the biological constitution of social insects such as ants and bees is relatively fixed and determines their social organization and behaviour. The evolution of *Homo sapiens*, too, has led our species to have a relatively fixed biological constitution but it is a constitution that makes individual members of the species heavily dependent on experience and learning. Humans *have* to learn in order to be able to function and survive, and it is this which makes it possible for human societies to have a history and to develop; that is, to undergo changes of form. According to Elias, however, although the *biological* evolution of *Homo sapiens* cannot be reversed – though the species could, of course, become extinct and, in the course of time, probably will[6] – our *social* development is reversible. As Elias expressed it:

> Change in human figurations is very closely bound up with the possibility
> of transmitting experiences gathered in one generation to subsequent gener-
> ations as acquired social knowledge.[7] This continuous social accumulation of
> knowledge plays a part in the changing of human society. But the continuity
> of the collection and transmission of knowledge can be broken. The increase
> in knowledge does not bring about a genetic change in the human race.
> Socially accumulated experiences can be lost.
>
> (Elias 1983: 13)

The terms 'biological evolution', 'social development' and 'history', says Elias,
denote layered yet separate sequences of change which occur at different rates. In
the long process of biological evolution, the species *Homo sapiens* probably emerged
as a distinct and recognizable species some 50,000 years ago. Its social development,
though fast by comparison with the rate at which significant biological evolution usually takes place, was, at first, comparatively slow, speeding up following
the agricultural and urban 'revolutions' and becoming even quicker following the
'scientific revolution' of the seventeenth century and the 'industrial revolution' of
the eighteenth. Nevertheless, though fast by comparison with biological evolution,
social developments are often so slow by comparison with an individual lifetime,
that people do not recognize them as occurring at all. In Elias's words once more:

> Measured by the length and rate of change of an individual human life, social
> developments often take place so slowly that they seem to stand still. It is
> possible that the social figurations formed by people change so little for a
> number of generations that they are regarded by those involved as immutable
> social forms. Thus, for a long period in the development of European Society,
> people are embraced over and over again by the figuration 'knight-page-priest-
> bondsman'. Today, and for a number of generations past in the developed
> industrial societies, people are repeatedly found in relationships such as 'worker
> – (white collar) employee – manager' or 'higher – middle – lower official'. The
> functional interdependence of these and all other divisions in a particular
> society entails . . . a certain exclusivity. Knight and bondsman would scarcely
> fit into an industrial figuration.
>
> (Elias 1983: 13)

Let us conclude this Introduction by briefly discussing Elias's contributions to
the sociology of sport. As will be seen, they are 'historical' or 'process-sociological'
in character.

The development of modern sport

According to Elias (1971, 1986a), the term 'sport' can be used in two main ways:
in a general sense to refer to non-work related forms of physical activity, with or
without an element of competition. In terms of this rather abstract usage, sport is
a socio-cultural universal. However, the term can also be used more concretely to

refer to a group of competitive physical activities which are specifically modern in key respects and which first began to emerge in England, Scotland, Wales and Ireland – 'the Atlantic Isles' – in the eighteenth and nineteenth centuries. Following Elias, figurational sociologists tend to favour the second definition.

It is Elias's contention that the word 'sport' first acquired its modern meaning in eighteenth-century England, the dominant member of 'the Atlantic Isles'. Aristocratic and gentry groups were centrally involved in this process of language development and it occurred, Elias suggested, correlatively with: (i) a change of habitus and, above all, conscience among these ruling groups; and (ii) a highly specific set of changes in English society at large.

Elias coined the process term 'sportization' as a shorthand way of conveying the central meaning of this complex set of changes which were, he claimed, closely connected with the English/British/Irish variant of the overall European civilizing process. More particularly, Elias used the term 'sportization' to refer to a process in the course of which the rules of sports came more and more to be written down, nationally (subsequently internationally) standardized, more explicit, more precise, more comprehensive, orientated around an ethos of 'fair play' and providing equal chances for all participants to win, and with reducing and/or more strictly controlling opportunities for violent physical contact. Non-playing officials such as referees, umpires, timekeepers and judges with an array of sport-specific sanctions ('penalties', 'free kicks', etc.) at their disposal also began to be introduced and, at the same time, participants began to be expected, in line with the direction of the overall civilizing process, to exercise stricter, more even and more continuous self-control both on and off the field of play. In the game contests that came to be known as 'sports', a flexible balance also began to be established between the possibility of obtaining a high level of pleasurable combat or contest tension and what was regarded as reasonable protection against the chances of injury.

Elias's explanation of why processes of sportization occurred first of all in England and, to an extent, also in the neighbouring countries which it dominated goes beyond the 'economistic' explanations offered by Marxists such as Rigauer (1981), and Brohm (1978) and by 'hegemony theorists' such as Hargreaves (1986). It also goes beyond Guttmann's (1978) hypothesis of a correlation between the 'sports revolution' and the 'scientific revolution' by adding references to comparative social structural and 'political' developments into the equation. More particularly, Elias notes how Germany and Italy remained relatively disunited until well into the nineteenth century, while France and England became relatively united nationally as early as the seventeenth and eighteenth centuries. France, however, had become highly centralized and its people subject to a form of 'absolutist rule', one aspect of which was that the right of subjects 'to form associations of their own choosing was usually restricted . . . if not abolished' (Elias 1986b: 38; Dunning 1999). In England by contrast, movement towards a highly centralized, 'absolutist' state was more or less destroyed in the seventeenth century by the Civil War (1632–49) and the so-called 'Glorious Revolution' (1688). One consequence of what were, in effect, early symptoms of democratization was the placing of restrictions on the powers of the monarch. Similarly, the reliance placed by the English on naval force meant that the large centralized bureaucracy required to coordinate an army geared to defending land frontiers did not develop. In ways such as these, a variety of processes contributed in England to the landed classes retaining a high degree of autonomy *vis-à-vis* the monarchical state and also, via parliament, sharing with the monarch in the tasks of ruling (Dunning 1999).

Further to this, according to Elias, as the feelings associated with the seventeenth century 'cycle of violence' began to calm down, the habitus of members of the English ruling classes underwent a 'civilizing spurt', a process marked most notably in the emergence of ritualized political party forms of ruling. In the words of Elias:

> Military skills gave way to the verbal skills of debate . . . rhetoric and persuasion . . . which required greater restraint all round. It was this change, the greater sensitivity with regard to the use of violence which, reflected in the social habitus of individuals, also found expression in the development of their pastimes. The 'parliamentarization' of the landed classes of England had its counterpart in the 'sportization' of their pastimes.
>
> (Elias 1986b: 34)

This initial sportization of pastimes occurred in two main waves: an eighteenth-century wave in which the principal pastimes that began to emerge as modern sports were boxing, cricket, foxhunting and horseracing; and a nineteenth century wave in which soccer, rugby, hockey, tennis, athletics and water sports such as rowing and swimming began to take on modern forms (Dunning 1992, 1999; Elias and Dunning 1986a). Members of the aristocracy and gentry were primarily responsible for developments in the first wave; while in the second, members of the bourgeoisie – the industrial middle classes – joined the landed classes in taking the lead. 'Clubs' were the organizational form of the first wave; 'associations' and 'unions' of the second (Dunning 1999).

'Sport' in the ancient and early modern worlds

During the 1960s, Elias and Dunning began to test the hypothesis that the early development of modern sports can be understood as a civilizing process by under-taking comparative and developmental examinations of the Ancient Greek and Roman equivalents of modern sports (Elias (1986a: 126–49) called them 'agonistic game contests'), especially boxing, wrestling and 'the pankration', an Ancient Greek equivalent of today's 'ultimate fighting'.[8] They also looked at the 'folk games' and other 'sports' of Medieval Europe, especially 'football', Cornish 'hurling', Welsh 'knappan' and their continental European equivalents (Dunning 1999). What these studies revealed was that the sport-like activities of people at earlier stages in a civilizing process were very different from the sports of today. Elias (1986a) demonstrated, for example, how the agonistic games of Ancient Greece were used as a direct training for war, involved higher levels of violence than are publicly permitted in sports today and were based on a warrior ethos rather than an ethos of fairness. This is the sort of thing that Elias's theory of civilizing processes would lead one to expect. The city states of Ancient Greece were patriarchal societies with slave economies. They went frequently to war, were characterized internally by high levels of physical and material insecurity, were ruled by warrior elites and involved patterns of clan feuding for purposes of what we today call 'justice' and 'crime control'. All this was reflected in the conscience and habitus of their people, above all the fact that most of them grew up with a lower threshold of repugnance regarding physical violence than tends to be the case among the peoples of Western Europe today.

In their work on the folk games of medieval and early modern Europe, Elias and Dunning (Dunning 1961; Elias and Dunning 1986a) painted a broadly similar picture. More particularly, they showed how such games were not highly regulated and were played according to localized, orally transmitted customs rather than centrally determined written rules. They were also played over open countryside as well as through the streets of towns. Further to this, the numbers of participants were indeterminate and not equalized between the contending sides. And finally, these games involved a higher level of open violence than would be tolerated in comparable games today. In fact, although they were 'mock' or 'play fights', they were considerably closer to 'real' or 'serious' fighting than their present-day counterparts are most of the time.

Elias and Dunning's work on the early development of football was extended by Dunning and Sheard in *Barbarians, Gentlemen and Players: A Sociological Study of the Development of Rugby Football* (1979). In this book, using rugby as their principal example but dealing also with the bifurcation of rugby and soccer, the authors tackled four main themes: (i) the development of 'more civilized' team games; (ii) the trend towards the commercialization and professionalization of top-level sport; (iii) the correlative trend towards the cultural centrality of sport and the increasing seriousness of player and spectator involvement; and (iv) 'football (soccer) hooliganism'. This latter theme was treated only hypothetically in that context but the hypotheses that were formulated served as the basis of the 1980s work on football (soccer) hooliganism by what came to be known as 'the Leicester School' (Dunning *et al.* 1988; Murphy *et al.* 1990; Dunning *et al.* 2002).

Conclusion

In *Sport Histories*, we have brought together ten case studies of the development of modern sports. Working with their understandings of the figurational approach, our contributors address both sports which have formed central foci of research and discussion in the sociology and history of sport – soccer (football), rugby, baseball, boxing and cricket – and others which have been relatively neglected – shooting, motor racing, tennis, gymnastics and Japanese martial arts. In a word, in this volume contact sports and non-contact sports are addressed, as well as individual and team sports, ball sports and non-ball sports, sports the modern forms of which began to develop in the eighteenth, nineteenth and twentieth centuries, and sports which were codified, not only in Britain, but also in France, the United States and Japan.

Through the studies that are offered in this collection, we think that new light is shed on such issues as: the influence of intra-national (e.g. class) conflicts relative to international conflicts in the development and spread of modern sports; the variable prominence of commercially led processes in different social contexts; the variable centrality of issues of violence, violence-control, pain and injury in the development of different sports and different countries; differences between elite-led and mass-led sports developments; and the part played by sports in the development of different social habituses (Elias 1991), perhaps especially those of different classes, national groups and males and females.

Horne and Jary (1987: 86ff.) suggested that the protagonists of figurational sociology claim that this perspective is 'unique'. That is not the case. We do, however, believe it to be representative of sociological 'best practice' in the field of historical sociology. It is also *distinctive* – not unique – in such respects as: (i) its focus on the emotional (affective) as well as the rational (cognitive) aspects of human behaviour; (ii) closely related to (i), its use of the model provided by Elias for studying humans 'body and soul' (Elias and Dunning 1966, 1971, 1986b); and (iii) its employment of the strategy recommended by Elias for circumventing such recurrent sociological (and philosophical) difficulties as the variably named 'individual v society'/'agency v structure'/'nominalism v realism' dilemma.

We think that the contributions in this volume illustrate the distinctiveness of the figurational approach in these and other respects. They also show its fruitfulness in generating more 'reality-congruent' depictions of the development of modern sports than have tended to be provided by protagonists of other perspectives. In addition, they alert students of sports history to the major underlying processes that have been involved in the development of modern sport, processes which should, in our view, underpin any serious scholarly analysis of the subject.

Let us add just one more comment in this Introduction. It is our hope that *Sport Histories* will make a small contribution to lowering the barriers which have been erected between sociology and history and the representatives of the different sociological paradigms or 'schools'. As Marx said, 'without conflict, no progress', and in sociology the 'paradigm wars' have undoubtedly contributed to the development of knowledge in various ways. In our view, however, the negative consequences of these academic struggles, many of them centred around philosophical-cum–ideological issues, have in recent years begun to outweigh the positive consequences. It is, we believe, high time for a return to the ethos and norms of *science* in this field; that is to free, open and honest debates in which discussion can be fierce but characterized by mutual respect. That is, like the core ideal of modern sport itself, debates in the sociology and history of sport should, in our view, exemplify an ethos of fair play and friendly rivalry. Who knows? Improving the academic study of sport in this way might even help us to contribute in a small way to comparable improvements in the field of sport itself.

Notes

1 Although the Vice-Chancellor described its work as 'distinctive' and 'distinguished', and although the CRSS is listed by the International Sociological Association on its website as one of the six leading centres in the world for the sociological study of sport, the Centre ceased to exist as a relatively independent entity in 2003 when it was 're-integrated' into the Leicester Department of Sociology, merged with the Sir Norman Chester Centre for Football Research and re-named 'The Centre for the Sociology of Sport'.
2 'Reification', writing of names and concepts as if they were 'things', is also called 'the fallacy of misplaced concreteness'. Philosophers deal with this issue under the heading of 'nominalism versus realism'.
3 *Dasein* is the German word for 'being' or 'existence' and literally means 'being there'.
4 Elias uses references to France quite frequently in his Introduction to *The Court Society* (1983) because the developing French court formed his main empirical example.
5 Elias adds a discussion of cosmic evolution to this set of overlapping sequences in *Involvement and Detachment* (1987b).
6 Our present level of understanding of physical evolution suggests that our sun will 'go supernova' after some 4,000 million years. In that context, *homo sapiens* will become extinct unless they have discovered a habitable planet or planets in some other sun system and some means of travelling over the vast distances involved.
7 Elias later spoke of 'social funds of knowledge' in this connection.
8 The emergence of 'ultimate fighting' appears to those who interpret Elias's theory of civilizing processes as postulating a necessary, unilinear and always 'progressive' development as negating his theory. However, that is a misinterpretation of the theory, which is about 'regressive' developments as much as 'progressive' ones. Moreover, as Marc Howes, a sociology MA student at the University of Aberdeen showed in 1997, state campaigns against 'ultimate fighting' in the USA and their success in curbing aspects of the violence which the campaigners find repugnant provide support for Elias's theory.

References

Andreski, S. (1974) *The Essential Comte*, London: Croom Helm.
Brailsford, D. (1991) *Sport, Time and Society: The British at Play*, London: Routledge.
Brohm, J.M. (1978) *Sport – a Prison of Measured Time*, London: Ink Links.
Dunning, E. (1961) 'Early Stages in the Development of Football as an Organised Game', unpublished MA thesis, University of Leicester.
—— (1977/2003) 'In Defence of Developmental Sociology: A Critique of Popper's *Poverty of Historicism* with Special Reference to the 'Theory of Auguste Comte', *Amsterdams Sociologisch Tifdschrift*, 4(3), 327–49. Reprinted in Eric Dunning and Stephen Mennell (eds), *Norbert Elias: Sage Modern Masters of Social Thought*, London: Sage, pp. 233–55.
—— (1992) 'Figurational Sociology and the Sociology of Sport: Some Concluding Remarks', in E. Dunning and C. Rojek (eds), *Sport and Leisure in the Civilizing Process: Critique and Counter-critique*, Basingstoke: Macmillan.
—— (1999) *Sport Matters: Sociological Studies of Sport, Violence and Civilization*, London: Routledge.
Dunning, E. and Sheard, K. (1979) *Barbarians, Gentlemen and Players: A Sociological Study of the Development of Rugby Football*, Oxford: Martin Robertson. A new edition with a new postscript is due to be published by Frank Cass, London, in 2004.

Dunning, E., Murphy, P. and Williams, J. (1988) *The Roots of Football Hooliganism: An Historical and Sociological Study*, London: Routledge & Kegan Paul.

Dunning, E., Murphy, P., Waddington, I. and Astrinakis, A. (eds) (2002) *Fighting Fans: Football Hooliganism as a World Problem*, Dublin: University College Dublin Press.

Elias, N. (1971) 'The Genesis of Sport as a Sociological Problem', in E. Dunning (ed.), *The Sociology of Sport: Selected Readings*, London: Frank Cass.

—— (1983) *The Court Society*, Oxford: Basil Blackwell.

—— (1991) *The Society of Individuals*, Oxford: Basil Blackwell.

—— (1992) *Time: an Essay*, Oxford: Blackwell.

—— (1986a) 'The Genesis of Sport as a Sociological Problem', in N. Elias and E. Dunning *Quest for Excitement: Sport and Leisure in the Civilizing Process*, Oxford: Basil Blackwell.

—— (1986b) 'Introduction', in N. Elias, and E. Dunning, *Quest for Excitement: Sport and Leisure in the Civilizing Process*, Oxford: Basil Blackwell.

—— (1987a) 'The Retreat of Sociologists into the Present', *Theory, Culture and Society*, 4(2–3), 223–47.

—— (1987b) *Involvement and Detachment*, Oxford: Basil Blackwell.

Elias, N. and Dunning, E. (1966) 'Dynamics of Sports Groups with Special Reference to Football', *British Journal of Sociology*, XVII(4), 388–402.

—— (1971) 'Dynamics of Sports Groups with Special Reference to Football', in E. Dunning (ed.) *The Sociology of Sport*, London: Frank Cass.

—— (1986a) 'Folk Football in Medieval and Early Modern Britain', in N. Elias and E. Dunning *Quest for Excitement: Sport and Leisure in the Civilizing Process*, Oxford: Basil Blackwell.

—— (1986b) 'Dynamics of Sports Groups with Special Reference to Football', in N. Elias and E. Dunning (1986) *Quest for Excitement: Sport and Leisure in the Civilizing Process*, Oxford: Basil Blackwell.

Giddens, A. (1984) *The Constitution of Society*, Oxford: Polity.

Goldthorpe, J. (1991) *On Sociology*, Oxford: Oxford University Press.

Goudsblom, J. (1977) *Sociology in the Balance*, Oxford: Blackwell.

Guttmann, A. (1978) *From Ritual to Record*, New York: Columbia University Press.

Hargreaves, J. (1986) *Sport, Power and Culture*, Oxford: Polity.

Horne, J. and Jary, D. (1987), 'The Figurational Sociology of Sport and Leisure of Elias and Dunning, an Exposition and Critique', in J. Horne, D. Jary and A. Tomlinson *Sport, Leisure and Social Relations*, Sociological Review Monography 33, London: Routledge & Kegan Paul.

Howes, M. (1997) 'A Good Clean Fight: The Civilising of Unarmed Combat Sports', unpublished MA dissertation, University of Aberdeen.

Murphy, P., Williams, J. and Dunning, E. (1990) *Football on Trial*, London: Routledge.

Popper, K.R. (1957) *The Poverty of Historicism*, London: Routledge & Kegan Paul.

Rigauer, B. (1981) *Sport and Work*, New York: Columbia University Press.

2 Boxing in the western civilizing process

Ken Sheard

Introduction

Many people in modern western societies may find the idea of the 'civilizing' of boxing a contradiction in terms. There is a tendency for many people in such societies to regard this form of fist fighting as a brutal, degrading, barbaric and physically and mentally damaging activity which scarcely deserves the designation 'sport'. Certainly many people are undoubtedly repelled and revolted by the direct infliction of physical damage and pain which are integral aspects of boxing. However, as I hope to demonstrate, it is possible to use the concept of 'civilizing processes', to shed meaningful light on the development of the sport (Elias 1978, 1982).

More specifically, this chapter has four major objectives:

1 briefly to spell out Elias's concept of civilizing processes;
2 to justify the apparently paradoxical claim that boxing has undergone a civilizing process by utilizing the framework established by Eric Dunning and myself in our study of rugby football (Dunning and Sheard 1979);
3 to lay bare the social processes involved in the development of boxing into the form in which we know it today; and
4 to argue that the identification of 'civilizing changes' in a sport – especially where the control of violence is concerned – does not imply that it has been rendered innocuous. While many of the changes that have occurred in boxing over the years have, indeed, reduced its dangers, it is also the case that some of these changes only *appear* to lessen the physical harm inflicted by boxers on each other. However, within the context of civilizing processes appearances are important, especially when people are freed by such appearances from the constraints of conscience which might otherwise have inhibited their actions.

Civilizing processes

Boxing, which is undoubtedly one of the more physically damaging and violent of contemporary sports, is an ideal vehicle for testing aspects of Elias's theory of civilizing processes (Elias and Dunning 1986: 13). A central part of Elias's argument is that there has occurred a long-term decline in people's propensity for obtaining pleasure from violence; that is, from both engaging in and witnessing violent acts. Moreover, there has been a tendency to push violence and other evidence of human animality and physicality 'behind the scenes'. People who enjoy taking part in or watching 'real' violence are fewer in number than they used to be, and those who do, often experience feelings of unease or even guilt. Consequently the devotees of violent sports often feel under pressure to counter the accusations of 'barbarism' and 'cruelty' to which their commitment gives rise and may feel constrained to construct ideological defences and legitimations in order to justify their participation, both to others and to themselves. The present levels of unease aroused by boxing – unease which is experienced by many of its supporters – as well as the demands of its opponents that boxing be banned, can be made more intelligible if such feelings and demands are situated and examined within the context of 'civilizing processes', using the term in the highly specific, non-evaluative sense employed by Elias.

Boxing, civilizing processes and the control of violence

It is necessary to stress that modern boxing and its associated violence which repels many citizens of contemporary Western European societies, constitute a carefully controlled, regulated and diluted form of violence compared with what had been common in earlier forms of the sport. Many boxing historians and journalists have attempted to legitimize the modern 'scientific' sport of boxing by 'inventing' an ancient tradition for it, searching for its origins in the sport-fighting of the Ancient Greeks and Romans.[1] Even at the end of the nineteenth and beginning of the twentieth centuries, part of the motivation behind such attempts appears to have been a desire to demonstrate just how 'tame' the modern activity was compared with the boxing of the ancient world. In this regard, the proponents of such arguments were correct! However, such comparisons were, and are, misleading for, as Elias pointed out, Greek and Roman boxing was based on principles very different from modern sport-boxing (Elias 1971; Elias and Dunning 1986: 126–49). The Greek and Roman activities were based on the military value of honour and not on modern notions of fair play, and boxers in the ancient world often fought with heavily bandaged hands reinforced on occasions – as in the case of the Roman 'caestus' – with wooden slats and spikes. They stood toe-to-toe and exchanged blows in turn, without taking evasive action or attempting to avoid punishment, for to do so would have been regarded as shameful and cowardly. Deaths and serious injuries were, not surprisingly, common.

The prize fighting of the eighteenth and nineteenth centuries was also different in many respects from boxing as we know it today. Over the last three centuries, the rules governing the sport have become increasingly complex, the bureaucratic organizations controlling it have become more powerful and the law of the land has become more intrusive, more protective, than ever before. The violence of boxing has been controlled and contained. Prize-fighting can be said to have gone through a 'sportization' process as it metamorphosed into boxing.

Using the framework developed by Dunning (1972/3) and Dunning and Sheard (1979: 33–4), the modern sport of boxing can be said to have become more 'civilized' by a number of interrelated processes which include the following:

1   Boxing in the early period of its development – i.e. from approximately the mid-seventeenth to the early decades of the nineteenth century – was by present standards an extremely violent, brutal and bloody activity. However this aspect of the sport has since become increasingly regulated by a complex set of formal written rules. These rules not only define and control the sorts of violence which are permitted, but also outlaw violence in certain forms. The type of violent blow permitted and the areas of the body allowed to be attacked have been carefully delineated. Thus in the early stages of the sport's development it was possible to use a variety of what we would now call 'wrestling' holds to subdue an opponent. For example the 'cross-buttock' throw, in which the opponent could be thrown over one's hip to the ground, was allowed (Brady 1946: 10). This could then be followed by a leap onto the fallen adversary, smashing one's knees into his exposed ribcage. Eyes could be gouged, hair pulled and the testicles attacked. The nature of the punch, and the permitted shape of the fist, have also been more carefully defined. The 'target' must be hit with the knuckle part of the hand. Hitting with an open glove – 'slapping' – is not allowed, possibly because it once permitted one's opponent to be injured by the lacing of the glove. 'Straight finger' blows to the eyes are also banned.

2   The rules also allow for penalties to be imposed on boxers who infringe these rules. For example, points may be lost by boxers who hit 'below the belt', use the head illegally, or who receive constant warnings for holding and hitting. Under modern conditions champions who refuse to defend their titles within a specified time period, or who turn up to defend their titles over-weight (see below), may have the titles taken from them.

3   Weight divisions have been introduced in an attempt to equalize conditions for all boxers. In the early days of the prize-ring, there were no weight divisions and men (and sometimes women) fought each other irrespective of poundage. It was not until the 1880s, after the widespread adoption of the Queensberry Rules of 1865, that a real effort was made to standardize weight divisions both in Britain and the United States. This innovation allowed boxing skill to have a greater impact on the outcome of a contest than extra weight or extra reach.

4   Boxing has also been civilized by having restrictions placed on the length of contests and the length of 'rounds'. Most professional championship contests in Britain now follow the lead given by the European Boxing Union and are fought over 12 rounds of three minutes each. In America until relatively recently the stipulated 'distance' was 15 rounds. And before this – in both the US and Britain – the usual distance was 20 rounds of three minutes each. By contrast, prior to the 1860s, a round ended with a fall, and fights would be fought to a finish or until one of the fighters could not continue for any reason. In Britain, the largest number of rounds to be fought under this system was the

276 fought between Jack Jones and Patsy Tunney, at Cheshire, England, in 1825 (Golesworthy 1983: 136).

5   Physical protection has been introduced to protect boxers from both the permitted and accidental violence they can inflict on each other. For example padded gloves, gum shields, headguards and groin-protectors have all been introduced over the years. Gloves are claimed to have been first introduced in 1747 when Jack Broughton, an ex-prize-fighter, early 'entrepreneur' and boxing tutor, and supposed originator of the first code of written rules governing the 'sport' of boxing, advertised the use of 'mufflers' to be used by his gentlemen pupils at his Haymarket Amphitheatre, London. The intention, it was said, was to secure them from 'the inconveniencing of black eyes, broken jaws and bloody noses' (*The Daily Advertiser*, 1747). The last heavyweight fight with bare knuckles for the British championship took place in 1885, and in America the last formal bare knuckle fight occurred in 1889 (Golesworthy 1983: 26). The whole subject of the use of gloves is an important and significant one and the full implications of their use and design for a civilizing process are discussed later.

6   Boxing has also been civilized by the introduction of outside controlling personnel whose job it is to ensure that a contest is properly managed and the rules observed. We take such personnel for granted nowadays, but in the past prize-fights were 'supervised' – if that is the correct word given that they had little or no formal influence/authority over the conduct of the fight – by the respective fighters' 'seconds', perhaps assisted by the 'stake-holder', the person delegated to guard the money wagered on the fight. If there was a 'specialist' referee, he was not necessarily highly trained or neutral. During the prize-ring days, the absence of a qualified referee did not necessarily matter as it was usually clear who the winner was: the person left standing at the end of the contest!

7   In Britain in the eighteenth and early nineteenth centuries there were no nationally centralized rule-making and rule-enforcing bodies of any note or effectiveness. The Amateur Boxing Association was not formed until 1880 and it was 1929 before a body designed to administer British professional boxing at the national level – the British Boxing Board of Control – got off the ground.

8   Finally, there was little that could be described as medical control of boxing until well into the twentieth century. Nowadays, boxers – especially, it is claimed, professional boxers – are subject to apparently stringent medical tests and controls. All the officials in British boxing would profess to put the safety of boxers before all other considerations, and they argue that fights will be stopped at the first sign that a boxer is unable to defend himself/herself.

A further sign of the civilizing of boxing relative to its forms in the eighteenth and nineteenth centuries, is that boxing contests nowadays are decided on points no matter how they end – even after a knock-out. The rules state that the boxer counted out shall receive no points for that round, while his opponent receives ten (Hugman 1985: 542–43). This represents a distancing from, or a formal underplaying of, the violence of the knock-out. The need for this arose at the end of the nineteenth century when deaths in the ring at the National Sporting Club led to club officials being arraigned for manslaughter. Consequently, there was great pressure on all officials and boxers to stress that boxers were not engaging in a 'fight' but a 'contest', and that the object of the exercise was not to inflict serious harm on the opponent but to use skill to amass points (Sheard 1992: 270–4).

Boxing and broader civilizing processes

Let us look now at some of the broader processes of which this civilizing of boxing was a part. In the majority of historical accounts of the development of boxing an Oxfordshire man, James Figg (1695–1734), is singled out as the person who 'invented' the sport. But given that semi-formalized fist-fighting was so obviously part of an amorphous folk tradition, why has Figg been singled out for special treatment? The answer seems to be that Figg was the first person to commercialize boxing and to develop it as a 'business' (Sugden 1984: 63) and that with the help of his patron, believed to have been the Earl of Peterborough, he set up a School of Arms in Tottenham Court Road, London, where he apparently made friends with the rich, the powerful and the famous. Figg proved to be a very capable tutor and, after a few years, was able to move to larger premises. Figg seems to have been one of the first entrepreneurs to appreciate the value of publicity and advertising and was one of the first men to place boxing on anything like a business footing. It is perhaps not without importance for the development of the sport in England that Figg was being patronized by the gentry and aristocracy at a time when their counterparts in what later became Germany, for example, were patronizing Bach and Mozart (Sheard 1992: 94).

It is also significant that Figg could not unambiguously be identified as a 'boxer', able to make a living for himself purely as a fist-fighter. Figg, as well as teaching boxing, taught the use of the broadsword and single-stick. There was at Figg's time, then, obviously a demand for training in the arts of 'attack and self-defence'. Increasingly, however, the trend was away from the more deadly swords and pistols and towards the use of fists and sticks. It is this trend, which encouraged the growth of the more 'civilized' sport of boxing, that needs explaining.

It also needs to be emphasized that Figg was better known as a *teacher* than as a prize-fighter. Figg only fought twice during the 15 years after he supposedly 'won the title' (Fleischer 1949: 4). It was as a teacher and exhibitor that Figg made his name and it was from among the younger members of the aristocracy and gentry that he apparently drew most of his clientele. These two points are of some significance for the development of the sport, and for the argument about civilizing processes being advanced here.

Instead of focusing on the personalities of Figg and others who built on his foundations (Wignall 1923: 35–42), as many historians of the sport have been inclined to do, a broader range of questions needs to be posed if a sociologically more adequate explanation of boxing's civilizing process is to be arrived at. Why, for example, was there a market for the sorts of skills that Figg offered to teach? Why was this market apparently growing at this particular time? Why was there a demand for training in the so-called 'scientific' use of the fists, when in earlier periods physical security had been defended, quarrels settled and honour satisfied by the use in duels of more deadly weapons such as the sword and the pistol?

An important strand in the sociological explanation of the complex processes involved in these developments is Elias's contention that the eighteenth century in Britain saw the end of a 'cycle of violence' (Elias and Dunning 1986: 26–40). This was a trend which he saw as related to important components of the developing British class structure. Elias suggested that the end of this cycle of violence, and the resulting 'parliamentarization' of political conflict, had important implications for the increasing 'sportization' not just of prize-fighting but of many British folk activities. The state, Elias argued, was becoming more effective in curbing the violence of the warrior nobility and people began to look for a more 'civilized' way of settling disputes than the potentially deadly duel. Consequently gentlemen increasingly came to want to learn to defend themselves and to attack others – as Elias notes, these men were not just concerned with 'self-defence' – by what we might call an 'educated use of the fists'.

However, it is unlikely that such a development, on its own, would have led to the development of a *sport* of boxing, for there were clearly other processes involved. It might be suggested that gentlemen and aristocrats did not wish to risk social degradation by taking part in prize-fights. Nor could they risk acquiring the facial features of 'the bruiser'. However, they could develop the required boxing skills for settling *private* grudges if they could be assured that their features would be protected. This, as we have seen, was part of the rationale for the introduction of gloves for sparring by Jack Broughton in the mid-eighteenth century. These gentlemen and aristocrats could also obtain excitement – in what was becoming an increasingly routinized society – by betting on the results of prize-fights. Or they could obtain this excitement by 'running' a fighter themselves, just as they ran stables of horses. Hence, a more civilized, sport-like activity, in which gentlemen directly participated, developed alongside the more brutal prize-fighting reserved for working men. These gentry and aristocratic groups increasingly got their excitement and thrills from the less *direct*, more civilized, activities of watching fights, betting on fights and running their own champions and less by direct participation in fighting.

However, it is clear that, in order to develop as a sport, professional boxing needed resources on which to draw. In the eighteenth century, urban boxing theatres such as the famous Fives Court in St Martin's Street, London, started to develop. These urban theatres could have provided a context for the development of a more restrained form of prize-fighting that might have provided a regular income for fighters and 'promoters' alike. However these venues gradually came to be regarded as offending against public sensitivities and changing standards of acceptable behaviour. They were also, because of their urban setting, more vulnerable to the control of magistrates and later, the police. In fact, an incipient move towards boxing becoming a 'false' sport, pre-arranged after the nature of twentieth century professional wrestling (Stone 1971), was nipped in the bud by the fact that prize-fighting was increasingly forced into rural areas where it came more closely under the control of the less 'respectable' members of the aristocracy and gentry.

The type of exhibition boxing which was starting to develop in the eighteenth century, with the odd 'serious' championship thrown in, provided a 'safer' foundation for the development of the sport, but also ran the risk of becoming relatively predictable and potentially boring for spectators – almost a branch of 'show business' – and, more to the point, completely unsuitable for the gambling with which it was so intimately connected. By the end of the century people like Daniel Mendoza (1766–1836), were making a good deal of money by either selling or 'exhibiting' their skills at their own 'schools' or by travelling the country on the theatre circuit, often in the company of comedians and actors (Wignall 1923: 55–8). This had its attractions, of course, for both entrepreneurs and boxers, in that it was much easier to charge for admission when prize-fighting or exhibition boxing were conducted within the confines of a hall, 'academy' or theatre. Gathering money from the vast crowds attracted to the big fights organized in the rural areas was a very different proposition. Mendoza, and other good fighters, made their reputations fighting for a 'title' and they were tempted to capitalize on this reputation by turning to the realms of teaching or giving exhibitions. Such activity was easier and safer than defending their titles in real fights against real challengers and running the risk of losing the very source of their status and monetary reward. This sort of theatrical activity was becoming a normal, and increasingly important, part of the career of famous fighters.

My contention is, then, that in the early days of the fairground boxing booth and urban amphitheatres – that is, in the first half of the eighteenth century – the boxers themselves were able to exercise some control over the punishment they meted out, and more importantly received, by engaging in exhibitions, and that the existence of these amphitheatres inhibited the development of boxing as a sport. Such a suggestion differs from the analysis presented by Brailsford (1988: 13–14). Brailsford argues that the closing of Broughton's amphitheatre, sometime around 1750, *stunted* boxing's development because London lost the opportunity to develop specialized boxing arenas, while boxing had to contend with all the problems of being an illegal activity. Moreover, it was in competition with legal activities like cricket and racing, and, later, football; sports which could establish permanent venues, advertise, charge for admission and pay reliable performers a steady if unspectacular income (Brailsford 1988: 13). Brailsford is certainly correct to suggest that none of this was possible for prize-fighting and that its development was inhibited as a consequence. However, as far as boxing's development as a 'true' sport was concerned – in which the outcome of contests remained uncertain – the effects of its illegality and the closure of the urban amphitheatres were not so unambiguously detrimental as Brailsford suggests.

I have already suggested that the urban boxing booths and amphitheatres were much *more* vulnerable to control by the nascent forces of 'law and order' than were prize-fights in rural areas. Moreover, these 'matches' and shows were becoming very predictable, more ritualized and controlled either by the pugilists themselves or by small-time entrepreneurs. Had boxing remained confined to the towns and cities at this time, and had it remained in the hands of a few 'showmen', then it is unlikely that it would have developed as a cult and national pre-occupation in the way that it did during the Regency period.[2] It had to come more directly under the influence of the aristocracy and gentry, who could develop it in accordance with *their* values, before this could happen. Moreover, because of the theatricalizing of boxing and the habits which it encouraged, urban prize-fighting was becoming unsuitable for the gambling with which it was so intimately connected. But in the country, under the influence and protection of the aristocracy, the prize-fight was developed primarily as a vehicle for gambling. It seems reasonable to suggest, in other words, that prize-fighting had to move or be 'driven' to rural or semi-rural settings before it could develop further as a 'genuine' sport. It was only in such settings that large crowds could gather relatively free from the increasingly hostile interference of the urban authorities, who more and more saw it as their brief to act in the interests of the emerging commercial and industrial middle classes. Furthermore, the authorities were under pressure from various religious and ethical societies to act against any activity which did not accord with the more 'civilized' standards then coming into effect. It seems unlikely, although this must remain speculation, that prize-fighting – indeed, any sort of pugilism – would have been allowed to develop as a serious, bodily contact and bodily damaging, inherently unpredictable sport given this combination of circumstances. If it was to develop along these lines it could only do so 'behind the scenes' and out of sight in what were becoming increasingly 'civilized' times. This was, in fact, part-and-parcel of the civilizing process as conceptualized by Elias, even though – and apparently paradoxically for those who misread or misunderstand Elias's theory – it added to the real ferocity and blood-letting associated with the sport.

It would appear on the surface that the direct patronage system was one factor working *against* the further civilizing of boxing, at least so far as the fighters themselves were concerned. However, this sort of prize-fighting was relatively 'civilized' in the broader sense suggested by Elias and as argued here. Not only did the regulatory influence of gambling make itself felt – in that the search for equality of odds made it essential that conditions were as 'equal' as possible for both fighters – but these men fought 'by proxy', as it were, on behalf of their aristocratic patrons. The old 'free knights' enjoyed direct fighting and bloodshed. They were direct participants. Increasingly, the aristocratic supporters of boxing were beginning to derive their main pleasure from *watching* other people fight in a manner that they laid down. For Elias such a transformation represents a significant 'spurt' in a civilizing process (Elias 1978: 202–3).

As far as the fighters themselves were concerned, prize fighting continued in rural areas as an extremely violent and bloody activity in which fighters were expected to continue their contests to the point of physical exhaustion. Boxing as a more 'genuine' – as opposed to a staged and pre-arranged – contest was perhaps saved by this development. But it also meant that a 'career' as a professional fighter was often short-lived, and hence the attraction of teaching. A career structure which offered *more* boxers the opportunity to make money over a *longer* time period and which was less physically damaging required prize-fighting to be legalized and that it be superseded by a more respectable, regulated form of fighting – by 'boxing'. It is impossible in the space available here to trace in its entirety the complex figuration of interweaving bonds and interdependencies involved in the civilizing of prize-fighting, but changes in the balance of power between the aristocracy and gentry, the rising bourgeoisie of the towns and an urban proletariat were all implicated (Sheard 1997).

During the nineteenth century the availability of increasingly effective means of social control – such as, after 1829, Sir Robert Peel's police force – meant that if boxing were to develop relatively unmolested, it was constrained to seek the protection of private clubs and to go even further 'behind the scenes'. In settings such as the National Sporting Club it came under the influence of a mixture of upper and middle class groups who formalized it further and fought some of the more important battles over its 'respectability' when early deaths in the ring nearly led to its demise (Deghy 1956: 145–61).

Violence control: reality and appearance

Let me conclude by making what may appear to be a controversial claim but one which is fully consistent with Elias's non-evaluative ideas about civilizing processes. I would like to suggest that civilizing processes in European countries have involved not only attempts to control or eliminate what have come to be seen as excessive physical harm and damage in sports and elsewhere, but that it has also become equally important – if not *more* important – that they should *appear* to be eliminated, or *appear* to be under stringent control. This concern with appearances may lead to the introduction into sporting and other activities of cosmetic changes which make those activities *appear* less dangerous but which, in reality, may make them *more* damaging, *more* harmful than before; however the *appearance* of reduced harm may satisfy 'public opinion' and the consciences of individuals.

Although the argument presented here is that boxing has been undergoing a civilizing process in the sense suggested by Elias, it has *not* been argued that boxing, as a result of such a process, has become *less* dangerous or *less* physically injurious, or less violent in an absolute sense, than previously. There now seems to be general agreement that boxing is indeed a violently dangerous activity, but there are those who would argue that it is no more so than comparable sporting activities such as rugby football, and that some of its potential benefits outweigh its risks. However, this is not to claim that boxing, as a result of this 'civilizing process', is unambiguously *less* dangerous than it once was. This may, in fact, be the case. It is difficult to say. Restrictions on the number of rounds and the length and number of contests, the introduction of weight limits, the supervizing of contests by referees, the regular medical checks, the use of padded rings and posts and protected ropes, the use of headguards, gum shields and padded gloves, all would *appear* to make the sport safer and would *appear* to protect the participants from undue damage and harm. But, at one level at least, appearances *may* be deceptive. Some of these innovations were introduced for other than safety considerations. Almost all Broughton's rules, for example, were introduced to protect gambling interests rather than the health of the fighters (Atyeo 1979: 162). His 'mufflers' were not introduced for 'proper' prize-fighting but to prevent gentlemen from giving and receiving 'degrading' cuts and bruises while receiving lessons. Gloves were not accepted for professional contests until late in the nineteenth century, and then only in order to defuse the abolitionist movement and to help establish the 'legality' of boxing. By this time they were not intended to protect the person being hit, but the hands of the hitter. This is an important point to which I will return shortly. Other innovations, as the following example demonstrates, were primarily designed to fit in with commercial interests and considerations, particularly the interests of television companies and producers.

It is often suggested that the number of rounds in professional boxing contests was reduced as a safety measure. Ellis Cashmore (1990), however, suggests that this was not the reason behind the change. In discussing what he sees as the effect of television on many sports, Cashmore points out that:

> Some argued that the decision of boxing's three main governing bodies to reduce championship contests from the traditional fifteen to twelve rounds was motivated not so much by safety reasons as by commercial demands. There was little conclusive evidence that the serious injuries associated with boxing were incurred in the final three rounds, but in the mid-1980s, the World Boxing Council, World Boxing Association, and International Boxing Federation all changed their rules. Fifteen three-minute rounds, as well as fourteen one-minute intervals, preamble and post-fight interviews amounted to an awkward seventy to seventy-five minutes. Twelve rounds yielded forty-seven minutes, as well as, say, thirteen for padding, which fitted perfectly into a one-hour time slot.
>
> (1990: 146–7)

It is possible to argue that in certain respects, boxing, as a consequence of undergoing a civilizing process – and particularly in comparison with bare-knuckle prize-fighting – may have become *more* physically injurious, not less so. This is only an *apparent* paradox. Here the distinction that Dunning (1986: 224–44) makes between 'affective' and 'instrumental' violence sensitizes us to the possibility that more 'civilized' violence may, in its calculation and premeditation, be more or as equally damaging as the affective violence that gives pleasure to its participants. In other words, to say that boxing has been civilized is not necessarily to imply that it has been rendered in all respects less harmful than it used to be. Similarly, to suggest – as it is possible to do – that modern war is more 'civilized' than it used to be, in that war is now conducted from a distance, and more often involves bombs and missiles rather than the 'face-to-face' combat of a previous era, or that fewer people positively enjoy killing, is not to deny the vast destructive power of such warfare.

Perhaps the best example to support the argument that certain innovations in boxing may have made the sport more, rather than less, dangerous, is the introduction of boxing gloves. It is popularly believed that one of the great leaps forward in the civilizing of boxing – or from changing it from prize-fighting into boxing – was the increase in the use of gloves, which followed the drawing up of the Marquess of Queensberry's rules in 1865. The introduction and gradual adoption of the Marquess of Queensberry rules, and the use of gloves that Queensberry mandated, was hailed at the time as a most important step so far as ridding prize-fighting of its more obvious barbarities was concerned. For example in the 1880s, the famous American boxer, James L. Sullivan, suggested that:

> The Marquess of Queensberry rules are the best, for under these rules a man can demonstrate his superiority without fear of the law; without showing unnecessary brutality, either to himself or to his opponent; without the great expense incidental to fighting under the London Prize-ring Rules, and also with better advantage to himself. The London Prize-ring Rules allow too much leeway for the rowdy element to indulge in their practices. Such mean tricks as spiking, biting, gouging, concealing snuff in one's mouth to blind an opponent, strangling, butting with the head, falling down without being struck, scratching with nails, kicking, falling on an antagonist with knees, the using of stones or resin, and the hundred other tricks that are impossible under the Marquess of Queensberry Rules, are under the others practised almost openly.
>
> (quoted in Wignall 1923: 219)

It is to say the least ironic, then, that the introduction of the Queensberry Rules and boxing gloves – which cut down on the amount of blood and gore – not only increased the popularity of boxing at a time when it was under sustained attack, but also increased the likelihood of brain-damage. The *Sunday Times* journalist, Nick Pitt, puts it like this:

> Little did the magistrates, who permitted glove-fighting contests to take place, or the public, whose conscience was spared by the comparative lack of blood, realise the trade-off they had condoned. Gone were the gore, the broken bones and bunged-up eyes of the bare-knuckle era, but in their place was a more brutal and insidious legacy that even today is difficult to measure or predict: brain-damage.
>
> (Pitt 1984)

Early prize-fighting was extremely bloody – much more so than modern boxing. An important aspect of the civilizing process as experienced in Europe up to now is that reminders of our animal natures have tended to get pushed behind the scenes. This has been the case since at least the Renaissance but sensitivities have changed over the centuries and the threshold of repugnance was higher in the past than it is now. For example, the English essayist, William Hazlitt, was fairly typical of his age in the care he took to describe the *bloody* nature of prize-fighting. In his classic description of the battle between Tom 'the Gas-man' Hickman and William Neate in 1821, Hazlitt (1822) wrote: 'All traces of life, of natural expression, were gone from him. His face was like a human skull, a death's head, spouting blood. The eyes were filled with blood, the nose streamed blood, the mouth gaped blood.'

Such bloody descriptions would, nowadays – especially in an AIDS-conscious age – probably only be written by anti-boxing writers whose intention was to sicken and disgust. Although the appearance of blood can still produce a frisson of excitement among modern boxing audiences (possibly because it signals that victory and defeat are in sight), the *dwelling* on blood to which writers in the early nineteenth century seem to have been prone appears nowadays to be much reduced or absent. The majority of modern audiences – despite what some of boxing's critics would suggest and certainly not in comparison with the past – do not like to watch boxers with bad cuts, or who appear to be taking too severe a beating.

It is ironic, then, that the introduction of gloves helped to save competitive boxing (they had previously been used for sparring and exhibitions) from the threat of extinction at the very time that the law, the public and many influential patrons were turning against it. Prize fighting with bare-knuckles was so *obviously* barbaric, so *obviously* bloody, as to be increasingly difficult to defend. In modern times, bare-knuckle fighting is presented as 'scandalous' and 'horrific'. However, as former British heavyweight champion, Henry Cooper (Cooper 1982: 31), has pointed out:

> The boxer whose hands are covered by only the minimum of protection would think twice before throwing a punch unnecessarily – as they did in the bare-knuckle days. There is a tendency now to regard that era of boxing as barbaric. That is a matter of opinion, but what is a matter of fact is that because of the risk of a boxer hurting himself, fewer punches were thrown. The big one didn't go in until the deliverer of the blow was virtually assured of hitting the target.

As long ago as 1942 the tenth Marquess of Queensberry (1942) drew attention to the circumstances in which the knock-out assumed its more central significance:

> Until gloves came into general use the probabilities were that the puncher would suffer more damage to his hand than the recipient of the blow. Certainly until my grandfather framed the new rules there was no point in knocking out your adversary. Remember, there was no count in those days. Merely because a fighter was wuzzy for a few seconds had no bearing on the final issue. It meant simply that his seconds dragged him to his corner, and did what was necessary to bring him round to his senses. Under such conditions it was stupid to apply the knock-out blow. All it meant was the end of another round – and another respite for the kayoed fighter . . .
>
> The bare-knuckle fighters delivered terrible blows on top of the head, behind the ear, on the chin, but seldom knocked out their man. Tom Cribb broke the negro Molyneaux's jaw by a blow on the point, but Molyneaux kept to his feet. Unquestionably if Cribb had been wearing gloves the negro would have been knocked out – the larger area of the padded fist being certain to find contact with the tiny nerve end which thus rudely jolted, produces momentary unconsciousness.

In fact, after the death in 1962 of the Cuban fighter Bennie Paret, who died after a professional fight in New York, the Committee on the Medical Aspects of Sport of the American Medical Association made a number of recommendations to provide 'optimum protection' for boxers. It not only recommended research into suitable types of protective headgear, but went on to suggest that:

> to prohibit wrapping the hands in protective bandages under the gloves would cut down the force of the blows, and so also would the removal of some of the padding from the gloves, because boxers would be more alive to the danger of damaging their own hands.
>
> (Committee on Medical Aspects of Sport 1962)

It is now generally recognized that the function of boxing gloves is to protect the hands of the puncher, *not* the head of the recipient. As Pitt (1984) has pointed out:

> Their luxurious padding appears to be designed to soften a blow, to protect the recipient. But really they protect the striker's hands, making the hitting of an opponent as painless as pulling a trigger. With the protection of the glove, it is possible to hit a person as hard and as often as you like (and the modern, trained, well-fed boxer hits very hard and very often) with impunity. Indeed, gloves add weight to a boxer's blows. They are in effect, weapons.

However, it is not just the weight of the gloves that is important – after all both amateur and professional boxers are encouraged to wear heavier gloves for sparring, and amateurs wear heavier gloves than professionals for contests – but what they allow to happen to the brain:

> If you placed your head in a vice and a strong man hit you on the head it would hurt, but it would be unlikely to damage your brain. If you removed the vice, and the strong man hit you so that your head spun, it might hurt less, but brain damage would be far more likely. For research into brain injuries has shown that it is rotational forces, those which cause the brain to swirl inside the skull, that are much the most dangerous.
>
> (Pitt 1984)

The introduction of gloves not only produced more brain damage, but led to new techniques of fighting – in bare-knuckle fighting, punches tended to be straight and cutting. A man using the hooks or slogging shots to the side or back of the head that gloves made possible would have run the risk of breaking his fingers. The introduction of gloves also led to more excitement in that there were more knock-outs, the knock-out being a euphemism for brain damage. Furthermore, the new ten-second knockout rule that the Queensberry rules introduced – a fighter had previously been allowed 30 seconds to regain the 'scratch' in the middle of the ring and recommence fighting – further encouraged clubbing blows because it was much easier to punch a man into ten seconds than into 30 seconds of unconsciousness

(Gorn 1989: 204–5). The concern with superficial appearances rather than truly effective safety measures is further illustrated, it is suggested, by the recent controversy over the introduction of headguards. Many boxers and managers believe that headguards, because they obscure vision and encourage carelessness, make boxing *more* dangerous, not less so. The 1984 British Medical Association (BMA) report admitted that headguards could protect against cuts and eye injuries but was at pains to point out that they were of little use in preventing brain damage (1984: 26), which tends to occur when the jelly-like substance of the brain is shaken around inside the skull. In fact headguards, by making the head heavier, are more likely to cause the swirling movement that can contribute to long-term damage to the brain.

The dangers inherent in using boxing gloves and headguards are only the two most obvious examples of innovations that apparently reduce injury but which may in reality contribute to more serious – although *hidden* – damage. Public pressure led to the introduction of both these 'safety measures', and public pressure would probably prevent their removal. Similarly, electro-encephalogram (EEG) examinations were introduced into the medical checks required for boxers even though medical personnel recognized that such examinations could not, and do not, reveal the likely long-term effects of concussive blows to the head. They were introduced as a cosmetic measure and not because doctors believed that they would be particularly effective in reducing the dangers of brain damage to boxers. Indeed one could argue that they were partly intended to divert attention from more dramatic and potentially more efficacious reforms; in this regard it might be noted that many people have, over the years, called for blows to the head to be banned (Wignall 1926: 21). This sort of action, were it to be implemented, would represent a huge advance in boxing's civilizing process and would certainly rid the sport of much of its current stigma. However, in the eyes of the majority of the sport's *cognoscenti* a ban of this nature would run the risk of 'emasculating' boxing beyond all recognition.

It has been argued here that, in the course of the British civilizing process physical functions generally came to be regarded with a new apprehension and sensitivity. The activity of prize-fighting was more appropriate to an earlier stage in this process and was gradually superseded by the more controlled and 'sportized' activities of amateur and professional boxing. As it became increasingly disreputable to be involved in an activity which caused damage or offence to others, so it became necessary to find ways of deflecting in advance adverse criticism and of handling the psychic discomfort of guilt. It also involved a genuine need or desire not to damage others or subject them to harm or to appear deliberately to harm them. One response to such pressures has been the introduction of changes into boxing, some of which apparently meet some of the objections to its 'barbarity' but which, in reality, may make boxing a more, rather than less, dangerous activity.

Notes

1 See in particular the works of Pierce Egan (1812, 1827). Egan's stories and claims were reproduced rather uncritically by, among others, Buchanan-Taylor and Butler (1947: 1–2, 5) and Brady (1946).
2 Technically speaking, the 'Regency period' refers to the years during which the Prince of Wales assumed the responsibilities of his father, George III, when his father was incapacitated by mental illness. However, John Ford (1971) refers to a longer period from 1787 to 1824 as 'The Age of Regency Boximania'.

References

Atyeo, D. (1979) *Blood and Guts: Violence in Sports*, New York: Paddington Press.

Brady, J. (1946) *Strange Encounters: Tales of Famous Fights and Famous Fighters*, London: Hutchinson's Library of Sports and Pastimes.

Brailsford, D. (1988) *Bareknuckles: A Social History of Prizefighting*, Cambridge: Lutterworth Press.

British Medical Association (1984) *Boxing: Report of the Board of Science and Education Working Party*, London: BMA.

Buchanan-Taylor, W. and Butler, J. (1947) *What Do You Know About Boxing?* London: Heath Cranton.

Cashmore, E. (1990) *Making Sense of Sport*, London: Routledge & Kegan Paul.

Committee on Medical Aspects of Sport (1962) 'Statement on Boxing', *Journal of the American Medical Association*, 181–242.

Cooper, H. (1982) *Henry Cooper's Book of Boxing*, London: Arthur Barker Ltd.

Deghy, G. (1956) *Noble and Manly*, London: Hutchinson.

Dunning, E. (1972/3) 'The Structural-functional Properties of Folk-games and Modern Sports: A Sociological Analysis', *Sportwissenschaft*, 3, 215–32.

—— (1986) 'Social Bonding and Violence in Sport', in N. Elias and E. Dunning, *Quest for Excitement*, Oxford: Basil Blackwell.

Dunning, E. and Sheard, K. (1979) *Barbarians, Gentlemen and Players, A Sociological Study of the Development of Rugby Football*, Oxford: Martin Robertson.

Egan, P. (1812) *Boxiana*, London: G. Smeeton.

—— (1827) *Anecdotes*, London.

Elias, N. (1971) 'The Genesis of Sport as a Sociological Problem' in E. Dunning (ed.), *The Sociology of Sport: Selected Readings*, London: Frank Cass.

—— (1978) *The Civilizing Process, Vol. 1: The History of Manners*, Oxford: Basil Blackwell.

—— (1982) *The Civilizing Process, Vol. 11: State Formation and Civilization*, Oxford: Basil Blackwell.

Elias, N. and Dunning, E. (1986) *Quest for Excitement: Sport and Leisure in the Civilizing Process*, Oxford: Basil Blackwell.

Fleischer, N. (1949) *The Heavyweight Championship: An Informal History of Heavyweight Boxing from 1719 to the Present Day*, London: Putnam & Co.

Ford, J. (1971) *Prizefighting: The Age of Regency Boximania*, Newton Abbott: David and Charles.

Golesworthy, M. (1983) *Encyclopaedia of Boxing*, London: Robert Hale.

Gorn, E. (1989) *The Manly Art: The Lives and Times of the Great Bare-knuckle Champions*, London: Robson Books.

Hazlitt, W. (1822) 'The Fight', *New Monthly Magazine*.

Hugman, B.J. (1985) *The British Boxing Yearbook*, Feltham: Newnes Books.

Pitt, N. (1984) 'Bare fists and the thinking fighter . . .', *Sunday Times*, 3 June 1984.

Queensberry, The 10th Marquess of (1942) *The Sporting Queensberrys*, London.

Sheard, K. (1992) *Boxing in the Civilizing Process*, unpublished PhD thesis, Anglia Polytechnic University, Cambridge.

—— (1997) 'Aspects of Boxing in the Western "Civilizing Process"', *International Review for the Sociology of Sport* 32, 1, 31–57.

Stone, G.P. (1971) 'Wrestling: The Great American Passion Play', in E. Dunning (ed.), *The Sociology of Sport: Selected Readings*, London: Frank Cass.

Sugden, J.P. (1984) *Urban Poverty, Youth Culture and the Subculture of the Boxer*, unpublished PhD thesis, University of Connecticut.

Wignall, T.C. (1923) *The Story of Boxing*, London: Hutchinson.

—— (1926) *The Sweet Science*, London: Hutchinson.

3 Public schools, status rivalry and the development of football

Eric Dunning and Graham Curry

Introduction

It will, we think, help the reader if we begin this discussion of the development of soccer as a world game by considering the origins and meanings of the terms 'football' and 'soccer'. That is because they are sometimes used as synonyms and sometimes not.

In almost every country it is usual to refer to the world's most popular ball game as 'football' or by the translation of that English word into the native tongue. Examples are: *Fussball* in German; *voetbal* in Dutch; *futebol* in Portuguese; *futbol* in Spanish and *fotboll* in Swedish. The only exception, at least in Europe, is in Italy, where the term *gioco del calcio* ('kicking game') is used to reflect the claim of *aficionados* of football there that Italy was the birthplace of the modern game. Such a claim is almost certainly false.

'Soccer' is derived from an abbreviation of the term 'association' and refers to the highly specific modern Association way of playing. Although not so widely used as 'football', in Britain and Ireland the term 'soccer' is widely understood. It is not so widely understood in continental Europe, Africa, Asia or Central and South America. In fact, the principal countries where the term 'soccer' is used are those of North America and Australia where its use is made necessary by the fact that Americans, Canadians and Australians use 'football' to refer to games which were produced in the nineteenth and early twentieth centuries by their citizens of European descent.

This discussion may seem needlessly pedantic. It is, however, essential, if only because it is commonly believed outside Australia, Canada and the USA that 'football' implies a mainly non-handling, primarily kicking and heading game, in which, during the course of play, only the goalkeepers are allowed to use their hands. Such a belief is erroneous. The term 'football' dates from at least 1314 when it was used to refer to a class of loosely regulated folk games in which handling and throwing as well as kicking were allowed. Some of these games were called by names other than 'football' and in some of them sticks could be used. More recently, 'football' has come to be a generic term which refers to a class of 'sportized'[1] ball games, central among them association football (soccer), rugby football (both union and league), American football, Canadian football, Australian football and

Gaelic football. There is an abundance of relatively strong data about the history of this class of games and, if properly interpreted, these allow one to form hypotheses about the game's development. In order to tease out and test such hypotheses, it is necessary to return to 1314 and begin our search.

Folk football in medieval and early modern Britain

In Britain, reliable evidence for the existence of a game called 'football' does not begin to accumulate until the fourteenth century. Between 1314 and 1667, orders prohibiting football and other popular games were issued by the central and local authorities on numerous occasions. Table 3.1 gives an idea of the frequency of such prohibitions, together with an indication of how widely in a geographical sense the folk antecedents of modern football were played.

The 1496 statute of Henry VII was re-enacted several times during the reign of Henry VIII (1509–47), the last English monarch to re-enact such legislation. It remained on the statute book until 1845 under the title 'The bill for maintaining artillery and the debarring of unlawful games' (Marples 1954: 43).

The prohibition of 1314 and that issued by Edward III in 1365 show the main reasons why the authorities wished to ban football and similar games. The order of 1314 was issued in the name of Edward II by the Lord Mayor of London and referred to 'great uproar in the City, through certain tumult arising from great footballs in the fields of the public, from which many evils perchance may arise'. It aimed 'on the King's behalf' to forbid the game 'upon pain of imprisonment' (Marples 1954: 439–41). Edward III's prohibition was connected with the belief that playing games like football was having adverse effects on military preparedness. It is significant that this was the time of the Hundred Years War between England and France, which broke out in 1338. The prohibition of 1365 reads:

> To the Sherriffes of London. Order to cause proclamation to be made that every able bodied man of the said city on feast days when he has leisure shall in his sports use bows and arrows or pellets and bolts . . . forbidding them under pain of imprisonment to meddle in the hurling of stones, loggats and quoits, handball, football . . . or other vain games of no value; as the people of the realme . . . used heretofore to practise the said art in their sports when by God's help came forth honour to the kingdom and advantage to the King in his actions of war; and now the said art is almost wholly disused and the people engage in the games aforesaid and in other dishonest, unthrifty or idle games, whereby the realm is likely to be without archers.
>
> (Marples 1954: 181–2)

It is clear that the state authorities in medieval Britain tried to suppress football and other traditional games because they regarded them as a waste of time and a threat to public order and national defence. As a result, they tried to direct the energies of the people into what they (the authorities) regarded as more useful channels such as military training.

Table 3.1 Selected list of prohibitions by state and local authorities of the folk antecedents of modern football

Year	Monarch, other responsible official or group	Place
1314	Mayor of London in the name of Edward II	London
1331	Edward III	London
1349	Edward III	London
1364	Synod of Ely	Ely
1365	Edward III	London
1388	Richard II	London
1389	Richard II	London
1401	Henry IV	London
1409	Henry IV	London
1410	Henry IV	London
1414	Henry V	London
1424	James I of Scotland	Perth
1450		Halifax
1454		Halifax
1457	James II of Scotland	Perth
1467	Leicester	
1471	James III of Scotland	Perth
1474	Edward IV	London
1477	Edward IV	London
1478	Lord Mayor of London	London
1488	Leicester	
1491	James IV of Scotland	Perth
1496	Henry VII	London
1533	Mayor of Chester	Chester
1570		Peebles
1572		London
1581		London
1594		Shrewsbury
1608		Manchester
1609		Manchester
1615		London
1636		Oxford
1655		Manchester
1660		Bristol
1666		Manchester
1667		Manchester

Sources: Magoun (1938), Marples (1954), Shearman (1887), Young (1968).

Note: Local rather than state authorities were responsible for those prohibitions where the name of a particular individual or group does not appear.

Official prohibitions may tell us about how the authorities in medieval and early modern Britain viewed folk football but they provide little information about the character and structure of such games. A detailed examination of Carew's seventeenth-century account of Cornish 'hurling' indicates that these folk antecedents of modern football and related modern sports were forms of intergroup combat-games which were closer to 'real' fighting than is usually the case with their twentieth-century 'offspring'.

According to Carew, hurling matches were mostly organized by 'gentlemen'. The 'goals' were either these gentlemen's houses or two towns or villages some three or four miles apart. There was, he said, 'neither comparing of numbers nor matching of men'. The game was played with a silver ball and the object was to carry it 'by force or sleight' (trickery) to the goal of one's own side. Carew described the game thus:

> Whosoever getteth seizure of this ball, findeth himself generally pursued by the adverse party; neither will they leave, til . . . he be laid flat on God's deare earth; which fall once received, disableth him from . . . detayning the ball: hee therefore throweth the same. . .to some one of his fellowes, fardest from him, who maketh away withall in like manner . . .
>
> The Hurlers take their next way over hilles, dales, hedges, ditches; yea, and thorow bushes, briers, mires, plashes and rivers whatsoever; so as you shall see 20 or 30 lie tugging together in the water, scrambling and scratching for the ball. A play (verily) both rude and rough, and such as is not destitute of policies, in some sort resembling the feats of warre: there are horsemen placed . . . on either party . . . and ready to ride away with the ball if they can catch it . . . But . . . gallop any one of them never so fast, yet he shall be surely met at some hedge corner, crosse-lane, bridge or deep water, which . . . they know he must needs touch at: and if his good fortune gard him not . . . he is like to pay the price of his theft, with his owne and his horses overthrowe . . .
>
> The ball in this play may be compared to an infernall spirit: for whoever catcheth it, fareth straightwayes like a madde man, struling and fighting with those that goe about to holde him: and no sooner is the ball gone from him, but he resigneth this fury to the next receyver and himselfe becometh peaceable as before. I cannot well resolve, whether I should more commend this game, for the manhood and exercise, or condemne it for the boysterousness and harmes which it begetteth: for as . . . it makes their bodies strong, hard, and nimble, and puts a courage into their hearts to meete an enemie in the face: so . . . it is accompanied by many dangers, some of which do ever fall to the players share. For proofe whereof, when the hurling is ended, you shall see them retyring home, as from a pitched battaile, with bloody pates, bones broken and out of joynt, and such bruses as serve to shorten their daies; yet al is good play, and never Attourney nor Crowner troubled for the matter.
>
> (Carew 1602; quoted in Dunning and Sheard 1979: 27)

Carew's account gives a good idea of the loose overall structure of this type of game. There was no limitation on numbers of participants, no stipulation of numerical equality between sides and no restriction on the size of the playing area. Hurlers did not play on a demarcated field but on the territory between and surrounding what were agreed on as the goals of the two sides; that is, the places to which custom decreed that they had, respectively, to transport the ball to win.

Cornish hurling was a rough but by no means unregulated game. One of the customary rules emerges from Carew's account: when tackled the player in possession had to pass the ball to a team-mate. There was also a rudimentary division of labour within each team into what Carew, using a then-contemporary military analogy, called a 'fore-ward', a 'rere-ward' and two 'wings'. This shows that use of the terms 'forward' and 'wing' to denote particular playing positions (a practice which survives in present-day soccer and rugby) has a long ancestry and military roots. Carew also mentioned a division between players on horseback and players on foot. This is interesting because it suggests that, in these folk games, elements of what were later to become separate games – in this instance, not only soccer and rugby but also hurling and polo – were rolled together into an undifferentiated whole.

The roughness described by Carew is what one would expect of games played by large numbers of seventeenth-century English people according to loosely defined oral rules. There was no referee to keep control and no outside body to appeal to in cases of dispute. That games of this type continued to be played until the nineteenth century emerges from an account of a kind of football that was played each Christmas Day in the early 1800s in South Cardiganshire, Wales:

> At Llanwennog, an extensive parish below Lampeter, the inhabitants for football purposes were divided into the Bros and Blaenaus . . . The Bros . . . occupied the high ground of the parish. They were nicknamed 'Paddy Bros' from a tradition that they were descended from Irish people. The Blaenaus occupied the lowlands and, it may be presumed, were pure-bred Brythons . . . [T]he match did not begin until about mid-day . . . Then the whole of the Bros and Blaenaus, rich and poor, male and female, assembled on the turnpike road which divided the highlands from the lowlands. The ball . . . was thrown high in the air . . . and when it fell Bros and Blaenaus scrambled for its possession, and a quarter of an hour frequently elapsed before the ball was got out from the struggling heap . . . Then if the Bros could succeed in taking the ball up the mountain to Rhyddlan they won the day; while the Blaenaus were successful if they got the ball to their end of the parish . . . The whole parish was the field of operations, and sometimes it would be dark before either party secured a victory. In the meantime, many kicks would be given and taken, so that on the following day the competitors would be unable to walk, and sometimes a kick on the shins would lead the two men concerned to abandon the game until they had decided who was the better pugilist . . . The art of football playing in the olden time seems to have been to reach the goal. Once the goal was reached, the victory was celebrated with loud hurrahs and the firing of guns, and was not disturbed until the following Christmas Day.
>
> (quoted in Dunning and Sheard 1979: 29–30)

Some authorities have been reluctant to use accounts of 'hurling', 'knappan', 'bottle-kicking' and similar games such as East Anglian 'camp-ball' (Moor 1823) (perhaps 'camp' in this case derives from or is cognate with the German *kämpfen* which means to fight, hence 'fight-ball') as evidence regarding the folk antecedents of modern football. That is understandable but arguably based on a failure fully to appreciate the nature of this type of games. They were played according to orally transmitted customs, not bureaucratically administered national rules; hence the chances of variation in names and playing customs between communities were great because there were neither written rules nor central organizations to unify the name or the manner of playing. Given that, references to football in medieval and early modern sources do not imply a game played according to a single set of rules. Identity of names is therefore no guarantee of identity of the games to which these names refer. By the same token, the differences between folk games that were given different names were rarely as great as those between modern sports. That is, as far as one can tell, the differences between hurling, knappan, camp-ball, bottle-kicking and, as referred to in the medieval and early modern sources, football, were neither so great nor so clear-cut as those between rugby, soccer, hockey and polo today.

Some of these games may have had different names because they were played with different implements. The 'knappan', for example, was a wooden disc. The 'bottle' in the Hallaton-Medbourne game is a wooden keg. 'Football' is the name which most frequently recurs, but references to it in some earlier accounts seem to be referring to a type of ball rather than to a type of game. For example, the London prohibition of 1314 referred to 'tumult arising from great footballs', not from 'playing football', while the Manchester prohibition of 1608 referred to playing '*with* the ffotebale' rather than to 'playing ffootbale' (Dunning and Sheard 1979: 22). As far as we have been able to ascertain, the type of ball to which this name was given was an inflated animal bladder, usually, but not always, encased in leather. Balls of this larger type probably lent themselves better than smaller, solid balls to kicking. This could explain the origin of the term 'football'. Alternatively, the term could have signified a game played *on* foot as opposed to horseback. Only gradually does it seem to have been used primarily with reference to a type of game. However, despite the increasing preponderance of this latter meaning, it would, we think, still be wrong to assume that, in folk games called 'football', the ball was only or mainly propelled by foot, or, conversely, that in games called 'hurling' or 'handball' it was only thrown or otherwise propelled by hand.[2] That is because prohibitions in these folk games were less clearly defined and less strictly enforceable than is the case in modern sports. Indeed, as we shall try to show, soccer, the minimal handling, mainly kicking game, and rugby, the handling, carrying and throwing game in which, relatively speaking, kicking is de-emphasized, are both products of the nineteenth century.

The folk antecedents of modern football were traditionally associated with religious festivals/holidays ('Holy Days') such as Shrovetide, Easter and Christmas. However, they could also be played on an *ad hoc* basis at any time in the autumn, winter or spring. They were played across country and through the streets of villages and towns and often by females as well as males. Except in *ad hoc* games one played as the ascribed member of a specific group against a traditional 'enemy' – for example, for Hallaton v Medbourne, the 'Bros' v the 'Blaenaus', the shoemakers v the drapers, the bachelors v the married men, the wives v the spinsters – rather than as the individual member of a club one had joined voluntarily and where the primary reason for associating was the choice of playing football. In these folk games, community identity took precedence over individual identity, and the degree of individual choice that players had was, compared with amateur footballers today, relatively small. This is not to say that such community identity was not often enthusiastically expressed.

Whatever their names, and whether associated with a particular festival or not, the folk antecedents of modern football were, relative to their present-day counterparts especially as played in the more developed societies of the West, openly emotional affairs characterized by physical struggle. Such restraints as they contained were loosely defined and imposed by custom as opposed to elaborate formal regulations that are written down, requiring players to exercise a high degree of self-control and involving the intervention of external officials when a deliberate foul is committed, a foul occurs accidentally or the self-control of the players breaks down. As a result, the basic game-pattern – the character of these folk games as struggles between groups, the open enjoyment in them of excitement akin to that generated in battle, the riotousness and the relatively high level of socially tolerated physical violence – was always and everywhere the same. In short, these games were cast in a common mould which tended to transcend differences of names and locally specific traditions of playing.

Folk football in continental Europe

As we suggested earlier, ball games similar to the British folk antecedents of modern football were also played in France. Just as in Britain, these folk games were prohibited by royal edict, for example by Philippe V in 1319 and Charles V in 1369 (Marples 1954: 25). Such attempts were made as late as the beginning of the Revolution, suggesting that the French authorities were just as unsuccessful at suppressing these games as their British counterparts. Similar edicts were enacted in colonial America showing that the earliest English settlers must have played such games as well and that they were similarly problematic (Gardner 1974: 96).

In Italy, a somewhat more regulated game, the *gioco del calcio*, had developed by the sixteenth and seventeenth centuries. The participants, we are told, were 'young Cavaliers of good purse', and two teams of 27 members per side played every evening in the Piazza di Santa Croce in Florence from Epiphany to Lent (Marples 1954: 67). That it remained a rough game is emphasized in an English translation, published in London in 1656, of a description by Boccalini. The beginning reads as follows:

> The noble Florentines plaid the last Tuesday at the calcio in the Phebean field . . . and though some, to whom it was a new sight to see many of these Florentine gentlemen fall down to right cuffs, said, that that manner of proceeding in that which was but play and sport, was too harsh, and not severe enough in real combat . . . [T]he Commonwealth of Florence had done very well in introducing the calcio among the citizens, to the end that having the satisfaction of giving four or five good round buffets in the face to those to

whom they bear ill will, by way of sport, they might the better appease their anger (than by the use of daggers).

(Young 1968: 88–90)

The presence of pike-carrying soldiers in pictorial representations of the game (Marples 1954: facing p. 21) suggests that the social control function attributed to *calcio* by Boccalini may not always have been performed. It seems reasonable to suppose that pikemen were regarded as necessary in case the excitement of the struggle led either the young noble players or members of the crowd to get carried away and lose their self-restraint (Guttmann 1986: 51).

The development of modern soccer

It has been suggested, for example by Bredekamp (1993: 53–4), that *calcio* formed the model on which soccer is based, but there is no direct evidence of such a process of diffusion. In support of his claim, Bredekamp cites just one piece of data: the fact that English people associated with the British Consulate in Livorno took part in a ceremonial game of *calcio* there in 1776. However, as evidence, this is very weak. In Bredekamp's account, the English people involved remain nameless; nothing is said about *how* they played *calcio*, *how familiar* they were with the rules, and *how many times* they played. More importantly, nothing is said about these people trying to introduce the game to friends and acquaintances back in England. In other words, the inferential component in Bredekamp's account is so strong and the evidential component so weak that it is better for the moment to suppose that the early development of soccer – and of rugby, too; they were socially co-produced – was a process which occurred autonomously in England or, more properly, in Britain and Ireland. Early in the twentieth century, other countries began to become involved as well, especially France. Three social processes that took place more or less simultaneously in Britain in the eighteenth and nineteenth centuries are of relevance in this connection: (1) the cultural marginalization of folk football, a process that began in the middle of the eighteenth century and gathered pace in the nineteenth; (2) the emergence of a thriving, primarily pub-related footballing sub-culture; and (3) the development of newer forms of football in the public schools and universities from about the 1840s. In our view, it was the latter that were to prove decisive for the future.

The cultural marginalization of folk football

Writing of football in 1801, Joseph Strutt argued that: 'The game was formerly much in vogue among the common people, though of late years it seems to have fallen into disrepute and is but little practised' (Strutt 1801: 168). Similar arguments were proposed by an anonymous Old Etonian in 1831 (Dunning and Sheard 1979: 21ff.) and by Scotsman, William Hone, in 1841 (Young 1968: 6). What they wrote undoubtedly reflected a then contemporary trend but recent research by Goulstone (2000, 2001) and Harvey (1999) suggests that these nineteenth century authors exaggerated its magnitude and extent. Indeed, since the folk forms of football never died out completely and variants of this tradition continue to be played in parts of Britain today – for example Ashbourne (Derbyshire) football, Hallaton (Leicestershire) 'bottle kicking', and the Kirkwall (Orkneys) 'ba' game' – it is, we think, better to speak of a process of cultural marginalization as having occurred in this connection.

Regarding the cultural marginalization of folk football, it is enough in the present context to note that these forms of playing seem to have fallen foul of the 'civilizing' and 'state formation' processes as they were experienced in eighteenth- and nineteenth-century Britain and that it was probably this that authors such as Strutt, Hone and the anonymous Old Etonian were picking up on. That is, increasing numbers of people were coming to regard the roughness of folk football with repugnance. At the same time, the formation of the new police force in the 1820s and 1830s placed in the hands of the authorities an instrument of social control more efficient than any previously available. The prohibitions which had begun in 1314 could thus be more rigidly enforced and 'the bill for maintaining artillery and the debarring of unlawful games' could be removed from the statute book. Another influence may also have been at work. It is possible that the survival of folk football in the face of centuries of opposition had been predicated in part on support from sections of the aristocracy and gentry. If that is, indeed, a reasonable supposition, then a further reason for the cultural marginalization of these antecedents of modern football may have been connected with the way in which industrialization and state formation involved an augmentation of the power of rising bourgeois groups. As a result, status competition between members of the bourgeoisie and the landed classes grew more intense, leading the latter to grow more status exclusive in their behaviour and to withdraw their support from the traditional sports of the 'common people'. Whatever the degree of adequacy of this hypothesis, it is certainly the case that public schools and universities were the central loci of the development of embryonic forms of soccer and the rival rugby code. Before we examine them, however, it is necessary briefly to examine the research of Goulstone and Harvey.

Football outside the public schools

Until recently, scholars working on the history of football have invariably accepted the opinion expressed by Strutt, Hone and the anonymous Old Etonian that football went into decline in the early part of the nineteenth century, surviving as a vigorous and regularly practised pastime only in the public schools. Goulstone and Harvey, however, have shown that these scholars and the authors of the nineteenth-century sources on which they relied were mistaken. Indeed, not only does the evidence amassed by Goulstone and Harvey suggest that football continued to flourish in the early nineteenth century; it also suggests that processes of limited modernization occurred in contexts *outside* the public schools. Goulstone, for example, cites the following newspaper announcement which appeared in 1838:

A match at football will be played at the cricket ground, Leicester, on Good
Friday next, between eleven (principally printers) from Derby and the same
number of Leicester. The winners to challenge an equal number from any
town in England, for a purse not exceeding £25.

(Goulstone 2001: 29)

Five years later, in 1843, the following match was described as having taken
place at Thurstone in the Holmfirth area of Yorkshire:

An excellent match at football took place at Thurstone lately, between six
of the celebrated players of that place and six from Totties, which ended with
neither party getting a goal. The latter is prepared to make a fresh match on
the following terms, viz. six or eight players on each side, two goals out of
three; to come off at Shrovetide, half-way between their respective homes, for
£5 a side. The money is always ready at Mr Charles Whitehead's, the Blue
Cap Inn, Totties. Thurstonland can also be accommodated on the same terms.
A letter will meet with attention.

(Goulstone 2001: 30)

For present purposes, these two examples must suffice as illustrations of the
compelling case recently offered by Goulstone and Harvey. What these authors
successfully show is that football matches between sides of equal, but variable and
not yet standardized, numbers were taking place in non-public school contexts at
least around the same time as comparable developments were occurring in the
public schools, and may even have preceded them. These non-public school
matches were generally pub-related, with stake money playing a significant part.
This suggests that, as in the cases of cricket, boxing and horse-racing in the
eighteenth century, one aspect of the initial modernization of football, the introduction of the practice of playing matches between sides of limited and equal
numbers, was partly connected with gambling and the incipient monetarization if
not yet the full-blown commercialization and professionalization of the game. That
said, however, the evidence points overwhelmingly to the public schools and
universities (particularly Cambridge) as having formed the principal institutional
loci where not only the incipient modernization of football but also, and more
importantly, the bifurcation into the soccer and rugby forms took place. In the
case of rugby, indeed, this is shown in the name. The evidence also suggests
that these rival forms were co-produced in a context of status rivalry between the
public schools. It is to developments in the public schools and universities that we
now turn.

The development of football in the public schools

Initially formed as charitable institutions for the education of 'poor and needy
scholars and clerks' or as local grammar schools, during the eighteenth and early
nineteenth centuries the public schools were transformed into boarding schools for

fee-paying pupils from the upper and upper middle classes (Dunning and Sheard 1979: 47–51). At least two consequences followed from this usurpation by the higher classes. The first was that the class discrepancy between masters (teachers) and pupils inherent in the structure of this type of schools where middle-class academics were attempting to cater for the educational needs of boys who mostly came from higher social strata than themselves, meant that masters were unable to prevent the emergence of forms of self-rule by the boys. The second was that this power and status discrepancy between masters and pupils led to a chronic lack of discipline and not infrequent rebellions by the boys. That use of the term 'rebellion' is apposite in this context is shown by the fact that the revolt at Winchester in 1818 could only be quelled by the militia using bayonets and by the fact that, in 1793, the boys there 'victualled the College for a regular siege, ransacking the shops for provisions'. They also 'provided themselves with swords, guns and bludgeons and . . . mounted the red cap of liberty and equality'. At Rugby in 1797, the headmaster's classroom door was blown off its hinges, his windows were smashed and his books were thrown on to a bonfire. Order was only restored with military help (Dunning and Sheard 1979: 51–3).

Youthful bravado probably played a part in these rebellions. Those in the 1790s were undoubtedly affected, at least superficially, by then-contemporary events in France. From a sociological point of view, however, the rebellions were the most obvious surface manifestations of a struggle between masters and boys in which, for a long time, neither party was able to establish effective dominance over the other. The result was the gradual crystallization of a system of dual control which later came to be known as the 'prefect–fagging system'. This was a system in which the rule of masters was granted a degree of recognition in the classroom in return for the reciprocal recognition of the right of 'prefects' – the leaders among the older boys – to exercise dominance as far as extracurricular activities were concerned.

The 'fagging' part of the system emerged as part of the same process. The fact that masters were unable to control the oldest boys meant they were unable to control them in relation to their younger fellows. As a result, there emerged a dominance hierarchy among the boys determined mainly by relativities of age and physical strength: the boys who were older and/or physically stronger 'lorded' it over those who were younger and/or physically weaker. The juniors were forced into the role of 'fags'; that is, into providing menial, ego-enhancing and possibly homosexual services for their seniors. The strongest held sway and, as one would expect of teenage males untrammelled by effective adult control, often exercised their power mercilessly.

The prefect–fagging system was central to the early development of football in the public schools. At each school the game was one means by which older boys asserted dominance over juniors. One of the customary duties which developed for fags was that of 'fagging-out' at football. This meant they were compelled to play and were restricted for the most part to the role of 'keeping goal', that is they were ranged *en masse* along the baselines. Thus it is suggested that, at Westminster in the early nineteenth century, 'the small boys, the duffers and funk-sticks were the goalkeepers, twelve or fifteen at each end'. 'Douling', the name given to football at Shrewsbury, was the same as they used for 'fagging'. It is reputedly derived from the Greek for 'slave'. At Winchester in the early nineteenth century, fags, one at either end, were even used as goalposts, the ball having to pass between their outstretched legs to score. Fags were also used as a means of boundary demarcation (Dunning and Sheard 1979: 55); that is, they were lined up around the pitch.

Just as in the folk antecedents, football in the public schools at this stage was governed by oral rules. This meant that the character of the game varied from school to school, differences being affected by decisions made in relation to the geographic peculiarities of particular playing areas – the game was not yet played on pitches constructed and marked out specifically for playing football – and by the accretion of locally specific traditions. Despite such differences, however, handling the ball as well as kicking was allowed at all the schools.

All forms of public school football at this stage were also rough. In the 'scrimmages' in Charterhouse 'cloisters football', for example, 'shins would be kicked black and blue; jackets and other articles of clothing almost torn into shreds; and fags trampled underfoot' (Dunning and Sheard 1979: 56). At Westminster, 'the enemy tripped, shinned, charged with the shoulder, got you down and sat upon you – in fact, might do anything short of murder to get the ball from you' (Dunning and Sheard 1979: 55). Furthermore, in Charterhouse 'field' football, there were a good many broken shins, for most of the fellows had iron tips to their very strong shoes and some freely boasted of giving more than they took' (Dunning and Sheard 1979: 56). Iron-tipped shoes were also used at Rugby where they were called 'navvies'. According to an Old Rugbeian reminiscing in the 1920s, navvies had 'a thick sole, the profile of which at the toe much resembled the ram of an ironclad'; that is, a battleship (Dunning and Sheard 1979: 55–7). They were used especially for purposes of 'hacking', the practice used for breaking up a scrummage, and an early form of tackling.

The development of written rules and the bifurcation of soccer and rugby

During the 1830s and 1840s, at a point when the cultural marginalization of folk football was beginning to reach its peak, newer forms of the game, more appropriate to the emergent social conditions and correlative values of an urbanizing and industrializing society in which state formation and civilization were correlatively advancing, began to develop in the public schools. Centrally involved in this process were: (1) the committing of the rules to writing; (2) a stricter demarcation and limiting of the size and shape of the playing area; (3) the imposition of stricter limitations on the duration of matches; (4) a reduction in the numbers taking part; (5) an equalization of the number of players on the contending teams; and (6) the imposition of stricter regulations on the kinds of physical force that it was legitimate to use. It was in the course of this incipient modernization – which seems to have been more comprehensive than the comparable (and perhaps in part related?) process taking place in the wider society, such as in the context of the pub football played for stake money so amply documented by Goulstone and Harvey – that the soccer and rugby ways of playing began recognizably to emerge out of the matrix of locally differentiated public school games. Rugby appears to have been the first to begin to take on its distinctive profile.

It remains widely believed that rugby resulted from a single deviant act by a single individual (Macrory 1991: 23–52). The individual in question was William Webb Ellis who is said in 1823, 'with a fine disregard for the rules of football' customary at Rugby School at the time, to have picked up the ball and run with it. There is no doubt that Webb Ellis was a pupil at Rugby in 1823. What is doubtful is this reductionist explanation of the emergence of the rugby game. It is socio-logically more plausible to suppose that rugby and soccer were co-produced. That is, they are best understood as having been produced, not simply within particular public schools in isolation, but within the wider social field formed by *all* the public schools at the particular stage of industrialization, urbanization, civilization and state formation reached in Britain between about 1830 and the 1850s. It was a stage when tensions between the landed classes and the rising bourgeoisie were growing more intense and, it seems reasonable to suppose, these intensifying class and status tensions were reflected in relations between the public schools, playing a part in the development of these in many respects diametrically opposite ways of playing football.

Assuming that the extant data provide a reliable guide, it seems that the first public school to commit its football rules to writing was Rugby. According to Marples (1954: 137) and Young (1968: 63), this process took place in 1846. In 1960, however, Eric Dunning came across a set dated 1845 in the Library at Rugby School (see Dunning 1961; Macrory 1991: 86–90). These were basically the same as those produced in 1846, except that they were preceded by a set of organizational and disciplinary rules which provide a clue as to why this process of codification may have taken place. The prefect–fagging system at Rugby had recently been reformed by Thomas Arnold, headmaster there from 1828 to 1842. Basically, what Arnold achieved – we are referring to his disciplinary not his academic achievements – was the transformation of the Rugby variant of the prefect–fagging system from a system of dual control which was conducive to persistent disorder, into a system of indirect rule which was conducive to greater harmony both in staff–student relations and in those between the boys. There is, however, no evidence that he was directly involved in the transformation of Rugby football which depended on this development. The rules were not committed to writing until three years after Arnold's death.

A crucial aspect of the reformed prefect–fagging system at Rugby as far as the development of football was concerned consisted of the fact that it permitted the masters to increase their power while simultaneously preserving a substantial measure of self-rule for the boys. A system of informal assemblies they called 'levees' grew up, the name presumably taken from the practice of Louis XIV of France of holding meetings while rising from bed. Significantly, it was a 'Sixth Form Levee' (an assembly of the senior boys) which produced the written rules of 1845 and the first section was concerned with tightening up and legitimizing the administrative role of prefects in relation to football.

Correlation, of course, does not necessarily imply causation. However, the fact that the available evidence points towards Rugby as having been both the first public school to achieve effective reform of the prefect–fagging system and the first to commit its football rules to writing suggests strongly that these two processes were linked. There is reason, furthermore, to believe that, besides Arnold's qualities as a teacher, the fact that effective disciplinary reform was first achieved at Rugby was connected with that school's relatively recent formation as a public school – it had been a local grammar school until the 1790s – and the fact that its pupils tended to come from lower ranks in the upper and middle classes than those at, for instance, Eton and Harrow. The status discrepancy between masters and pupils would thus have been lower at Rugby, making that school correspondingly easier to control and reform (Dunning and Sheard 1979: 74–5).

If the surviving evidence is a reliable guide, the second public school to commit its football rules to writing was Eton, located next to Windsor and with associations with the royal court. Written rules were produced there in 1847, two years after the Rugbeians had committed their football rules to writing.[3] Evidently the size of teams was customary and taken for granted by Etonians at that time for there is no mention of it in the 1847 rules. However, Young claims that eleven-a-side football was played at Eton as early as 1841 (Young 1968: 67–8). The fact that matches between limited, equal numbers – 15 or 20 per side – also began at Rugby in 1839 or 1840, although matches between uneven sides continued to predominate, suggests the possibility that there were forms of communication between the public schools as far as football matters were concerned (Dunning and Sheard 1979: 90). There may also have been some borrowing and modelling by the public schools in this regard from pub games in the wider society.

Four among the thirty-four rules laid down at Eton in 1847 are of special interest. They are:

8. The goal sticks are to be seven feet out of the ground: a goal is gained when the ball is kicked between them provided it is not over the level of the top of them.
9. The space between each goal stick is to be eleven feet.
22. Hands may only be used to stop the ball, or touch it when behind. The ball must not be carried, thrown, or struck by the hand.
29. A player is considered to be sneaking when only three, or less than three, of the opposite side are before him and may not kick the ball.

The first three of these rules were diametrically opposite to their counterparts at Rugby where carrying the ball and scoring by kicking above H-shaped posts were legislated for in the rules of 1845. They can thus be considered as legislating for an embryonic form of soccer. So can rule 29, the rule regarding 'sneaking' (the evocative Eton term for 'offside') even though the Field Game continues today to resemble rugby in that its rules do not allow deliberate forward passing. Use of the term 'sneaking', with its moralistic flavour, is indicative of how strongly the boys at Eton felt at that stage about this particular form of gaining an unfair advantage. The 'rouge', another Eton practice, is comparable to the Rugby 'try'.

Marples (1954: 140) speculated that the first schools where a non-handling game developed were Westminster and Charterhouse. However, the available evidence suggests that he was wrong. For example, writing in 1903, Captain F. Markham, a former Westminster pupil, remembered that 'running with the ball (Rugby fashion) ... and "fist-punting" were both allowed in Westminster football until 1851 or 1852' (Dunning and Sheard 1979: 55). In other words there seems to have been an interval of four to five years between the virtual abolition of handling at Eton and the outlawing of such a practice at Westminster. Perhaps after a period of experimentally introducing a Rugby element into their football, the Westminster boys were following Eton's lead? Similarly, when written rules were produced at Charterhouse for the first time in 1862, stopping the ball with one's hands and catching were allowed (Dunning 1961: 104). Furthermore, according to Shearman (1887), the rules at Harrow included four governing the use of hands as late as 1887. It would thus seem that Eton was the first public school to impose a virtual taboo on the use of hands. It follows accordingly that the Eton Field Game was probably the earliest prototype of soccer.[4]

Why should the boys at Eton have wanted to produce such a game? One doubtful possibility is that the Etonians produced an almost entirely kicking game completely oblivious to what was happening at other public schools. However, this is unlikely. They considered their school to be the leading public school in all respects. It was the second oldest, only Winchester being able to take pride in a longer pedigree. Having been founded by Henry VI in 1440, Eton was also able to boast about being a royal foundation. Moreover, being located next to Windsor, it continued to have connections with the royal court and to recruit its pupils mainly from the highest social strata. One can easily imagine how the Eton boys would have reacted to the development of a distinctive way of playing football at Rugby, in their eyes at the time an obscure Midlands establishment which catered primarily for parvenus.

Under Arnold, the fame of Rugby School had begun to spread and, with it, the fame of their form of football. The Rugby boys, it seems reasonable to suppose, were hoping to draw attention to themselves by developing such a distinctive game. However, it would seem similarly not unlikely that, by developing a form of football that was equally distinctive but in key respects diametrically opposite to the game at Rugby, the Etonians were deliberately attempting to put the 'upstart' Rugbeians in their place and to 'see off' this challenge to Eton's status as *the* leading public school *in all respects*. As Elias (2000) showed, status competition between upper-class and rising middle-class groups has played an important part in the civilizing processes of Europe. More particularly, in 'phases of colonization' members of the latter would adopt the manners and standards of the former, leading these upper-class groups in 'phases of repulsion' to develop, as means of status demarcation and exclusion, more refined standards involving the imposition of a demand for the exercise of even greater self control. The hands are among the most important bodily implements of humans and, by placing a virtual taboo on their use in a game, the Etonians were demanding that players should learn to exercise self-control of a very high order. In a soccer playing society today where children learn to kick the ball and not to use their hands from a young age, this might not seem a particularly difficult demand. However, when it was first introduced, it must have been equivalent to being required to balance peas on the back of one's fork. Indeed, we hear that when Etonians and others first tried to introduce the non-handling game to members of the working class, the latter were required to play holding a shilling and were allowed to keep it if they succeeded in not using their hands.

The emergence of soccer as a national game

Starting in the 1850s, the embryonic soccer and rugby games spread into the wider society. Two more general social developments underpinned this process: an expansion of the middle classes which occurred correlatively with continuing industrialization, urbanization, state formation and civilization; and an educational transformation usually referred to as the 'public school games cult' (Marples 1954: 119). There is no need to analyse these wider developments here. It is enough to note that the games cult help to establish social conditions conducive to the spread of football in its embryonic modern forms, above all playing a part in transforming what were destined to become soccer and rugby into status-enhancing activities for adult 'gentlemen'.

This process of diffusion involved the spread of these newer football forms, in the first instance especially rugby, to the new public schools which began to be set up. It also involved the formation of clubs specifically for playing one or another form of football. However, in the absence of unified national rules, inter-school and inter-club matches were difficult if not entirely impossible to play. An example of the sorts of difficulties that were faced is provided by the following letter which was written in 1861. As one can see, it is supportive of the view that Eton–Rugby rivalry constituted *a*, if not *the*, major axis of tension in this regard:

> What happens when a game of football is proposed at Christmas among a party of young men assembled from different schools? . . . The Eton man is enamoured of his own rules, and turns up his nose at Rugby as not sufficiently aristocratic; while the Rugbeian retorts that 'bullying' and 'sneaking' are not to his taste, and that *he* is not afraid of his shins, or of a 'maul' or 'scrimmage'.
> (*The Field: The Country Gentleman's Newspaper*, 14 December 1861: 525)

In such a situation, pressure began to grow for the establishment of common, national rules. John Charles (J.C.) Thring, the Old Salopian Assistant Master at Uppingham, one of the new public schools, issued a compromise code in 1862 which he entitled 'The Simplest Game'.[5] In 1863, a veritable flurry of forthright opinions championing the various school games were expressed in letters to *The Times* by representatives of a number of public schools. However, what one might call 'school particularism' was great in that period and this correspondence seems to have served only to accentuate the differences between the rival codes. Any practical initiative to break the impasse was going to have to come from outside the public schools or from public school old boys who would have been able to approach the issue of football rules in a relatively detached manner.

Writing to the *Daily Telegraph* in September 1863, a correspondent suggested that a 'Football Parliament' should be established (Macrory 1991: 166). Shortly afterwards, more particularly, starting on 24 October 1863, John Dyer Cartwright published a series of ten articles on this specific subject in *The Field* dealing with: 'The value of the Game, its present position, and the discussion concerning the rules' (*The Field*, 24 October 1863: 413) (for an in-depth analysis of Cartwright's role, see Curry 2003). Two days after the publication of Cartwright's first article, the inaugural meetings of what was to become 'The Football Association' began at the Freemason's Tavern, Lincoln's Inn Fields, London. It is, we think, best to assume that these meetings were held, not in response to the suggestions of particular individuals such as Cartwright, Thring or the *Telegraph* correspondent, but rather in response to the general climate of opinion to which they contributed.

In this situation, support began to polarize around the rugby model and what we can now recognize as its embryo soccer counterparts. Besides the Eton Field Game, which was dominant in this regard, the latter included its equivalents at Charterhouse, Harrow, Shrewsbury, Westminster and Winchester. In a word, the bifurcation of soccer and rugby which appears to have been set in motion principally by Eton–Rugby rivalry in the 1840s was perpetuated at a national level, leading to the formation of separate ruling bodies, the Football Association (FA), as previously noted, in 1863 and the Rugby Football Union (RFU) in 1871. Only the formation of the FA need concern us here. In order to present a more complete picture, two partly autonomous developments are of relevance in this connection: the formation of the earliest independent clubs; and the growth in the importance of football as a leisure activity at the universities of Cambridge and Oxford.

The first reliable record of a football club in England comes from Sheffield, Yorkshire, where Sheffield Football Club issued a constitution in 1857 and a set of rules in 1858.[6] Another club is recorded in the Sheffield suburb of Hallam in 1860 and, within two years, there were 15 clubs in the district. Numbers 5 and 6 of the rules formulated by the Sheffield Committee in 1858 show that Sheffield football was modelled on one or more of the embryo soccer games. These rules were:

5. Pushing with the hands is allowed but no hacking or tripping up is fair under any circumstances whatsoever.
6. Holding the ball excepting in the case of a free kick is altogether disallowed.

During the early years of the Football Association's existence, Sheffield FC administrators and players were to provide vital support for the fledgling national body. Indeed, for a short while in the late 1860s there were more clubs playing a non-rugby form of football according to unified and centrally administered rules in the Sheffield area than there were clubs in London playing according to FA rules (Dunning and Sheard, 1979: 125–6). Nevertheless, the data suggest that many early clubs were founded in the South of England, particularly in and around London. For example, Forest Football Club, which played at Snaresbrook, Essex, was founded in 1859 by a group of Old Harrovians, prominent among them Charles William and John Forster (J.F.) Alcock, originally from Sunderland but by 1858 resident in Chingford, Essex (Booth 2002: 8–9). Both were soon to figure prominently in the formation of the FA. Forest had become Wanderers by 1864 but maintained the Harrow connection. Another early club with Harrow connections was N.N. [No Names] Kilburn, though the date of its formation remains at present unknown. Other clubs known to be in existence by 1863 include Blackheath (1858), Richmond (1859) and Harlequins (1859), all three playing variants of rugby. Also founded by that date were the following embryo soccer clubs: Crystal Palace (1860), Barnes (1862) and, from outside the London area, Notts County (1862).

The significance of the universities of Cambridge and Oxford for the development of soccer – there is far more relevant evidence that emanates from the former – lies principally in the fact that it was at those institutions that young upper- and middle-class adult males began for the first time regularly to play the newer forms of football. These forms began to be played by undergraduates in the late 1830s in conjunction with the spread of the 'games cult' to the universities, a fact which is hardly surprising since the majority of students came from public schools. Sport, of course, was already established as a university institution. What happened in conjunction with the games cult was that ball games, together with rowing and track and field athletics, began to replace sports such as hunting at the top of the prestige hierarchy of university sports. It was, in other words, a largely civilizing development in Elias's sense. Cricket and rowing were the first to become established but, from about 1850, devotees of football began to vie for a higher position on the ladder of university sporting prestige for their game. As it gained acceptance, men from different schools, brought up according to different football traditions, were thrown together. Since only relatively small numbers from particular schools found themselves in the same college at any one time, in order to secure regular and meaningful contests it was necessary for 'old boys' (former pupils) of different schools to play together. However, the absence of common rules meant that such matches were often full of conflict. For example, we are told how, during a match at Trinity College, Cambridge in 1848, 'Eton men howled at the Rugby [men] for handling the ball' (Letter to the FA from Henry Charles Malden, dated 8 October 1897). This provides further support for the hypothesis we outlined earlier regarding tension between Etonians and Rugbeians. It was a desire to avoid such tensions and to widen the field of football competition that led to attempts to construct common rules.

Common rules were produced at Cambridge in 1838, 1846, 1848, 1856 and 1863, the frequency with which new rules had to be constructed suggesting that none of them really caught on. Of the 26 framers of these five sets of rules, 17 were undergraduates or fellows at Trinity College, a favoured college with Eton 'oppidans' who constituted a high percentage of the students there (see Curry 2002 for a more detailed discussion). This suggests that the influence of Etonians on the Cambridge football community in those years was strong, thus helping to explain why the rules of 1856 and 1863, the only ones that have survived, resemble the Eton Field Game in incorporating a virtual taboo on handling and an absolute taboo on hacking. Only the rules of 1863 had lasting consequences. That was because when, later in the same year at the inaugural meetings of the fledgling FA, an attempt was made to impose unified rules containing a large rugby component, supporters of an embryo soccer form used the Cambridge rules in a way that helped to perpetuate the emergent bifurcation. The 1863 Cambridge rules were produced in October by a committee comprising undergraduates from six schools. Eton, Harrow and Rugby each had two representatives; Marlborough (a rugby-playing school), Shrewsbury and Westminster one apiece. The 6–3 majority on the committee in favour of the embryonic soccer-playing schools led, not surprisingly, to the adoption of rules which mirrored their preferences. Those governing use of the hands and violent play – the most important areas of disagreement – read as follows:

13. The ball, when in play, may be stopped by any part of the body, but NOT be held or hit by the hands, arms or shoulders.
14. All charging is fair, but holding, pushing with the hands, tripping and shinning are forbidden.

(Dunning and Sheard 1979: 105)

These rules would probably have remained of local significance only had it not been for the series of meetings held in London towards the end of 1863 that we have alluded to already. These were the inaugural meetings of the FA and deserve detailed consideration.

On the surface, the first three meetings of the new association proceeded smoothly. Draft rules of the game were agreed and printed. However, they embodied significant elements of rugby and, had they been accepted, would have legitimized the closely related practices of 'hacking' and 'carrying' in the new game over which the nascent FA was hoping to preside. The fourth meeting was held on 24 November and the conflict inherent in the incipient bifurcation of soccer and rugby broke into the open. Until that point it had remained dormant at least as far as officially recorded business was concerned. What happened between the third and fourth meetings was that the 1863 Cambridge rules came to the notice of supporters of the embryo soccer game and they were impressed, especially by the rules which prohibited 'carrying' and 'hacking'. Encouraged by support from such a prestigious quarter, they went on the offensive. Support also came from the Royal Engineers Football Club, Chatham, and from William Chesterman of Sheffield FC. According to Chesterman, the FA's recently printed draft rules were 'directly opposed to football and . . . more suggestive of wrestling' (Green 1953: 28). The tide was beginning to run in favour of the embryonic soccer model.

Shortly after the opening of this fourth meeting, J.F. Alcock, one of the two Old Harrovian brothers, proposed 'that the Cambridge rules appear to be the most desirable for the Association to adopt'. His motion was defeated. So was one by Francis Maule (F.M.) Campbell of Blackheath Football Club to the effect that the Cambridge rules were merely 'worthy of consideration'. Eventually, an amendment was passed stipulating 'that the rules of the Cambridge University embrace the true principles of the game with greatest simplicity, and therefore, that a committee be appointed to enter into communication with the committee of the University to endeavour to induce them to modify some of their rules'. Before the close, however, a motion was carried by a majority of one instructing the Association Committee 'to insist upon hacking' in its negotiations with the University (Green 1953: 26). This suggests that, at that stage, some people attending the inaugural FA meetings were still striving to negotiate a truly composite game. It also suggests that, for the moment, neither those in favour of the embryonic soccer code nor those in favour of its rugby rival enjoyed a decisive advantage.

It was thus the fourth meeting of the fledgling FA that witnessed the first open clash between the advocates of what were shortly to become the rival national football codes. On 1 December 1863 at the fifth meeting, this conflict was completely revealed. Discussion centred again on the contentious draft rules regarding 'carrying' and 'hacking'. The Secretary-elect, Ebenezer Cobb Morley, said that he did not personally object too strongly to 'hacking' but felt that to retain these rules would seriously inhibit the development of football as an adult game. The President-elect, Arthur Pember, supported him, referring to a 'fifteen' he had organized for a match: 'I was the only one who had not been at a public school', he said, 'and we were all dead against "hacking"' (Green 1953: 29). F.M. Campbell of Blackheath FC, the principal advocate at these meetings of the rugby code, replied that, in his opinion, 'hacking' was essential if an element of pluck was to be retained in football and threatened that, if 'carrying' and 'hacking' were excluded from the Association game, his club would withdraw. The supporters of the rugby code were heavily defeated in a vote and the contentious rules were struck out. Close examination of the lists of those present at each meeting suggests that adherents to the embryo soccer game had plotted to ensure that they would be in a majority when the critical vote was taken. On 8 December at the sixth and final inaugural meeting, Campbell rose to say that, although his club approved of the FA and its aims, the rules adopted would emasculate football. Blackheath was unwilling to be party to such a game and wished to withdraw. By this action, the Blackheath club paved the way for the final and irrevocable parting of the ways between soccer and rugby.

'Laws' 9 and 10 of the rules adopted by the newly formed FA in 1863 marked the decisive development of soccer away from the rugby practices of 'hacking' and 'carrying'. They were:

9.   No player shall carry the ball.
10.   Neither tripping nor hacking shall be allowed. . .

The civilizing intent of the drafters of these rules emerges further from Law 14 which reads:

14.   No player shall be allowed to wear projecting nails, iron plates, or gutta-percha on the soles or heels of his boots.

That the game at this stage continued to involve a handling component emerges from Law 8, the start of which reads:

8.   If a player makes a fair catch, he shall be entitled to a free kick, providing he claims it by making a mark with his heel at once.

Despite this dichotomization of the game of football, both the association and rugby codes thrived. However, during the latter part of the twentieth century, it was to be soccer that emerged as not only the preferred form of football but also the world's most popular team sport. The reasons for its comparative success are not difficult to find. It requires little equipment and is comparatively cheap to play. Its rules – apart perhaps from the offside law – are relatively easy to understand. Above all, these rules regularly make for fast, open and fluid play, and for a game which is finely balanced among a number of interdependent polarities such as force and skill, individual and team play, attack and defence (Elias and Dunning 1986: 191–204). As such, its structure permits the recurrent generation of levels of excitement which are satisfying for both players and spectators. At the heart of this lies the fact that matches are physical struggles between two groups governed by rules that allow the passions to rise yet keep them – most of the time – in check. To the extent that they are enforced and/or voluntarily obeyed, the rules of soccer also limit the risk of serious injury to players. That is another respect in which it can be said to be a relatively 'civilized' game. Soccer played at top level also has a 'ballet-like' quality and that, together with the colours of the players' clothing and spectacular modes of presentation, helps further to explain its wide appeal. Of course, other sports possess some of the characteristics listed here but arguably only soccer has them all. That, it is reasonable to believe, is why it has become the world's most popular team sport.

Notes

1 The concept of 'sportization' was developed by Norbert Elias as a means of denoting the social process in the course of which modern forms of sport arose. See Elias and Dunning (1986).
2 The possibility that primarily kicking games were, as it were, more generally 'in the air' is suggested by the fact that there was a special form of East Anglian 'camp ball' called 'kicking camp' (Moor 1823). It would not, of course, have had the prestige of the Eton Field Game (see our later discussion) and thus would have been far less likely to spread.
3 When Dunning and Sheard first wrote *Barbarians, Gentlemen and Players* in 1979 they believed that the boys at Eton had initially committed their football rules to writing in 1849. Since then, the 1847 Eton rules have come to light, strengthening the Eton–Rugby status-rivalry hypothesis by making the Eton response to the Rugbeians' provocative act swifter and more immediate than first seemed to have been the case.
4 It is, we think, useful to view the various school football games in this period as differentially located on a continuum stretching between, at one end, an imaginary game with no handling at all, and, at the other, an imaginary game with no restrictions on the use of hands whatever. Seen in these terms, the Eton Field Game would be positioned fairly close to the former end, the Rugby game close to the latter. The games of the other main public schools – Charterhouse, Harrow, Shrewsbury, Westminster and Winchester – would, in no particular sequence, be ranged between the two. However, they would all be closer to the end of the continuum occupied by the Eton Field Game than the position of Rugby. This is because the boys of each of these schools favoured a mainly kicking rather than a handling and carrying form of football. But let us reiterate our major point: if we are right, it was the Eton and Rugby games that were most innovative and which diverged most from the range which constituted the early nineteenth century norm.

5   J.C. Thring – he was normally addressed as Charles – was the younger brother of Edward Thring, the Old Etonian Fellow of King's College, Cambridge, who became Headmaster of Uppingham School in 1853. J.C. was initially educated at Shrewsbury School and subsequently attended St John's College, Cambridge, where he was involved in developing a compromise set of football rules in 1846. He went on to be an Assistant Master at Uppingham from 1859 to 1869.
6   Our data relating to football in Sheffield have been obtained from the Football Club Records of Sheffield Football Club in the Sheffield City Archives and from Sheffield Central Library.

References

Booth, K. (2002) *The Father of Modern Sport: The Life and Times of Charles W. Alcock*, Manchester: The Parrs Wood Press.

Bredekamp, H. (1993) *Florentiner Fussball: die Renaissance der Spiele*, Frankfurt/M: Campus.

Curry, G. (2002) 'The Trinity Connection: An Analysis of the Role of Members of Cambridge University in the Development of Football in the Mid-nineteenth Century', *The Sports Historian*, 22(2), 46–73.

—— (2003) 'Forgotten Man: The Contribution of John Dyer Cartwright to the Football Rules Debate', *Soccer and Society*, 4(1), 71–86.

Dunning, E. (1961) 'Early Stages in the Development of Football as an Organised Game', unpublished MA thesis, University of Leicester.

Dunning, E. and Sheard, K. (1979) *Barbarians, Gentlemen and Players: A Sociological Study of the Development of Rugby Football*, Oxford: Martin Robertson.

Elias, N. (2000) *The Civilising Process*, revised translation edited by E. Dunning, J. Goudsblom and S. Mennell, Oxford: Blackwell.

Elias, N. and Dunning, E. (1986) *Quest for Excitement: Sport and Leisure in the Civilising Process*, Oxford: Blackwell.

Gardner, P. (1974) *Nice Guys Finish Last*, London: Allen Lane.

Goulstone, J. (2000) 'The Working-class Origins of Modern Football', *International Journal of the History of Sport*, 17(1), 135–43.

—— (2001) *Football's Secret History*, Upminster: 3-2 Books.

Green, G. (1953) *The History of the Football Association*, London: Naldrett.

Guttmann, A. (1986) *Sports Spectators*, New York: Columbia University Press.

Harvey, A. (1999) 'Football's Missing Link: The Real Story of the Evolution of Modern Football', *European Sports History Review*, 1, 92–116.

Macrory, J. (1991) *Running with the Ball*, London: Collins Willow.

Magoun, F.P. (1938) *A History of Football from the Beginnings to 1871*, Cologne: Änglistische Arbeite.

Marples, M. (1954) *A History of Football*, London: Collins.

Moor, E. (1823) *Suffolk Words and Phrases*, Woodbridge: J. Loder.

Shearman, M. (1887) *Athletics and Football*, London: Longmans & Co.

Strutt, J. (1801) *The Sports and Pastimes of the People of England*, London.

Young, P. (1968) *A History of British Football*, London: Stanley Paul.

4 Rugby union football in England

Civilizing processes and the de-institutionalization of amateurism

Andrew White

The history of rugby union football in England is closely associated with the institutionalization, and in more recent times de-institutionalization, of amateurism. The first of these processes, and the attendant conflicts, ultimately led to the bifurcation of rugby football into union and league forms in 1895, and have been explored by Dunning and Sheard (1979), Collins (1995, 1996, 1998), Delaney (1984) and Williams (1989). Greenhalgh (1992) and Delaney (1984) have also made important contributions with their analyses of the ways in which the fledgling rugby league authorities, the Northern Union (NU), attempted to regulate and control the institutionalization of professionalism after 1895.

For figurational sociologists, of course, the work of Dunning and Sheard (1979) is seminal. In *Barbarians, Gentlemen and Players*, they conclude by signalling the rise of rugby union football as a gate-taking sport which, in the context of the accelerating commercialization of rugby, was eroding a central principle of amateurism, the proscribing of payment for playing. Elsewhere (White 1994) I have attempted to continue the analysis of Dunning and Sheard, tracking the components and shifting power relationships associated with the transition to professionalism. The decision announced at an interim meeting of the International Rugby Football Board (IRFB) – the 'Paris Declaration' – on 27 August 1995, and subsequently ratified at a full meting of the IRFB in Tokyo in September, effectively enabled national organizing bodies to administer a professional game and represented a landmark in the formal de-institutionalization of amateurism in rugby union.

The two key moments in the history of rugby football in England, although separated by 100 years, are intimately associated with the institutionalization and de-institutionalization of amateurism. Indeed, Sheard (1997) has identified striking parallels between the policies of the NU after the 1895 bifurcation and those of the Rugby Football Union (RFU) after 1995 with both processes emerging 'dialectically'. In the last quarter of the nineteenth century the meanings of amateurism relative to professionalism were worked out in the context of a set of increasingly intense social pressures. In the late twentieth century, accompanying the domestic and global expansion of rugby as a modern sport, there was again a largely unintended and unplanned erosion of the principles, ethos and organizing structures of amateurism. In short, the process of de-institutionalizing amateurism re-emerged in a different, broader and global context. In the light of these preliminary observations, this chapter seeks to build on the figurationally informed accounts of the development of rugby union by assessing some of the more recent historical works in this regard and, by extending the analysis to encompass more contemporary developments, to provide a comparative analysis of the figurationally specific patterns and events associated with the two major transitions in rugby football.

'Folk' football: decline and adoption by the English public schools

Dunning and Sheard (1979) have identified the origins and development of rugby union football in England up to the late 1970s as occurring in five overlapping stages. In the first stage, from the fourteenth century into the twentieth century, the generic name of 'football' (sometimes called 'mob' or 'folk' football) is given to variants of a range of wild, rough, mass participant folk-games in pre-industrial Britain that were the antecedents of modern rugby (union and league) and association football (soccer). Although there were regional variations – Knappan in Wales, Cornish variants of 'hurling' and camp-ball in Norfolk and Suffolk – they had a number of common characteristics. They were often *ad hoc*, although some were associated with Saints or 'holy days' and rural community festivals. Participant numbers were often unspecified but frequently included a variety of occupational and status groups as well as, in some areas, members of the aristocracy and landed gentry. Games had unwritten and loosely defined oral rules and, with high levels of violence, were akin to 'mock battles' and symbolic struggles for territory within and between communities. Dunning (1993: 53) has pointed out that the high levels of violence in these folk antecedents of modern rugby, 'reflected the comparatively non-advanced "threshold of repugnance" with regard to witnessing and engaging in violent acts'.

The second stage, from about 1750 to 1840, involved a 'modernizing' of the folk antecedents of football by boys in the English public (i.e. private, fee-paying) schools. Folk football itself declined during this period. Dunning and Sheard (1979) suggest that this was only partly due to the effects of industrialization and agrarian reform with migrants to urban-industrial settings increasingly subject to a tightening of labour discipline, limitations of time and space and a growing disengagement from their rural traditions. In addition, folk football was forcibly suppressed. Members of the aristocracy and landed gentry withdrew their support, becoming more 'status-exclusive' in the face of twin threats to their dominance from rising bourgeois power and increasingly restive lower classes. In urban contexts there were now more effective instruments of social control, for example Sir Robert Peel's police force, to suppress, although not without some resistance, the transfer of folk football traditions to the towns and cities.

The types of football adopted by the public schoolboys were local adaptations of folk football. However, the games were intimately bound up with the structure and development of authority relations in the public schools, the 'prefect–fagging' system. The 'prefect–fagging' system, to a degree, resolved the power struggle between the masters (socially inferior to the majority of pupils) and the older boys (prefects) who would often exercise brutal forms of control and discipline over the younger boys (fags). Additionally, and importantly for the development of football, in return for recognition of the rule of the masters in the classroom, the prefects extracted from the masters the right to exercise dominance over their leisure activities. Prefects made football compulsory for the junior boys, assigning them minor defensive roles, incorporating and reinforcing the traditions of roughness inherent in their folk football antecedents. Indeed, at Charterhouse and Rugby schools iron-capped boots ('navvies') were worn to enhance 'hacking', the practice of kicking an opponent's shins in an attempt to drive a ball on the ground through a mass of players. These rough and physically dangerous games were thought to reinforce virtues of manliness and physical courage (Dunning and Sheard 1979: 58–9).

Towards the end of this period, from about 1830 to 1860, distinctive forms of football in the public schools began to emerge. This third phase was characterized by a rapid transition with both formal control and self-regulation distinctive features of an 'incipient modernization' of 'Rugby' football. The practice of carrying the ball grew, was increasingly tolerated in the 1830s, and by 1845 'running-in' with the ball was incorporated into the rules of football at Rugby. It appears that this was still a dangerous practice; the 'runner-in' could be subject to a range of violent measures to impede his progress. Nevertheless, handling the ball and running with it was emerging as a distinctive feature of the Rugby school variant of football (see Dunning and Sheard, 1979: 59–62 for a discussion of the Webb Ellis origin 'myth').

The codification of 'rugby' football

The fourth stage in the development of rugby occurred during the last half of the nineteenth century when public school football spread into the wider society. The period also encompasses the formation of the Football Association (FA) in 1863, the Rugby Football Union (RFU) in 1871 and the bifurcation of rugby into league and union forms in 1895. The start of the period is characterized by the spread of the public school games cult and a growing polarization around the Rugby 'handling' and Eton 'kicking' variants of football. Williams (1989: 309) summarizes this as,

> the byproduct of a conflict between established and ascendant classes in the public schools. Older, impeccably aristocratic establishments like Eton, Winchester, Harrow and Shrewsbury could adopt a 'new' form of popular street football with impunity, but the headmasters of more recent foundations like Cheltenham, Marlborough, Wellington, Clifton and Haileybury, as well as re-endowed old grammar schools like Sherborne, Sedburgh and Tonbridge opted for the game they themselves had learned as masters or pupils at Arnold's Rugby, a school like theirs that had come into existence to cater for a thrusting industrial and commercial middle class anxious to put as much distance as

possible between themselves and the lower orders from which they might be thought to have sprung.

Variations within these two game types depended on the topography of school boundaries and traditions. Diversity in the playing of football became problematic when men from these schools went to university and/or formed independent clubs and began to play against each other. A number of attempts were made at Cambridge University from the late 1830s to construct unified rules. The 1863 rules excluded key components of the 'Rugby' model, in particular handling the ball and the rougher elements of 'tripping up' and 'hacking'. In consequence, the rugby-playing Cambridge students began to play in isolation.

At the same time the growth of independent clubs and competitive matches was assisted by improvements in transport and communication. This enabled the predominantly upper middle-class men who formed these clubs to become, through the expanding newspaper industry, nationally renowned 'footballers and gentlemen'. With increasing demands for inter-club and inter-school matches came further pressures for unified rules. Conflict over which of the two models' rules should be adopted came to a head in December 1863 at the fifth meeting of the embryo Football Association. At this meeting 'running in' and 'hacking', the two most violent aspects of the rugby model, were excluded from the rules. Supporters of the 'Rugby' model subsequently withdrew from the FA on the grounds that, without these key features, football would be emasculated. The 'Cambridge Rules' accelerated the separate development of Association football (soccer) and Rugby football (rugger), further formalized in 1871 with the formation of the RFU. Factors contributing to a need for a central governing body and for unified rules were: the growing popularity of soccer over rugby because of its simpler rules and more open game dynamics; the appearance of variants of 'rugger'; and internal and external pressures regarding what was perceived as the 'barbarous' practice of hacking. Dunning and Sheard (1979) interpret the 1871 prohibition of hacking and tripping, along with an ethos of gentlemanly behaviour of voluntarily abiding by the rules under the authority of the captain and of exercising self-restraint in robust physical encounters, as evidence of developments moving rugby in a 'civilizing' direction.

The democratization and institutionalization of amateurism

The rapid national diffusion of soccer and rugby entailed a process of democratization, as middle-class men who had not been to public school and members of the working class began to play in greater numbers. Both groups brought with them their own sets of values and, along with the traditional values of the public school elite, created a 'melting pot' of social relations. The diffusion of rugby down the social ladder was more pronounced in the North of England, and in Lancashire and Yorkshire particularly. Lancashire tended to have proportionately more 'socially exclusive' clubs than the latter, probably due to the relative numbers of club founders and members having attended public school. In Yorkshire there were relatively more socially 'open' or 'mixed' clubs, a product, Dunning and Sheard (1979: 136) suggest, of lower status middle-class groups who had not received a public school education. Moreover, the social arrangement of factory relations in Yorkshire and Lancashire at this time meant that the 'industrial' middle class exhibited a relatively low degree of social exclusiveness. In effect, as Holt (1989: 114) points out, 'an educated elite that was merged with land, and a business class, which received little in the way of official approval' characterized the structure of the middle class in late Victorian Britain. The latter group was able to enhance their status through their support and association with local sport.

Barlow (1993) and Russell (1994) both draw attention to the significance of these industrialized contexts. In his study of the growth of rugby football in Rochdale between 1868 and 1890, Barlow (1993: 65) focuses on the interplay between middle-class sporting idealism and an emerging industrial-urban working-class culture and cautions against over-emphasizing the influence of the middle class in this context. Many of the parochial 'works' and street teams were the result of the efforts of working men, founded on competitiveness and community pride and characterized by a relatively limited adherence to the ethos of 'fair play'. Russell's broader study of the adoption of rugby and association football in the West Riding of Yorkshire and Lancashire also suggests that, despite some localized differences, the middle and upper classes played a crucial role in establishing the local football code. He also points to the influence of working-class groups in developing technical aspects of the game. In making this point he offers an additional explanation to that of Dunning and Sheard (1979) who argue that the appeal of rugby was based on the relatively high level of 'roughness', which was consonant with traditional standards of working-class masculinity.

Working-class participation, as players and spectators, was further facilitated by an increase in spare time as working hours shortened, and by growing financial surpluses. In large part, as both Barlow (1993) and Collins (1995, 1998) have shown, working-class participation often took place under the tutelage, organizational and financial support of middle-class groups. Nevertheless the proliferation of clubs in the industrial North of England, along with the growth of sports spectatorship, was a product of, and further generated, a sense of collective identity and civic pride expressed through sporting representatives. These developments contributed to what Dunning and Sheard (1979: 145) have interpreted as a process of 'proletarianization' of rugby, particularly evident in the counties of Yorkshire and Lancashire (a similar process was evident in the development of rugby in the West Country (White 2000)). This process explains, to a degree, the pressure for the inauguration of the Yorkshire Challenge Cup competition in 1877, and its success in terms of its spectator appeal and as a stimulus for the foundation of new clubs. Dunning and Sheard (1979: 145) further suggest that, concomitantly, a related process of 'bourgeoisification' was evident in the formalization of competitions and 'monetization' of aspects of the game (e.g. the emergence of 'gate-taking' clubs, cash payments to players, etc.).

These developments, and the growing financial and playing strength of the Yorkshire and Lancashire clubs, alarmed the RFU establishment who felt they had proprietorial rights over the way the game should develop. Though officials of both the Yorkshire and Lancashire unions often assisted the RFU in regulating the development of the game (Collins 1998), an ideological battleground, between the RFU and their Northern allies, developed over the concept of amateurism; rugby became 'a site of conflict between the expression of working class cultural practices and the dominant cultural codes of the public school ethos' (Collins 1998: 61).

Amateurism as an ideology was relatively undeveloped prior to the 1880s. Indeed, as Holt (1989: 103) points out, the term 'professional' came into use in the 1850s and the term 'amateur' in the 1880s. Up to this period amateurism was an amorphous, loosely articulated set of values regarding the functions of sport and the standards believed necessary for their realization (Dunning and Sheard 1979). It was the threat of professionalism, not only in Rugby football but also in other sports, that prompted the public school elite to crystalize the ideology of amateurism, and accompany it with voluntary, bureaucratic, administrative structures (Holt 1992). The ethos stressed adherence to a code of 'gentlemanly' behavioural standards of self-restraint and fair play and viewed participation in sport as a moral end in itself (rather than a source of material gain). This amateur ideology emerged 'dialectically'; that is, in opposition to the encroachment of professionalism and the commercialization of sport through gate-taking (Dunning and Sheard 1979: 147). In rugby a number of financial and non-financial rewards began to emerge. These included 'broken-time' payments to reimburse players for wages lost through playing or training, inducements to move clubs, voluntary collections or 'testimonials' for star players and rewards in kind (e.g. gifts of food, drink, seaside trips, etc.) (Collins 1995; Delaney 1984: 27–41). The public school elite generally opposed such practices, expressing concerns over the potential increases in levels of violence associated with an emphasis on winning and the behaviour of large gatherings of highly partisan working class supporters at a time of rising class tensions.

The bifurcation of 'rugby' football into 'union' and 'league' forms

In the broader context of conflictual class relations, the formalizing of the amateur ethos formed the basis from which the ultimate bifurcation of rugby into union and league forms would emerge. Collins (1998), Delaney (1984) and Dunning and Sheard (1979) all discuss the mechanics of the split, but differences emerge in the interpretation of the social dynamics of the process. Accordingly, it is to these interpretations that attention is turned.

Dunning and Sheard (1979: 198) suggest that the bifurcation of rugby was 'doubly determined'. The rugby establishment were drawn from relatively low status public schools. Their insecure and marginal membership of the public school elite generated a striving for status-exclusivity, particularly with regard to members of the working class. Amateurism was an ideology through which their own status could be emphasized. In contrast, a significant number of the representatives and officials of the Yorkshire and Lancashire gate-taking clubs were members of local elites drawn from the business and industrial bourgeoisie. These men, it is suggested, were predisposed to achievement orientation and monetizing personal and social relations. Thus they had few reservations regarding commercializing rugby through cup and league competitions and, given the structure of factory and community relations at the time, little status anxiety in their dealings with the working class. Furthermore, due to their close contact with supporters of amateurism in their own county unions – many of whom had not attended public school and had a weak attachment to the amateur ethos – officials of gate-taking clubs were able to exert pressure for compromises over the establishment of leagues and, importantly, the introduction of 'broken-time' payments. The gate-taking clubs were successful to the extent that the Yorkshire County Union proposed a motion at the 1893 RFU General Meeting supporting compensation for *bona fide* loss of time. This motion was defeated and the RFU subsequently enshrined in its constitution the requirement that only clubs, 'comprised entirely of amateurs shall be eligible for membership'. Even more restrictive amateur regulations were to follow, particularly with regard to broken-time payments, and were policed with draconian penalties for offenders. Faced with these circumstances, the sympathies of these men, as well as their relative autonomy at local level and their high degree of commercial self-confidence, all predisposed them to support their local connections rather than those with the RFU, and form the breakaway Northern Rugby Football Union in 1895.

Collins (1995, 1996, 1998), in large part concurring with Delaney (1984), amends and refines the analysis of Dunning and Sheard, suggesting that members of the northern industrial bourgeoisie *par excellence* were implicated in devising and enforcing amateur regulations in the County Unions of Yorkshire and Lancashire. Collins (1996: 37) argues that, 'these men unequivocally shared the instincts, aspirations and philosophies of their colleagues living in the South'. On this basis Collins suggests that in order to explain the 1895 bifurcation rather more emphasis needs to be placed on the split within northern rugby, and the relative influence of the 'North–South' divide downplayed. Finally, Collins argues that it was initially working-class players, rather than members of the industrial bourgeoisie, that pressed for payment for playing. Bourgeois groups may well have been sympathetic, as Dunning and Sheard suggest, but the success and stability of clubs was dependent on the expansion of revenue generating opportunities from cup and league competitions and the control over wage payments (Collins 1998: 130–7). The RFU along with leading representatives of the Yorkshire and Lancashire county unions were highly suspicious of new competitions (e.g. the Yorkshire Senior Competition, formed in 1892) which had been formed by the senior clubs, largely independently of their respective county unions. While there was a general consensus that professionalism *per se* would lead to rapid 'wage inflation', gate-taking club officials viewed 'broken time' payments as essential for working class participation and thus revenue from spectators.

Expediency and the economics of gate-taking clubs clashed head on with the enforcement of amateurism. The increasing rigour with which amateur regulations were being applied threatened the commercial viability of the gate-taking clubs through the loss of gate revenues. The potential loss of working-class players and the decline of the sport as a component of civic identity, were other key concerns. The senior Yorkshire clubs and nine Lancashire clubs met in 1894 for 'their mutual protection' after the circulation of the RFU 'Manifesto' on professionalism that year. They met again in January 1895 to discuss the possibility of forming a joint 'Northern League'. The rules of the new competition and organizational details of the administrative 'Union' between the Yorkshire and Lancashire clubs were submitted to the RFU for approval. They were rejected and the proposed union was forbidden (Delaney 1984: 62–4). In conjunction with the RFU's draft proposals for even more stringent anti-professional legislation in 1895, the administrators and officials of the leading gate-taking clubs felt they had no choice but to break away from the national union. As Collins (1996: 38) notes, the 'initial bourgeois consensus over amateurism therefore fractured when it became clear that, in order to impose amateurism, working class players had to be driven out'.

On Thursday 29 August 1895, at the George Hotel in Huddersfield, senior clubs from Yorkshire and Lancashire, in response to the RFU's proposed anti-professionalism regulations and pressure from their county unions on the issue of promotion to and relegation from league competitions, formed the Northern Football Union. They pledged themselves 'to push forward, without delay, its establishment on the principle of payment for *bona fide* broken-time only' (Collins 1998: 148). In this interpretation the resignation of the northern clubs was more a reaction to RFU intransigence than, as Dunning and Sheard (1979) suggest, a proactive expression of the relative autonomy and self-confidence of the 'northern businessmen' associated with the gate-taking clubs.

In summary, the diffusion of rugby football from the public schools into the wider society, was accompanied by shifting power ratios associated with lengthening and strengthening chains of interdependency. One of the consequences of these processes was to reduce violence in the game. Additionally, the expansion of the figuration brought with it the competing interests of working-class spectators and players, an increasingly powerful industrial bourgeoisie and the public school elite that dominated the rugby establishment. Relationships between these groups were at the root of the conflicts over the development of rugby. The RFU establishment along with their allies in the North displayed stronger affective attachment to amateurism than other groups in the figuration. In order to protect their 'we-group' identity and their perceived proprietorial rights over the development of the game, they refused to compromise with lower status groups on key issues. In so doing they precipitated the bifurcation of rugby football into the amateur 'union' and the professional 'league' forms.

The 'de-institutionalization' of amateurism

Goudsblom (1997: 149) has observed that 'yesterday's unintended social consequences are today's social conditions of intentional human actions'. In rugby union the amateur ethos and organizational structures institutionalized in 1895 guided developments for around the next one hundred years. Salient features during this period were:

- antagonism to professionalism;
- distrust of spectators;
- emphasis on 'player-centredness' and character-forming aspects, despite changes in playing laws designed to raise spectator interest;
- an increasingly bureaucratized governing body;
- transformation of the game into a rationalized 'achievement-orientated' pursuit;
- conflict between leading clubs and the 'governing body', the RFU.

From around the 1960s a process of de-institutionalization of amateurism became increasingly evident. This process accelerated as the pace of the commercialization of rugby quickened until, in 1995, the IRFB legitimized professionalism. This event marked the end of the fifth stage identified by Dunning and Sheard.

Dunning and Sheard (1979: 232–68) identified 'a number of unintended and unforeseen consequences' accompanying the expansion of rugby union towards the end of this fifth stage: the growth of bureaucratic control; the development of a rank hierarchy of clubs; and the rise of gate-taking clubs. They claim that the ethos of the game changed towards a 'spectator', rather than a 'player-centred' ethos necessitating ideological changes in attitudes to amateurism. Furthermore the playing of rugby union football, particularly at the top levels and through the 'junior' clubs, has become more 'serious', leading to a growing 'scientific' management of the playing side and evidence of an emerging professionalization of administrative functions. Finally, the organization of the game has come to be based on formalized domestic and international competitions. This pattern of development, they suggest, was instrumental in a growing crisis within the sport, centred on the emergence of a syndrome of characteristics associated with professional rather than amateur sport. Dunning and Sheard also emphasized that:

> At a deeper level . . . money and professionalism is what is at stake. In our view, that is necessarily the case for, in capitalist societies, there is an inexorable tendency for sports to be bound up with money values.
>
> (1979: 234)

There were at least six strands in this monetization process. First, there was the gradual institutionalization of direct, if disguised, payments to players. Second, indirect payments to players (housing, employment, kit, etc.) grew in extent and importance. Third, there was the development of an informal transfer market at elite level. These components, alongside the growing seriousness of participation, contributed to the emergence of 'attitudinal professionalism' among the top players. The policy response of the RFU can be characterized as a mixture of tightening amateur regulations (e.g. on player transfers), compromise (e.g. on permitted sources of earnings), and turning a Nelsonian 'blind-eye' to some regulation breaches. In England the situation came to be described as one of 'shamateurism', a concealed form of monetization and, for gate-taking clubs and the RFU, a means of extracting surplus value from players that, in similar fashion to 'broken-time' payments in the 1890s, assisted in avoiding wage inflation. The best players would gravitate to the clubs able to offer the most attractive packages and to manage the 'grey areas' of financial accountability.

Fourth, the increasing complexity of running a gate-taking rugby club as a business led to a significant expansion of managerial, coaching and administrative functions increasingly headed by professional staff. Fifth, there was an increasing formalization of player/club, player/governing body, and club/governing body relationships. Sixth, at both club and international levels, sponsorship and marketing grew increasingly significant (Malcolm *et al.* 2000: 65–6). In conclusion, there appeared to be, in the development of rugby union during the early 1990s, a movement along the amateur–professional continuum, illustrated in Table 4.1.

However, it was the development of global and international competitions (i.e. the Rugby World Cup and the Tri-nations tournament), increasing media and commercial interest, and growing competition from rugby league which were the critical factors in the transition to professionalism. Entrepreneurs, such as Australian David Lord, sought to capitalize on the situation. Rumoured to have the backing of officials of the South African Rugby Board, Lord attempted to gather together a 'professional troupe' of players to tour the globe, playing in specially staged competitions. By April 1983 Lord claimed that 136 players from seven countries had signed 'preliminary optional contracts'. Ultimately the scheme failed due to the disclosure that Lord was an undischarged bankrupt, the reticence of the South African rugby authorities (involvement would have lessened the chances of their returning from international sporting isolation imposed because of the apartheid system in South Africa), and the refusal of sponsors Adidas and Pernod to underwrite the venture.

Table 4.1 The amateur–professional continuum

	Amateur	*Professional*
Ethos	Play-like; moral qualities, e.g. fair play, sportsmanship, etc.	Work-like
Performance	Emphasis on player-centred production of pleasure, i.e. process as important as outcome	Emphasis on the production of pleasure for players *and* spectators; importance of outcome
Economic relationship	Large degree of autonomy from working life; sport as leisure-time activity	Contractual wage and ownership relationships; sport as occupation; 'commercialization' of the sport's performance and performer
Management	Volunteer basis of organization	'Professional-business' organization

Note: The features listed are not absolute but are an attempt to indicate the interrelated characteristics of more or less amateur/professional sports.

A similar scheme, attempted some 12 years later during the 1995 World Cup in South Africa, was, however, instrumental in the final phase in the development to full professionalism. At this time the southern hemisphere unions perceived as a threat the new transnational rugby league competition, 'Super League'. Financed and televised by Rupert Murdoch's News Corporation, it was felt that this competition would attract rugby union players and spectators to the rival code. To alleviate these dangers South Africa, New Zealand and Australia sold the television broadcasting rights to their 'Tri-nations' tournament and a competition between 12 regionally based teams (the Super-Twelve's tournament) to News Corporation for a reported £360 million over ten years. This 'deal' was announced on the eve of the 1995 World Cup Final in South Africa.

Among competing commercial interests present was the World Rugby Corporation (WRC). Its organizers included the former Australian Rugby Union official and international forward Ross Turnbull, television interests represented by Kerry Packer, as well as the ESPN pay-per-view television network and the South African Broadcasting network. The aim of the WRC was to recruit players to play in a two-tier tournament involving eight 'national' teams (Australia, South Africa, New Zealand, Western Samoa, England, Scotland, France and Wales) and up to 22 'provincial teams' to be sold as franchises. Turnbull, as Packer's agent, reportedly offered top players signing-on fees of £175,000 and salaries at a similar level. Key players such as Brian Moore and Rob Andrew of England, Sean Fitzpatrick of New Zealand and Phil Kearns of Australia, and Francois Pienaar, the captain of World Cup winners South Africa were approached. These high profile individuals, all nearing the end of their international careers, were then to recruit their teammates; indeed Pienaar successfully recruited virtually the whole South African World Cup winning side.

For the southern hemisphere unions the threat was now not so much from rugby league but from within rugby union. In the event, enhanced professional contracts for South African, Australian and New Zealand players, financed by revenues from the News Corporation deal, induced players to remain with their respective unions. WRC's rivalry finally collapsed, leaving News Corporation holding the television broadcasting rights to both the rugby union and the rugby league codes in the southern hemisphere. In the process, the unions also successfully secured monopoly contracts over their players.

The competition for playing resources represents the most significant impetus in the transition to professionalism. In contrast to events leading to the bifurcation of rugby in 1895, international rather than intra-national factors were the key drivers, but a similarity exists in the presence of entrepreneurial business interests, aware of the commercial value of rugby union and confident in their abilities to manage the game, if necessary, outside the control of governing bodies. Ironically, in contrast to the position of the entrepreneurial businessmen associated with the gate-taking clubs in 1895, it was the unions that believed they had 'no choice' but to pay their players. By the latter half of 1995, the IRFB would sanction the full-scale professionalization of rugby union football.

The institutionalization of professionalism

In August 1995 the IRFB 'Amateurism Working Party' produced a report which marked the culmination of an important stage in the development of rugby union football. The report was discussed by the IRFB Council at a three-day meeting in Paris which concluded on Sunday 27 August with the announcement that rugby union was to become an 'open', professional game.

The IRFB, at a full board meeting in Tokyo during September 1995, repealed the amateur regulations and framed new ones for an 'open' game. The RFU was faced with similar imperatives at domestic level now that, as Tony Hallett, the Secretary of the RFU stated, the 'veil of shamateurism' had been lifted (*Daily Telegraph*, 28 August 1995). Under the 'permissive' regulations of the IRFB, the RFU could exercise a significant degree of autonomy in framing domestic regulations. In September 1995 the RFU took advantage of these, declaring a one-year moratorium on full professionalism in England. There was, among dominant groups at the RFU, a reluctance to embrace a fully professional domestic game. Indeed, England's two IRFB representatives, Peter Brook and John Jeavons-Fellows, were criticized for apparently ignoring their RFU mandate to vote against the loosening or repeal of amateur regulations. Furthermore, it was recognized that the payment of players at club and international level would have to be financed from additional sources of finance, a problem exacerbated by the £34 million loan which the RFU had recently taken out to redevelop the national stadium (Twickenham). A 'breathing space' was therefore needed. A seven-man RFU Commission was given the task of addressing issues associated with the transition to professional rugby in England, its principal considerations being the structures for international and national rugby, new 'professional' regulations, a code of conduct for professional players and financial and marketing imperatives.

In summary, the lengthening and widening of chains of interdependency associated with the globalization of rugby union involved the incorporation of groups into a rapidly expanding figuration that did not have the same degree of affective bonding to the principles, structures and ethos of amateurism as did members of the RFU. Increasing reciprocal dependencies led to expanding multi-polar controls such that no one group, such as the RFU, was capable of determining outcomes. The RFU mandate to resist the developments in Paris was symptomatic of their structural and ideological ill-preparedness to respond to the legitimation of professionalism. The need for a 'moratorium' in England can be interpreted as an aspect of what Elias called a 'double-bind' (1987), which Dunning (1993: 48) described as follows:

> the less amenable a sphere of events is to human control, the more emotional and fantasy-laden people's thinking about it tends to be. . . . [and] . . . the less capable they are of constructing more object-adequate models of its connections and hence of controlling it.

In the context of rugby union football, the strong affective attachment to amateurism, alongside the RFU's rapidly fading role in rugby's global figuration, were among the root causes of 'emotionally laden' thinking in their initial responses to the legitimation of professionalism.

Contemporary patterns of development

The remainder of this chapter briefly highlights some of the discernible characteristics of an incipient sixth stage in rugby union's development. There is an emerging process involving the 're-institutionalization' of a nexus of values, beliefs, behaviours and organizational structures associated with professionalism (O'Brien and Slack 1999: 40; Skinner *et al.* 1999: 188–9). Among elite clubs there was an initial move to replace the amateur-volunteer management committees which proliferated under the period of shamateurism with hierarchical structures of professional administrators and coaches. As Thibault *et al.* (1991) and Slack (1997: 43–65) suggest, this was accompanied by increasing specialization, formalization and decentralization of functional roles to professional staff ultimately responsible to an amateur elected board representing the membership. This transitional phase was not without conflict due to the different expectations and values of each of the groups and jurisdictional ambiguity over their respective responsibilities, a phenomenon consistent with those observed by Amis *et al.* (1995), Slack *et al.* (1994) and Inglis (1997a, 1997b) in similar contexts.

At a number of clubs the resolution of conflict involved the emergence of 'dual structures' with the ambassadorial and social functions of club membership in the hands of amateur, elected committee members and executive commercial and playing decisions undertaken by professional staff. This transition was facilitated by the change from a membership 'club' to a limited company corporate structure which protected members and management from financial liability. However, it also placed the assets and/or shares of the majority of the elite clubs in the hands of entrepreneurial investor-owners (Malcolm *et al.* 2000: 68–71). Again there are echoes of the development of gate-taking clubs in the 1880s and 1890s that also used limited companies to secure funds, in this instance mainly for ground developments (Delaney 1984; Collins 1998; White 2000). In essence, one bourgeois organizational form replaced another as elite clubs, in their own ways and to varying degrees, moved through stages in the process of structural transition from what Kikulis *et al.* (1989, 1992, 1995) have defined as 'Kitchen Table', 'Boardroom' and 'Executive Office' 'archetypes'.

Associated with this transition has been the transfer of club ownership, mergers between rugby union clubs, between rugby union and rugby league clubs, and between rugby clubs and football clubs. Financial imperatives have also placed additional emphasis on initiatives to attract new audiences. The construction of 'match-day experiences' involving fireworks, popular music and various forms of 'entertainments' has, in essence, involved the choreographing of what Elias (1986: 44) has termed a pleasurable, 'controlled, de-controlling of the emotions'.

The RFU followed a similar (if initially more rapid) path to the clubs recruiting professional staff and reorganizing personnel consistent with a transition to a 'Boardroom archetype' with control vested in the elected membership, represented by the 57 members of the RFU Council and later a smaller, elected, amateur official dominated Management Board. One outcome of this development has been conflict within the RFU between the professional administrators and the amateur elected representatives over respective powers and roles. Moreover, there has been considerable conflict, negotiation and accommodation between the RFU and the elite clubs because the latter have moved rather more rapidly to an 'Executive Office' archetype whereas the RFU, constrained by their constitution, retain significant characteristics of the 'Boardroom' archetype. These structural arrangements slowed decision making and angered club owners and administrators due to the constant need for decisions to be ratified by the RFU board. The partial transition of the RFU to an 'Executive Office' structure involved the adoption of a management company structure, England Rugby Limited (ERL), a joint venture comprising professional and amateur representatives from the RFU and representatives from Premiership Rugby Partnership (PRP), itself an alliance of elite clubs and the Professional Rugby Players Association. ERL would be responsible for the development of the professional game with the power to negotiate financial, organizational and player-related issues. The evidence again suggests the emergence of a dual structure of management at governing body level, with the development of the amateur game in the hands of the RFU and the development of the professional game predominantly in the hands of ERL. Conflict with the Celtic unions ensued when the RFU's professional administrators attempted to break with the tradition of negotiating television rights collectively for the Six-nations tournament and independently negotiated a deal with BSkyB to broadcast England's home fixtures. Conflict within the RFU followed as professional administrators were accused of transgressing the traditional 'collective' component of the amateur ethos that had been the basis of previous negotiations regarding broadcasting rights.

In summary, structural-organizational transitions in the administration of rugby union football, which are characteristic of an emerging sixth stage in the development, resulted from conflictual relationships and shifting power balances. Although evident prior to the legitimation of professionalism, conflicts became more acute and acrimonious post-1995 as commercial imperatives came to dominate. This was particularly true for the elite professional players. The attitudinal professionalism and eroding voluntarist participation of shamateurism quickly gave way to the structures, values and behaviours associated with a professional rugby-playing career. Additional impetus came from those players who had crossed codes from rugby league to union and those who joined English clubs from overseas, particularly those from the southern hemisphere. Wage inflation followed as players, with the assistance of agents, became aware of their market value. Elite clubs were alarmed by the prospect of accelerating wage costs at a time when the distribution of central funds from the RFU, sponsorship and spectatorship had yet to be regularized. The RFU were far from isolated from this shift in power relations. In November 2000, players in the England squad threatened strike action after the RFU prevaricated over a review of their basic fees, bonuses and intellectual property rights as international players.

The substantial salaries of professional players were accompanied by proliferating regimes of surveillance and control over physical and mental preparation, skill development and playing performances. The 'scientization' of match preparation (Malcolm *et al.* 2000: 77) has involved use of medication that ranges along a continuum of dietary supplements to the use of banned performance-enhancing substances. Medical and physiotherapy support has increased markedly (Malcolm and Sheard 2002). Players, as Malcolm *et al.* (2000) point out, are now expensive assets the management of which requires the reconciliation of the players' and clubs' long- and short-term interests. Finally, a process of 're-masculinization' has been observable involving a transition, particularly among the forwards, away from traditionally valued vigorously aggressive, robust and combative masculinity to the skilled, muscularized, conditioned 'rugby athlete'.

These developments have contributed to a growing structural differentiation between professional and amateur players. While, as former England coach Dick Greenwood observed, the 'amateur has an inalienable right to play like a pillock' (*The Times*, 4 November 1985), this 'luxury' is increasingly unavailable to professional players. Professional administrators and coaches are, of course, subject to similar pressures. While power relations have shifted in favour of players and coaches, the lives of both groups, and administrators, are increasingly subjected to the rigours associated with the institutionalization of a professional sports management ethos.

A further theme emerging from the institutionalization of professionalism is a general reduction in the level of violence. This has largely been due to the ubiquity of television cameras making acts of foul play difficult to conceal; increased surveillance by match officials with extended powers; the 'citing' of players after the game for acts of violence missed by match officials; the appointment of professional referees, the professionalizing of disciplinary processes and the increasing encroachment of criminal law; and an increasing internalization by players of the financial and career impacts of foul play. The game has also changed as a result of alterations to the laws governing the ruck and tackle. These changes were made for reasons reminiscent of the development of the 'play the ball' rule by the Northern Union in 1899 and 1906, namely to raise levels of tension excitement by making physical contact between players more visible for both spectators and match officials (Sheard 1997: 131; Delaney 1984; Collins 1998). Additionally, new spectator groups, perhaps with a lower threshold of repugnance to witnessing acts of violence traditionally associated with rugby, needed to be attracted and retained. However, this had to be accomplished without compromising aspects of robust masculinity – the giving and taking of 'hard knocks' – an important component of the sport's spectator appeal.

While a review of contemporary developments would be incomplete without recognizing the rapid growth of women's rugby, a detailed analysis lies outside the scope of this chapter. The women's game in Britain and female participation in mini-rugby, have both been areas of considerable growth in recent years. It would appear that many of the developments in the male game such as the emergence of professional administrative structures, domestic and global competitions and professionalization of players, although contoured by gendered relationships, are similarly evident in the development of women's rugby. Labelled the 'fastest growing women's sport' in England in the early 1990s, women's rugby had, by 1995, been organized into five club divisions with regional sub-divisions at lower levels, and two student divisions. Cup and league competitions were instituted, the National Cup being sponsored by vodka distillers 'Vladivar' to the tune of £10,000. Further development of competitive structures post-1995, accompanied by funding from the National Lottery, has generated increased 'attitudinal' professionalism among elite international and club players similar to that in the era of 'shamateurism' in the men's game. Alongside this growing 'seriousness' of participation Wheatley (1994) provides evidence to suggest that some groups of rugby-playing women have reworded and appropriated male rugby songs as a sub-cultural style or 'bricolage', thus transforming aspects of male rugby 'style' in the specific cultural space of women's rugby.

Women's rugby is currently played in 20 countries and the inaugural Women's World Cup was staged in 1990 (England were runners-up in the first and champions in the second event in 1994, and runners-up again in 2002). These developments have been reflected at IRFB level through the production of a Strategic Development Plan for women's rugby. In England, the development of the Rugby Football Union for Women (RFUW) has involved growth in professionally staffed administrative and coaching structures alongside an amateur, volunteer, elected Executive Committee. Finally, similar to developments in male rugby at governing body level, there appears to be a transition towards a 'Boardroom' archetype of structures and relationships. This is characterized by a dual structure of professional staff and an elected executive to manage an emerging 'dual' structure of amateur, and at this stage, quasi-professional elite participation.

Conclusion

Rugby union's institutionalization of amateurism in the 1890s, and its de-institutionalization in the 1990s, were both unintended consequences of a shift in power relations associated with a widening and lengthening of chains of inter-dependency in the rugby football 'figuration'. Goudsblom's (1997: 147) observation that, over time 'more people are forced more often to pay more attention to more and more others' is apt in this context. The figurational sociological approach of Dunning and Sheard (1979), drawing on this tenet, unearthed five stages in the development of the sport. A sixth stage is now apparent and it is suggested that the principles of a figurational approach can be used to move towards an under-standing of the processes associated with this latest phase.

References

Amis, J., Slack, T. and Berrett, T. (1995) 'The Structural Antecedents of Conflict in Voluntary Sport Organizations', *Leisure Studies*, 14, 1–16.

Barlow, S. (1993) 'The diffusion of "Rugby" Football in the Industrialized Context of Rochdale, 1808–1890. A Conflict of Ethical Values', *The International Journal of the History of Sport*, 10(1), 49–67, London: Frank Cass.

Collins, T. (1995) '"Noa Mutton, Noa Laaking": The Origins of Payment for Play in Rugby Football, 1877–86', *International Journal of the History of Sport*, 12(1), 35–50.

—— (1996) 'Myth and Reality in the 1895 Rugby Split', *The Sports Historian*, 16, 33–41.

—— (1998) *Rugby's Great Split. Class, Culture and the Origins of Rugby League Football*, London: Frank Cass.

Delaney, T. (1984) *The Roots of Rugby League*, Keighley: Delaney.

Dunning, E. (1993) 'Sport in the Civilising Process: Aspects of the Development of Modern Sport', in E. Dunning, J. Maguire and R. Pearton (eds), *The Sports Process: A Comparative and Developmental Approach*, Champaign, IL: Human Kinetics.

Dunning, E. and Sheard, K. (1979) *Barbarians, Gentlemen and Players*, Oxford: Martin Robertson.

Elias, N. (1986) 'Introduction', in N. Elias and E. Dunning *Quest for Excitement: Sport and Leisure in the Civilizing Process*, Oxford: Blackwell.

—— (1987) *Involvement and Detachment*, Oxford: Basil Blackwell.

Goudsblom, J. (1997) *Sociology in the Balance*, Oxford: Blackwell.

Greenhalgh, P. (1992) '"The Work and Play Principle": The Professional Regulations of the Northern Rugby Football Union 1898–1905', *The International Journal of the History of Sport* 9(3), 356–77.

Holt, R. (1989) *Sport and the British: A Modern History*, Oxford: Clarendon Press.

—— (1992) 'Amateurism and Its Interpretation: The Social Origins of British Sport', *Innovations*, 5(4), 19–31.

Inglis, S. (1997a) 'Roles of the Board in Amateur Sports Organizations', *Journal of Sports Management*, 11, 160–76.

—— (1997b) 'Shared Leadership in the Governance of Amateur Sport: Perceptions of Executive Directors and Volunteer Board Members', *Avante*, 3(1), 14–33.

Kikulis, L., Slack, T., Hinings, B. and Zimmerman, A. (1989) 'A Structural Taxonomy of Amateur Sports Organisations', *Journal of Sports Management*, 3, 129–50.

—— (1992) 'Institutionally Specific Design Archetypes: A Framework for Understanding Change in National Sports Organisations', *International Review for the Sociology of Sport*, 27(4), 343–68.

—— (1995) 'Sector-specific Patterns of Organisational Design Change', *Journal of Management Studies*, 32(1), 67–100.

Malcolm, D. and Sheard, K. (2002) '"Pain in the Assets": The Effects of Commercialization and Professionalization on the Management of Injury in English Rugby Union', *Sociology of Sport Journal*, 19(2), 149–69.

Malcolm, D., Sheard, K. and White, A. (2000) 'The Changing Culture and Structure of English Rugby Union Football', *Culture, Sport and Society*, 3(3), 63–87.

O'Brien, D. and Slack, T. (1999) 'Deinstitutionalising the Amateur Ethic: An Empirical Investigation of Change in a Rugby Union Football Club', *Sport Management Review*, 2, 24–42.

Russell, D. (1994) 'Sporadic and Curious: The Emergence of Rugby and Soccer Zones in Yorkshire and Lancashire, c. 1860–1914', *The International Journal of the History of Sport*, 185–205, London: Frank Cass.

Sheard, K. (1997) '"Breakers Ahead!" Professionalisation and Rugby Union Football: Lessons from Rugby League', in *The International Journal of the History of Sport*, 14(1), 116–37.

Skinner, J., Stewart, B. and Edwards, A. (1999) 'Amateurism to Professionalism: Modelling Organizational Change in Sporting Organisations', *Sport Management Review*, 2, 173–92.

Slack, T. (1997) *Understanding Sport Organisations. The Application of Organisational Theory*, Champaign, IL: Human Kinetics.

Slack, T., Berrett, T. and Mistry, K. (1994) 'Rational Planning Systems as a Source of Organisational Conflict', *International Review for the Sociology of Sport*, 29(3), 317–28.

Thibault, N., Slack, T. and Hinings, B. (1991) 'Professionalism, Structures and Systems: The Impact of Professional Staff on Voluntary Sport Organisations', *International Review for the Sociology of Sport*, 26(2), 83–99.

Wheatley, E. (1994) 'Subcultural Subversions: Comparing Discourses on Sexuality in Men's and Women's Rugby Songs', in S. Birrell and C. Cole *Women, Sport and Culture*, Champaign, IL: Human Kinetics, pp. 192–211.

White, A. (1994) 'The Professionalisation of Rugby Union Football in England: Crossing the Rubicon?', unpublished MSc thesis, University of Leicester.

—— (2000) 'The "civilising" of Gloucester Rugby Football Club. A Historical Sociology of the Development and Management of an Elite, English Rugby Union Football Club, 1873–1914', unpublished PhD thesis, University of Leicester.

Williams, G. (1989) 'Rugby Union', in T. Mason (ed.), *Sport in Britain; A Social History*, Cambridge: Cambridge University Press.

5 Cricket

Civilizing and de-civilizing processes in the imperial game

Dominic Malcolm

In Jamaica on 29 January 1998, an international (test) match between England and the West Indies was abandoned on account of the state of the wicket (playing surface). Although on Christmas Day 1997 a limited-overs match between India and Sri Lanka had been abandoned for similar reasons, such an incident is unique in over 120 years of test cricket. Specifically, it was the unevenness of the ball's bounce off the wicket that was deemed to be hazardous to the players (slightly harder than a baseball, a cricket ball weighs between 155.9 and 163 grams and, at international level, is usually delivered at speeds of up to 90 miles per hour). In the 56 minutes of play prior to abandonment, England's physiotherapist was called to the field to treat injured players on six separate occasions (equating to approximately once every 12 balls bowled). It was this that led the umpires, in consultation with the team captains and the match referee, to decide that the wicket was too dangerous to play on.

British tabloid newspapers used headlines such as 'Son of a Pitch' (*The Sun*, 30 January 1998) and 'Killing Field' (*The Daily Mirror*, 30 January 1998) to describe the events. Match referee, Barry Jarman, was 'totally horrified' and thought that 'someone would have definitely been badly hurt if play had continued'. Umpire, Jack Bucknor, was 'worried the batsman could be hit every ball', and England physiotherapist Wayne Morton claimed, 'It was like war out there' (*The Sun* 30 January 1998). *The Times* editorial (30 January 1998) argued that, 'Somebody could have been killed. Test cricket is not a game for fainthearts. But neither should it be turned into an intimidatory dice of death.' Others, though fewer in number, argued that the game should have continued. Former England batsman Brian Close[1] argued, 'I should have imagined that in my day they would have gone on with it and made the best out of it' (*The Guardian*, 31 January 1998). These events provided part of the stimulus for researching this chapter. *Pace* Close, how have violence and injury, and perceptions of what levels of violence and injury are deemed tolerable in cricket, changed over the years? More particularly, what light does evidence from the sport of cricket shed on Elias's theory of civilizing processes and vice versa?

My previous work in this area has focused on spectator disorder in eighteenth- and nineteenth-century cricket (Malcolm 1999) and the relatively violent tenor of early (pre-1850s) cricket (Malcolm 2002). Through an examination of the development of the game's structural features (laws, customs, physical environment), I have argued that processes relating to the standardization, codification and national diffusion of cricket, like comparable processes in relatively violent sports such as football, rugby and boxing, represent something of a civilizing spurt. Yet, with this developmental pattern established, one is left with something of a conundrum. As the Jamaican test illustrates, a central tactic in modern cricket 'involves deliberately aiming the ball directly at the heads of opposing players, ostensibly in the hope of intimidating them and increasing the chances that they will play a false stroke' (Dunning 1992: 271). Yet this tactic is a relatively recent innovation. Roundarm and overarm bowling (essential in order to make the ball rise to head height) only became legal in 1835 and 1864 respectively and their introduction was marked by some considerable debate.[2] In addition to these developments, the 'Bodyline' controversy of 1932–3,[3] and the West Indian dominance of world cricket in the 1970s and 1980s, largely based on a reliance on short-pitched fast bowling (Malcolm 2001), appear to be developments which, in Elias's terms, represent 'de-civilizing spurts'.

One way in which we can account for these apparently de-civilizing changes is in terms of a shift in the balance between affective and instrumental forms of violence. In 'Social Bonding and Violence in Sport', Dunning (1986) attempted to address the idea that modern sports are becoming increasingly violent and that, correlatively, this represents a partial refutation of Elias's theory of civilizing processes. Dunning developed a typology of violence and demonstrated a historical shift in the balance between affective and instrumental forms of violence. In attempting to account for this pattern, Dunning argued that the external and internal pressures which contribute to civilizing processes have, in turn, increased people's propensity to use foresight, planning and rational strategies in everyday life. Hence, the 'dampening of Angriffslust' that has led to a reduction in 'affective' violence has been matched by changes to personality structures that have resulted in the development of an ability to use violence in a more rational or instrumental way. Modern sports therefore (and Dunning uses rugby, soccer and boxing as examples), may not be characterized by an increase in violence *per se* but, rather, by a relative increase in forms of violence that serve as a means for achieving certain goals, and a relative decrease in forms of violence based on high degrees of emotional spontaneity. If, in modern sports, 'the balance between rational and affective violence has changed in favour of the former' (Dunning 1986: 231) we can locate the cited cricketing developments in terms of this more general shift.

It is, however, important to avoid viewing the shifts in this balance as 'evolutionary' or 'unilinear'. Empirical evidence suggests that such trends have occurred in cricket, but this is not to say that we can dismiss potentially de-civilizing spurts as therefore unproblemtic. A similar point is made by Dunning *et al.* (1992) who note that Elias sometimes wrote as though, once a monopoly over violence is established, violence becomes more or less eliminated from society at large, except during times of war or revolutionary upheaval. While such an approach is useful in some contexts, they suggest that when working on a smaller time-scale – as indeed most present-day figurational sociologists inevitably are – 'we must seek to identify the sources and forms of continuing violence within societies which have a relatively stable and effective state monopoly of physical force' (Dunning *et al.* 1992: 10). To this end, they argue, first, that the manner in which the state monopoly over violence is used is a significant influence on the overall pattern of violence in a society; second, that certain sections of a society are more protected by this monopoly, while others are 'less subject to the sorts of civilizing constraints' (1992: 12) that most readily affect members of the higher classes; and third, they contend that:

> while Elias is correct to emphasize the close interconnection between functional democratization – processes of equalization that result from equalizing shifts in the balance of power – and civilizing processes, it should also be noted that functional democratization, since it involves a change in established patterns of dominance and subordination between groups, may also lead to a heightening of tensions and to increasing violence. Thus functional democratization, as it relates, for example, to the relationships between classes, between men and women and between different racial or ethnic groups may actually be associated with increases in violence, at least in the short term.

This passage forms the basis of the theoretical framework employed and examined here. More specifically, while the notion of a shift in modern cricket from affective towards instrumental forms of violence has, I argue, some validity, the notion of functional democratization gives greater analytical purchase in terms of explaining some of the shorter term increases in violence evident in the game. Thus, though the game is markedly less violent than it tended to be two or three hundred years ago, short term de-civilizing spurts can be theorized as follows: the development of roundarm and overarm bowling developed in the context of professional–amateur, upper class–lower class relations; the bodyline controversy is most understandable in the context of the shifting international balance of power between Australia and England; and the West Indian dominance of world cricket in the 1970s and 1980s can most adequately be viewed in terms of the development of neo-colonial 'racial'/ethnic relations. It is to these developments, and the relationship between violence and functional democratization, which I now turn.

The development of overarm bowling

Elias and Dunning, in their analysis of the dynamics of sports groups, contend that

> the whole development of most sport-games . . . centred to a very large extent on the resolution of this problem: how was it possible to maintain within the set game-pattern a high level of group tension and the group dynamics resulting from it, while at the same time keeping recurrent physical injury to the players at the lowest possible level.
>
> (1966: 395)

As the following account illustrates, with regard to cricket, this problem was most apparent in relation to attempts to ensure that the contest between batting and bowling remained relatively even.

Although the initial codification of cricket took place in the early to mid-eighteenth century, Sandiford (1994: 128) argues that the game cannot be said to have assumed its 'modern character' until 1864, the year in which overarm bowling was legitimized. In the early years of cricket the bowling of the ball along the ground in a fashion similar to modern bowls, was replaced by 'lob bowling'. The influential cricket historian, the Revd Pycroft, writing in 1851, recalled that under these relatively genteel conditions:

> the principle [sic] injuries sustained [by batters] are in the fingers . . . The old players in the days of underhand bowling played without gloves; and Bennett assured me he had seen Tom Walker [see below – DM], before advancing civilisation made man tender, rub his bleeding fingers in the dust . . . [Now, however], with a good pair of cricket gloves no man need think much about his fingers; albeit flesh will blacken, joints will grow too large for the accustomed ring, and finger nails will come off.
>
> (cited in Rae 2001: 86)

During the nineteenth century, however, bowling was revolutionized. Largely resulting from the innovation of leading batsmen who ran towards the high tossed lob in order to hit the ball before it bounced (also termed 'giving her the rush' (Altham and Swanton 1948: 65)), batting grew to dominate bowling and games became increasingly protracted. Bowlers responded accordingly. Tom Walker, playing for the Hambledon club circa 1788, 'made an attempt to introduce the new "throwing" style' but was censored by senior members of the club (Altham and Swanton 1948: 65–6). But it was John Willes in particular who was in the vanguard of these developments. The former Surrey player, W.W. Read (1898: 86–7) cites a report of a match held on 20 July 1807 which appeared in the Morning Herald, in which it is claimed that, the 'straight-armed bowling, introduced by J. Willes Esq. was generally practised in the game'. But, as the Morning Herald continues:

> Mr Willes and his bowling were frequently barred in making a match and he played sometimes amid much uproar and confusion. Still he would persevere until 'the ring' closed in on the players, the stumps were pulled up and all came to a standstill.
>
> (Pycroft cited in Birley 1999: 64)[4]

The issue of Willes's bowling came to a head in 1822 when, opening the bowling for Kent against the Marylebone Cricket Club (MCC), Willes was no-balled,[5] 'threw down the ball in disgust, jumped on his horse, and rode away out of Lord's and out of cricket history' (Altham and Swanton 1948: 66). Though admittedly speculative, Birley (1999: 64) claims that it was Lord Fredrick Beauclerk (perhaps the most influential aristocrat cricketer of his day and subsequently MCC president) who had persuaded the umpire to no-ball Willes.

The response to Willes's actions can only be understood within the broader structure of power relations in eighteenth-century cricket. The MCC made the laws (rules) and was largely content with the dominance of batting; their membership, consisting of predominantly upper-class amateur batsmen, stood to gain most from this trend. It was the professionals, often the employees of MCC members, who bowled and whose livelihoods depended on results. Thus, despite their relative lack of formal influence, professional bowlers had much to gain from pursuing new bowling techniques. They were, effectively, seeking to improve their market position in the face of harsher times (improved batting techniques, better prepared, more even, pitches). Two Sussex professionals, William Lillywhite and James Broadbridge, became the leading proponents of the new style: 'Where Willes could be dismissed as an eccentric amateur, here were two professionals clearly determined to take bowling on to a new level of proficiency' (Rae 2001: 100).

So successful was Lillywhite that he became known as the '*Non pareil*' and Sussex became the leading side in the country. That various players deployed roundarm bowling, despite its formal illegality, demonstrates the relatively limited authority of the MCC at this time. Whilst defeated opponents objected to their methods, Lillywhite and Broadbridge had an influential ally in G.T. Knight, a leading MCC member who was himself a roundarm bowler. After trying, and failing, to invoke a change in the laws, Knight persuaded the MCC president, H. Kingscote, to sanction three 'experimental matches' between Sussex and All England in 1827. After Sussex won the first two, the nine All England professionals (indicating that this was no straight batsmen–bowler, amateur–professional, class conflict) refused to play the final match, unless the Sussex bowlers 'abstain from throwing' (Altham and Swanton 1948: 67). The side was altered (the batting strengthened by the inclusion of two further amateurs), and with Knight's roundarm bowling particularly successful, the All England team secured victory in the final match.

The experimental matches provided no solution but Knight, through a series of letters to *The Sporting Magazine* in 1827–8, continued to set out the case for legitimating roundarm bowling. His argument was that the dominance of batting in the game was detrimental, that attempts to regulate roundarm bowling had continually failed because of the difficulties in defining what was, and what was not, a 'throw', and that other proposals to correct the imbalance between bat and ball (such as increasing the size of the wicket), would be retrograde steps. Furthermore, he claimed that this style of bowling was not at all new, that historical precedent existed (citing Tom Walker of Hambledon as one example) and, finally, that there was nothing to fear about the new style, because it 'makes it quite impossible to bowl fast and dangerously'. Mr Denison, replying for the MCC, stated that the change would lead to scientific play being replaced by chance hits, that the new style was throwing, 'pure and simple', and finally that 'It must lead to a dangerous pace, such as cannot be faced on hard grounds, save at the most imminent peril'.[6] The MCC resisted this particular challenge and modified Law X to clarify the existing position (Rait Kerr 1950: 76). Yet, in the face of the rising power of professionals in the game (though this is not to say that either the professionals or the amateurs acted in unison), the law was altered in 1835, 'legitimizing any ball not thrown or jerked in which the hand or arm did not go above the shoulder' (Birley 1999: 67).

A major unintended consequence of this law change, however, was that bowlers were effectively granted further licence to innovate. William Lillywhite experimented by raising his hand higher and higher and continued to dominate games and inflict injuries but such was Lillywhite's reputation, and his economic power as a cricketer spectators would pay to see, that few umpires were prepared to declare his style illegal. As leading umpire William Caldecott noted, '[umpires] thought that what Lillywhite did must be right . . . it was cruel to see how he would rattle either the knuckles or the stumps' (Brookes 1978: 95). Not surprisingly, others followed Lillywhite's lead.

During the 29-year period between the legalization of first roundarm and then overarm bowling, the Laws of cricket were regularly altered in both overt and covert attacks on new styles of bowling (see Rait Kerr 1950: 32). In 1845 Law X was reformulated allowing umpires to call 'no ball' whenever the bowler came *so close* to infringing that the umpire had doubts about the ball's legality. Penalties for no balls and wides began to be accredited to the bowler and leg byes were introduced in an attempt to curb bowlers' zeal.[7] The LBW laws[8] were revised so that, for the batter to be out, the ball had to pitch in a straight line between the wickets (restricting roundarm bowlers' chances of obtaining such a dismissal). Finally, in a move which might be seen as an attempt to swing the balance back towards the batter, attempts to improve the quality of the playing surface continued to be made (Malcolm 2002: 49–51).

This period was also notable for the development of professional touring teams such as William Clarke's All England XI. Matches were often one-sided affairs and Clarke's two fast bowlers, George 'Tear 'em' Tarrant and John 'the Demon' Jackson regularly intimidated the opposition. Tarrant's bouncers 'frighten[ed] timid batsmen . . . causing them to change colour and funk at the next straight one', while Jackson would bowl a 'deliberate head high full-toss' to batsmen who scored runs off his bowling (cited in Rae 2001: 88–9). But as unequal as these contests may have been, the issue of legitimate and illegitimate bowling did not resume centre stage until August 1862 when Edgar Willsher opened the bowling for All England against Surrey at the Oval. As Willsher, a professional with Kent, began his third over, he was no-balled by the umpire. His following five balls were also no-balled at which point he, and the eight other All England professionals, walked off the pitch (the two amateurs remained). Play was abandoned for the day but, presumably following overnight discussions, the game resumed the following morning, with the 'offending' umpire replaced.

This incident led to considerable debate in the press, an MCC vote to retain the existing laws 12 months later, and finally the revision of the law in June 1864. In the decisive meeting, R.A. Fitzgerald, Secretary of the MCC, opposed any rule change because he considered that 'high bowling' had led to high scores and a *lowering* of the general standard of bowling. Among those in favour of alteration were the Hon. F.S. Ponsonby who argued that the existing law was not, and could not be, enforced. Moreover, he noted that while some people were concerned that a change in the law might lead to greater dangers to the batsmen, greater care of the pitches could reduce these problems (*The Times*, 11 June 1864). The amendment was passed 27 to 20, 'amid much cheering', though in Birley's view, 'the belated relaxation of Law X had changed nothing' (1999: 101).

These bowling innovations could, on the one hand, be interpreted as a shift in the balance between affective and instrumental violence of the type discussed earlier. The development of this style of bowling was characterized by relatively high degrees of forethought and planning. The social tensions in the game, heightened by the developing marketplace in which professionals took increasing control over employment opportunities, the increasing popularity of such matches and the growing significance of revenue derived from paying spectators, provided impetus to the search for new tactics and techniques. It is difficult, if not impossible, to assess the motives and emotions of participants in these developments but it does seem that these strategies were employed not necessarily to inflict injury or increase violent play, but in a goal-oriented (i.e. playing success) manner. Indeed, we must presume that the professionals had, as much as anyone, an (occupational/financial) interest in limiting the occurrence of injury; their protests during the 1827 experimental matches perhaps being an indication of this. That such innovations should have led to a style of play which, taken in isolation, was likely to increase the occurrence of injury, was largely an unintended outcome of the shifting balance of power between competing groups in the game. The rising influence of the professional class of players we might fruitfully term a process of functional democratization. Groups of varying power became more closely intertwined, more functionally interdependent, such that 'every action taken against an opponent also threatens the social existence of its perpetrator; it disturbs the whole mechanism of chains of actions of which each is a part' (Elias 2000: 318). In this context, Lillywhite and Broadbridge's interdependence with G.T. Knight is a telling example.

The international diffusion of cricket

As the nineteenth century drew to a close, the number of actors in what might be termed the 'cricket figuration' was to increase further with similar, equally wide-ranging, effects. Throughout the Victorian era, cricket had played a prominent role in English public schools with many arguing that the game inculcated notions of gentility and manliness. Logically extrapolating from this notion, educators and leading cricket administrators alike argued that cricket could be used to 'civilize' the people of the Empire and strengthen the bonds between the colonized and the 'Mother Country'.

Yet, as I have argued elsewhere (Malcolm 1997), cricket developed in radically different ways in the various territories of the Empire. Though the diffusion of cricket to the Indian sub-Continent, South Africa, New Zealand and elsewhere is significant in terms of the alliances and power balances which subsequently influenced debates, an exhaustive account of the diffusion of the game is not within the scope of this chapter and discussion will be limited to cricket in the Caribbean and Australia only. In the Caribbean, according to Yelvington (1990: 2), the history of cricket is a tale of 'the gradual supplanting of whites by blacks on the field and in society'. Initially, members of the military played between and among themselves. However, during the period of slavery, blacks had been encouraged to use what 'leisure time' they had 'constructively' and became slowly incorporated into the game. Whites in the Caribbean used cricket to demonstrate loyalty to the Crown, to show that the heat of the tropics had not led to a degeneration of English stock and (once slavery was abolished in 1838) to distance themselves from the 'uncivilized' indigenes (Malcolm 2001: 265). Yet, significantly, the white desire for success in inter-island and international competitions entailed a process of functional democratization through the increasing reliance of whites on black players (and black fast bowlers in particular).

In Australia, though Aborigines played an important part in cricket's develop-ment, British immigrants held the most powerful positions in the game and established the first clubs (the Military Cricket Club and the Australian Cricket Club, both formed in 1826). Here, cricket symbolized the cultural unity of the so-called 'Anglo-Saxon race' within the Empire, and early Australian cricket was highly nostalgic with clubs adopting English names (e.g. the Mary-le-bone Club formed in Sydney in 1832) and grounds designed to replicate the English rural environment (Cashman 1998: 34). Inter-city rivalry contributed to the diffusion of cricket and the elite schools, run for the sons of the colonial gentry, aspired to develop boys' manly virtues through the game. As in the Caribbean, playing cricket served to demonstrate loyalty to the Empire and the continued strength and vigour of white men in hot climates (see Bale 2002 for a broader discussion of the influence of notions of 'environmental determinism'). Victories over England supported claims for (a degree of) equality in the two nations' dealings more generally.

The global diffusion of cricket was an aspect of the lengthening chains of interdependency and the functional democratization of the Imperial cricket figuration. Though initially subservient, as will be demonstrated, groups in the colonies increasingly sought to challenge the right of the English to define the way in which the game is played. Moreover, this challenge had consequences for the relative levels, and types, of violence evident in the game.

Bodyline

Given the differing patterns of relations in the respective colonies, it is not surprising that Australian self-assertion should predate its Caribbean counterpart. It was during the winter of 1932–3 that fast bowling was again to become the dominant issue within cricket. By this time, cricket and cricketing issues were placed in the Imperial context, where '"progress" was measured essentially by success in British terms against British standards maintained by British institutions' (Stoddart 1979: 126). 'Bodyline' undoubtedly represented a further shift towards the instrumental use of violence in the game. However, a more detailed account of events demonstrates the contemporary tolerance towards/repugnance of physical injury and violence, and the importance of lengthening interdependency ties (in the form of shifting class power balances and developing international/Imperial relations) for understanding such changes.

Australia's victory over England in 1930 was largely attributed to the batting of Donald Bradman. Presciently the Surrey captain, Percy Fender, wrote that 'something dictated by the result of reasoning' was needed to curb Bradman, 'something . . . along the lines of a theory' (cited in Rae 2001: 120). That theory was initially termed 'fast leg theory', though Australian journalists are thought to have invented the term 'bodyline' to economize on their cables to England (Stoddart 1979: 124). The main English protagonists were the captain Douglas Jardine, and his fast bowlers Voce, Bowes, Allen and, most importantly, Harold Larwood. That fast bowlers used short-pitched deliveries (bouncers) in order to disconcert the batsman was not a particularly new technique, for players from various countries had done this since overarm bowling became legitimate. Moreover, various individuals on the English county circuit had intermittently employed the kind of field settings characteristic of bodyline. Bodyline was different, however, in terms of the sustained nature of the attack through the persistent bowling of the ball at the batter's body or legs (or wide of the leg stump) thus restricting the batter's scoring opportunities, the regular deployment of five or more fielders on the leg side, the lack of compassion with which the tactic was used (e.g. persisting with bowling bouncers at batters who were visibly shaken having been hit) and, perhaps most importantly of all, because of the social context in which the matches took place.

Though the two nations were in the depths of an economic depression when the tour took place, the social significance of the games was such that record crowds were attracted. With England set to take a two to one lead in the best of five test match series, and with the Australian public becoming particularly enraged when wicketkeeper (i.e. not a specialist batter) Bertie Oldfield was hit by a Larwood bouncer, the Australian Board of Control sent a telegram to the MCC. Bodyline, they claimed, '[made] protection of the body by the batsman the main consideration. This is causing intensely bitter feeling between the players as well as injury. In our opinion it is unsportsmanlike' (reported in *Wisden* 1934: 328).[9] The MCC defended their team but offered the Australians the option of cancelling the tour. Jardine insisted that the accusation 'unsportsmanlike' be retracted, which it was (reluctantly) on the first morning of the next match. England went on to win the series four games to one.

The planning that lay behind the development of bodyline is symptomatic of the high degree of forethought characteristic of sport in relatively civilized societies. That the English sought to use the neutral term 'fast leg theory' demonstrates an attempt to underplay violent and physically injurious aspects (similar, perhaps, to the desire to push acts of a repugnant nature 'behind the scenes' which Elias (2000) identified). Indeed, Larwood always claimed that his bowling did not cause injury and was, in fact, less dangerous than 'conventional' fast bowling (Rae 2001: 139). Counter to this, while the Australian media, through the adoption of the term bodyline highlighted physical danger, the official response of the Australians took a somewhat different tack. In the Board of Control's telegram 'injury' was a secondary consideration to the 'intensely bitter feeling' between the players.

Underscored by the accusation that such tactics were unsporting rather than irresponsible, violent or dangerous (that is to say, such tactics made the ball difficult/impossible to score from), and by the highly vocal spectator response, the Australians 'challenged the imperial tradition that Britain set the standards for civilized behaviour' (Stoddart 1979: 126). The stances assumed by the respective parties illustrate a delicate balance of repugnance/tolerance towards violence at this time. Larwood and the MCC (see below) recognized that violence was a central issue, but the Australians, owing to their subservient status, were constrained from identifying the injuries sustained as their main objection, as this would have undermined the very notions of manliness which they sought to demonstrate through cricket participation. Their challenge to the dominant group's status took the form of questioning the 'right' of the English to define standards of behaviour; effectively a kind of surveillance and pressure from 'below'. Following a summer during which bodyline bowling was widely deployed in the English county game, and by the West Indian team touring England, *Wisden*'s editor came to condemn bodyline as a 'noxious form of attack' (*Wisden* 1936: 339–40). Even Arthur Carr, Larwood and Voce's county captain who had helped pioneer 'fast leg theory', acknowledged that 'Somebody is going to get killed if this sort of bowling continues' (cited in Rae 2001: 140–1). Before the 1935 season began, the MCC finally clarified their condemnation of bodyline, declaring illegal 'persistent and systematic bowling of fast, short-pitched balls at the batsman standing clear of his wicket' and issued instructions to umpires on sanctioning offenders (Birley 1999: 251).

One of the key features of the figuration enabling this challenge to be made was the weakening of English dominance due to the prior playing success of the Australians and the functional democratization evident within English cricket. Douglas Jardine was 'an amateur who looked and played like a professional' (Stoddart 1979: 131). Although firmly rooted in the elite classes, and felt by many to be particularly aloof, Jardine assumed the behaviour and cultural mores of his social 'inferiors' in an attempt to realize his goal of defeating Australia. Tellingly, shortly after his appointment as England captain, Jardine met Larwood, Voce and Carr to plan their attack. As Birley claims, 'the version [of events] preferred by Australians, of innocent professionals manipulated by wicked amateurs, though understandable, can scarcely be entirely correct' (1999: 103). Neither would it be correct to view bodyline as the professional bowlers' challenge to the dominant cricket conventions as defined by the amateur-elite. Rather, the development of bodyline tactics demonstrates a commingling of class cultures characteristic of an equalizing of power chances within the English game, and the social significance that the test series was to acquire can only be understood in terms of the international functional democratization characteristic of early twentieth-century post-Imperial, Anglo-Australian, relations.

Beyond bodyline

Post bodyline, short-pitched fast bowling continued to be a prominent feature of the game though it remained a tactic largely used against specific, prolific-scoring batsmen. During the 1951–2 test series against the West Indies, the Australians regularly deployed bouncers to undermine the batting of the '3 Ws' (Clyde Walcott, Everton Weekes and Frank Worrell) (Rae 2001: 151). Similarly, during the 1957–8 South African series against Australia, one 56-ball spell of bowling by Heine and Adcock of South Africa included a total of 53 bouncers (Williams 2001: 128). Criticisms were raised periodically; Rae (2001: 151) describes *Wisden* taking 'its traditional dim view' of events in 1951–2. In 1964, *Wisden*'s editor talked of bouncers as 'one of the curses of modern cricket' (1964: 92) and two years later the editor reiterated his feelings, arguing that treating cricket like 'warfare' had led to various controversies, including 'the use of the bumper to frighten and threaten the batsman with bodily harm' (1966: 78–9). But prior to the mid-1970s, short-pitched fast bowling was rarely used against the weaker batters. There was commonly thought to be a 'fast bowlers union' – an informal, unspoken agreement that fast bowlers would not bowl bouncers at each other. The decline of this convention was widely (though not entirely accurately) perceived to have been propagated by the West Indian team.

A number of commentators have discussed the development of a neo-Imperial, black West Indian cricket style based on a mix of 'flamboyant', 'contemptuous' batting and 'attacking', 'violent', fast bowling (see Malcolm 2001 for a more detailed discussion). Despite the contravention of certain cricketing conventions which this style posed, for many years West Indian cricketers remained somewhat constrained to behave according to the dominant, English norms and to practise forms of self-policing. During the 1926 England tour to the West Indies, England bowled bouncers to the (white) West Indian captain, H.B.G. Austin. When the West Indies' Learie Constantine retaliated in kind and bowled bouncers at the England captain, the Hon. F.S.G. Calthorpe, he was implored by his colleagues to stop. James (1963: 111–12) recalls:

> 'Stop it, Learie!' we told him. He replied: 'What's wrong with you? It is cricket.' I told him bluntly: 'Do not bump the ball at that man. He is the MCC captain, captain of an English county and an English aristocrat. The bowling is obviously too fast for him, and if you hit him and knock him down there'll be a hell of a row and we don't want to see you in any mess. Stop it!'

Constantine also recalled the 1933 West Indian tour to England, during which he resented 'the blindness of some of our critics who professed to see danger in those balls [bouncers] when we put them down and not when English players bowled them' (cited in Marqusee 1998: 167). Twenty-five years later Ray Gilchrist was sent home from the tour of Pakistan and India for bowling that the West Indian cricket administrators deemed to be counter to the spirit of the game.

But despite this long history, events from the mid-1970s represent a dramatic escalation in the use of, and the controversy surrounding, short-pitched fast bowling. Although the West Indian team were to become 'the most vilified and maligned [team] in sporting history' (Williams 2001: 117) the origins of this phase in the game are more properly located in England's tour to Australia and New

Zealand in 1974–5. The English players suffered at the hands of a new Australian pairing of fast bowlers, Dennis Lillee and Jeff Thomson:

> Dennis Amiss and Bill Edrich had their hands broken; David Lloyd's box was, in his own words 'completely inverted'; Luckhurst, Fred Titmus and Derek Underwood all took crunching blows; and Thomson got a ball to cannon into the covers via Keith Fletcher's skull. Lillee bowled a beamer[10] at Bob Willis, while the bumper he bowled at Geoff Arnold was described by Jim Laker as the most vicious ball he had ever seen. Willis, Underwood and Arnold were all established tail-enders.
>
> (Rae 2001: 158)[11]

Some (though not all) of these injuries occurred when batters faced short-pitched fast bowling. England also bowled short and fast and, like the Australians, targeted the weaker batsmen. When the team moved on to New Zealand, debutant and tail-end batsman Ewan Chatfield's life was only saved by the rapid use of mouth-to-mouth resuscitation and heart massage.

These matches clearly involved a high number of injuries, some of them particularly dramatic. However, they also represented something of a sea change in tactics and (again) a new context in which such actions took place. First, it became clear that weaker batsmen were no longer to be spared from having to deal with short-pitched fast bowling. Second, in contrast to the general air of disapproval that characterized previous episodes of on-field violence, crowds in Australia took an active role in encouraging their fast bowlers with chants such as 'Kill, kill, kill, kill'. Third, as Rae argues, fast bowlers clearly became 'less reticent about their aggressive agenda' (Rae 2001: 149). Lillee and Thomson were particularly outspoken. Shortly before the 1974–5 Australia vs. England series, Lillee wrote 'I bowl bouncers for one reason, and that is to hit the batsman and thus intimidate him . . . I want it to hurt so much that the batsman doesn't want to face me anymore' (cited in Wilde 1994: 36). Thomson, in a magazine interview stated: 'The sound of the ball hitting the batsman's skull is music to my ears' (cited in Rae 2001: 157).

England's matches in Australia and New Zealand inspired the editor of *Wisden* to address the issue of short-pitched fast bowling in *four* separate pieces in the Editor's Notes section of the 1975 edition. A piece on the 'History of the Bouncer' was accompanied by 'Nauseating Remarks' which discussed the comments of Lillee and Thomson. Under 'Menace of Short Pitched Bouncers' the editor argued that 'Action should be taken before someone is seriously hurt'. Most alarmingly, in 'Bad Example to Juniors' the former chairman of the Cricket Society, Dr R.W. Cockshutt was cited as reporting that 'in one year [by implication, 1974] nine men had been killed in junior cricket' due to cricket balls hitting the skull (1975: 96–7).

But the use of short-pitched fast bowling continued and many (Swanton 1978; *Wisden* 1979: 80; Wilde 1994: 68–9) attributed this development to Australian media baron Kerry Packer. Packer, as a consequence of his failure to secure the rights to televise Australian test cricket, recruited players for his own, rival, competition. Packer glamorized the confrontational and dangerous aspects of the game through aggressive marketing campaigns, leading at least one commentator to describe him as 'the Godfather of fast bowlers' (Wilde 1994: 68–9). Injuries occurred regularly. England's Dennis Amiss stated that 23 batsmen were hit on the head during Packer's first season (Wilde 1994: 69); Ray Robinson (1978: 29), writing in *The Cricketer*, counted a mere 16 during the Australian 1977–8 season as a whole. Yet it would be misleading to place Packer too centrally in these developments for not only did this type of bowling precede his involvement in cricket, but it was also subsequently to become inextricably bound to the West Indies cricket team and the assertion of a West Indian 'national' identity.

As Packer's influence over world cricket gradually waned, the West Indies refined short-pitched fast bowling into the 'most efficient form of attack yet devised' (Wilde 1994: 10). Both Wilde and Williams identify the West Indian desire to shed the image of 'happy go lucky' (Wilde 1994: 51), talented but 'less cautious and more flamboyant' cricketers (Williams 2001: 116) as a significant motivational force behind this development. A key turning point, however, was the West Indian defeat by India in Jamaica in 1976. Clive Lloyd declared the West Indian second innings, leaving India to score what at the time seemed an impossible 403 to win the game.[12] But India achieved this score and calls for Lloyd's resignation soon followed. Determined to win the next game, Lloyd replaced a spin bowler with an additional fast bowler (making three in total). The trio repeatedly bowled bouncers, hitting the Indian batsmen several times. Indian captain Bishen Bedi declared their first innings closed with four batsmen still to come to the crease and had five players 'absent hurt' in the second innings, in what was 'the nearest anyone has come to surrendering a test match' (Wilde 1994: 55).

It thus appears that the shift towards the use of instrumental violence was closely connected to the desire for competitive success and the desire to shed the ('racial') stereotypical image of West Indians and their cricket. These twin goals, and the relative power balances required to enable such a challenge, can be more usefully understood, again, in the context of the lengthening and strengthening of interdependency ties entailing processes of functional democratization in the neo-colonial setting. The fast bowling of blacks has played a central role in the 'gradual supplanting' of whites in Caribbean cricket (Malcolm 2001: 264–71), and in the period of cricket history more dominated by fast bowling than any other, West Indian fast bowling was pre-eminent. From 1980 to 1994 the West Indies won an unprecedented 79 per cent of all tests which they played and won 16 out of 24 test series (Wilde 1994: 176). Furthermore, of the 88 batsmen who retired (or were absent) hurt due to injuries inflicted by fast bowlers in test matches between 1974 and 1994, 40 incurred their injuries while playing against the West Indies (data adapted from Wilde 1994: 212–14).

It is perhaps not surprising that these events generated considerable controversy within the game. However, the nomenclature of the debate is also revealing. 'Brutal', 'vicious', 'chilling', 'thuggery', 'vengeance' and commonly, 'violent', were terms that regularly appeared in the English mainstream and specialist cricket press.

The West Indian slip catchers became known as 'Death Row' and their bowlers acquired nicknames such as 'Whispering Death' (Michael Holding) or were referred to, for example, as 'a cold blooded assassin' (Malcolm Marshall) (cited in Williams 2001: 117). *Wisden* carried articles, pictures, or Editor's Notes commenting on short-pitched fast bowling in eight of the ten issues between 1975 and 1984 and thrice more in the next eight years. In 1979, for instance, the editor noted: 'In modern times, the act of deliberate intimidation to make the batsman fearful of getting some severe injury has become almost systematic with all countries, except India, exploiting this evil deed' (1979: 79–80). In 1984, the editor added 'the viciousness of much of today's fast bowling is changing the very nature of the game'. West Indian players objected to the implication that their success was 'based not on skill but on intimidation and brute force' (Holding and Cozier, cited in Williams 2001: 119) and, as the early excesses of 1976 were not subsequently repeated, we can only assume that elements of West Indian self-censorship continued. But the weight of opinion, led by English, Australian and Indian cricket officials, sought to curb the use of short-pitched fast bowling (and thus West Indian success) through rule changes and the deployment of new forms of protective equipment.

The bodyline controversy ushered in new laws to deal with bowling deemed to be intimidatory but, while umpires did occasionally issue warnings (e.g. against the West Indies in Jamaica and at Old Trafford in 1976), they were criticized for not exercising their powers effectively. In 1975 *Wisden*'s editor recognized the 'heavy and onerous responsibility' resting with the umpire and suggested that Australian umpires' failure to implement the law effectively during the winter of 1974–5 may have been 'because the huge crowds urged Thomson and Lillee to maintain their assault and battery' (1975: 97). The following year *Wisden*'s editor had come to believe that 'too much responsibility' was placed on the umpires and that 'responsibility surely lies with the captains' (1976: 63).

Support for the umpires eventually came in 1976 when the International Cricket Conference (ICC) condemned the intimidation of batsmen, urged umpires to enforce the law more rigorously, and insisted that test match sides should attempt to bowl a minimum of 17.5 six ball overs per hour (curbing a development concomitant with the dominance of fast bowling, which led to both an intentional – to reduce the batting team's rate of scoring – and unintentional – ironically fast bowlers take longer than slow bowlers to complete their overs – reduction in the number of overs bowled). The following year the ICC accepted a recommendation that countries could mutually agree to restrict the number of bouncers to two per over and not more than three in any two consecutive overs (Williams 2001: 124) but this, and a similar scheme introduced in 1979 (*Wisden* 1979: 80), faltered when players unilaterally abandoned their agreements during play. A 'bouncer immunity' scheme for non-specialist batsmen was tried but again faltered due to problems of defining which batsmen should, and which should not, be covered under the scheme and in defining how long the immunity lasted for tail-end batsmen who scored a significant number of runs (Wilde 1994: 78). All such regulations remained voluntary until 1991 when the ICC introduced a three-year experimental scheme that limited bowlers to one short-pitched delivery per over (defined as any ball that would pass over the batsman's shoulder). In 1994 the law was revised to permit two bouncers per over, a regulation which still stands and runs in conjunction with the rulings on intimidatory bowling.

Concomitantly we see the development of more, and a wider range of, protective equipment for the batter. When England played against Australia in 1974–5, players rarely used chest guards, arm guards, inner thigh pads, or helmets. Colin Cowdrey, called up as a replacement for injured players, 'had the foresight' to have rubber sewn into his vest (Wilde 1994: 63). In 1976 Tony Greig was pictured with a motorcycle-style helmet and *Wisden* reported that Australian players, 'warning that somebody might get killed . . . [are] pleading for the introduction of headguards' (1976: 62). The helmet eventually became 'regard[ed] as acceptable' in test cricket after Rick McCosker's jaw was broken in 1977 (Robinson 1978: 29). Shortly after this incident, Greig's successor as England captain, Mike Brearley, experimented with a skull cap (Wilde 1994: 71) and the motorcycle-style crash helmet was piloted in 1978 in test cricket by Graeme Yallop, and in English county cricket by Dennis Amiss. *Wisden*'s editor described the development as a 'sartorially and aesthetically . . . objectionable trend . . . Yet if their use saves cricketers from serious injury, they must be allowed.' Warning that helmets might lead to an increased use of bouncers, the editor concluded: 'The helmet, it seems, has come to stay – an unsightly adjunct to an increasingly dangerous game.'

Though it took a number of years, the rate of player injury did ultimately subside. The objections to bouncers, the concern over the injuries and the action taken are all indicative of a 'civilized concern' and a 'civilized intervention'. The players, for instance, did not want the scars, and so on, to prove that they were men (see Sheard, Chapter 2 in this book, for a discussion of similar processes in boxing). The West Indians objected to the new laws, perceived to have been imposed as a challenge to their cricketing style and success. West Indian cricket captain, Vivian Richards, speaking of racism and hypocrisy stated: 'I know damn well that there are people at the top of the cricketing establishment who feel that the West Indies have been doing too well for too long' (Wilde 1994: 195). In 1991 the *Caribbean Times* asked whether there had been 'a white supremacist plot to undermine the West Indies long-standing status as kings of cricket' (cited in Williams 2001: 125). Whether or not such allegations of conspiracy were true, the debate over short-pitched fast bowling during the 1970s and 1980s had a distinctively 'racial' dimension. West Indian cricket, and black West Indian cricketers, had grown in influence in the cricket world and their ascent was closely related to the neo-colonial assertion of a West Indian national identity. It simultaneously represented a challenge to the traditional balance of power. Thus, once again, we can see that an equalizing of power balances went hand in hand with a higher incidence of (predominantly instrumental) violence in the game.

Conclusion

This chapter has sought to address the apparent conundrum identified in my introductory remarks, namely how can we understand the development of increasingly violent tactics in cricket? For while we might say that there has been an overall civilizing development in cricket in terms of a shift from affective to instrumental violence, and indeed if we look over a number of centuries, even in terms of the overall level of violence in the game, there have clearly been some very significant de-civilizing spurts during the last century and a half. My argument here has been that because functional democratization necessarily involves a change in the established pattern of dominance and subordination, heightened tensions and increasing violence may, and indeed in the instances outlined here did, occur. Consequently de-civilizing spurts within the game of cricket occurred due to the equalizing shifts in the balance of power, characteristic of the development of a more complex, global, social world.

Notes

1   Famously Brian Close played for England against the West Indies at Old Trafford in 1976. As discussed in the following text, this match is widely regarded as one of the modern era's most violent games. According to England bowler Bob Willis, Brian Close (with his batting partner John Edrich) received, 'the most sustained barrage of intimidation' he had ever seen (cited in Rae 2001: 162).
2   As discussed later, roundarm bowling involved permitting bowlers to raise their arms to shoulder height when delivering the ball to the batter. Overarm bowling essentially removed all restrictions on how high the arm could be raised when bowling.
3   Bodyline involved the persistent use of short pitched fast bowling at the body of the batter, and the positioning of a relatively large number of fielders on the 'leg' side.
4   The idea of making the 'ring' was taken from boxing where it was used as a means of separating contestants from spectators (see Malcolm 1999).
5   Balls that an umpire decides are unfair are called 'no-balls'.
6   This correspondence is reproduced by Denison in his *Sketches of the Players* (1845), which itself is reproduced in Arlott (1948).
7   A wide – defined as a ball which the batter does not have a fair chance of reaching – was punished by the award of one run to the batting team but was not initially included in the figures that recorded how many wickets, for how many runs, a bowler got. Leg byes are the runs made after the ball hits the batter's legs rather then his/her bat.
8   LBW or 'leg before wicket' laws enable a batter to be dismissed if it is their legs, rather than their bat, which stops the ball from breaking the wicket and thus a batter being bowled.
9   *Wisden Cricketers' Almanack*, first published by John Wisden in 1864 is often referred to as the Bible of cricket such is the reverence with which it is generally held.
10   A beamer is a ball that is bowled directly (i.e. does not bounce) at the batter's head.
11   'Tail-ender' refers to the final cricketers in a team's batting order and thus, normally the weakest.
12   The current laws of cricket allow for a captain to end his/her team's innings at any time; a tactic normally used to give a side sufficient time to bowl out the opposition.

References

Altham, H.S and Swanton, E.W. (1948) *A History of Cricket*, 4th edition, London: George Allen and Unwin.

Arlott, J. (ed.) (1948) *From Hambledon to Lords: The Classics of Cricket*, London: Christopher Johnson.

Bale, J. (2002) 'Lassitude and Latitude: Observations on Sport and Environmental Determinism', *International Review for the Sociology of Sport*, 37(2), 147–58.

Birley, D. (1999) *A Social History of English Cricket*, London: Aurum Press.

Brookes, C. (1978) *English Cricket: The Game and its Players Through the Ages*, London: Weidenfeld and Nicolson.

Cashman, R. (1998) 'Australia', in B. Stoddart, and K.A.P. Sandiford (eds), *The Imperial Game: Cricket, Culture and Society*, Manchester: Manchester University Press.

Denison, W. (1845) *Sketches of the Players*, London: Simpkin Marshall.

Dunning, E. (1986) 'Social Bonding and Violence in Sport', in N. Elias and E. Dunning *Quest for Excitement*, Oxford: Basil Blackwell.

—— (1992) 'Figurational Sociology and the Sociology of Sport: Some Concluding Remarks', in E. Dunning and C. Rojek (eds), *Sport and Leisure in the Civilizing Process: Critique and Counter-critique*, Basingstoke: Macmillan.

Dunning, E., Murphy, P. and Waddington, I. (1992) *Violence in the British Civilising Process*, Discussion Papers in Sociology S92/2, Leicester: University of Leicester, reprinted in E. Dunning and S. Mennell (2003) *Norbert Elias*, Vol. 3, London: Sage.

Elias, N. (2000) *The Civilizing Process, Sociogenetic and Psychogenetic Investigations*, Oxford: Basil Blackwell.

Elias, N. and Dunning, E. (1966) 'Dynamics of Sports Groups with Special Reference to Football', *British Journal of Sociology*, XVII (4), 388–402.

James, C.L.R. (1963) *Beyond a Boundary*, New York: Pantheon.

Malcolm, D. (1997) 'Stacking in Cricket: A Figurational Sociological Reappraisal of Centrality', *Sociology of Sport Journal*, 14(3), 263–82.

—— (1999) 'Cricket Spectator Disorder: Myths and Historical Evidence', *The Sports Historian*, 19(1), 16–37.

—— (2001) '"It's not Cricket": Colonial Legacies and Contemporary Inequalities', *Journal of Historical Sociology*, 14(3), 253–75.

—— (2002) 'Cricket and Civilizing Processes: A Response to Stokvis', *International Review for the Sociology of Sport*, 37(1), 37–57.

Marqusee, M. (1998) *Anyone but England: Cricket, Race and Class*, 2nd edn, London: Two Heads Publishing.

Pycroft, J. (1851) *The Cricket Field*, London: Longmans.

Rae, S. (2001) *It's Not Cricket: A History of Skulduggery, Sharp Practice and Downright Cheating in the Noble Game*, London: Faber and Faber.

Rait Kerr, R.S. (1950) *The Laws of Cricket: Their History and Growth*, London: Longmans, Green and Co.

Read, W.W. (1898) *Annals of Cricket: With My Own Experiences*, London: Sampson Low, Marston & Co.

Robinson, R. (1978) 'Helmet History', *The Cricketer*, April 1978.

Sandiford, K. (1994) *Cricket and the Victorians*, Aldershot: Scholar Press.

Stoddart, B. (1979) 'Cricket's Imperial Crisis: The 1932–33 MCC Tour of Australia', in R. Cashman and M. McKernan (eds), *Sport in History*, Queensland: University of Queensland Press.

Swanton, E.W. (1978) 'Helmet Heresy', *The Cricketer*, August 1978.

Wilde, S. (1994) *Letting Rip: The Fast-bowling Threat from Lillee to Waqar*, London: H.F. & G. Witherby.

Williams, J. (2001) *Cricket and Race*, Oxford: Berg.

Wisden (various years).

Yelvington, K. (1990) 'Ethnicity "Not Out": The Indian Cricket Tour of the West Indies and the 1976 Elections in Trinidad and Tobago', *Arena Review*, 14(1), 1–12.

6 Baseball

Myths and modernization

Daniel Bloyce

Simple bat-and-ball games were played in the United States of America (USA) early in the nineteenth century. During the 1840s–1860s three games, Philadelphia 'town ball', New York 'base' or 'round ball' and cricket, competed for ascendancy. Cricket, already codified and well established in England, waned in popularity while, concomitantly, baseball emerged in a developed and refined modern form. In 1907, a Commission that had been established to examine the origins of baseball published a report stating that the origins of baseball were owed entirely to the innovation of a single American, Abner Doubleday, in 1839. While these claimed origins have since been shown to be a fabrication, they nonetheless constitute a powerful sporting myth, crystallized in the minds of succeeding generations of Americans, apparently wanting to believe that 'their' national sport was entirely conceived within the USA. Using a figurational sociological approach, this chapter endeavours to explain the processes underlying the development of baseball and the processes involved in the creation of the 'Doubleday myth'.

There are numerous accounts of the development of baseball but a significant shortcoming of this body of historical work is that many authors provide simplistic, mono-causal explanations for the development of the game. Prominent among these explanations is the argument that baseball successfully emerged from the group of competing bat-and-ball games being played in the USA at that time because it was 'naturally' suited to the 'American temperament' (Story 1989; Wittke 1952). Others have suggested, with a rather higher degree of reality-congruence, that industrialization and urbanization processes led to the modernization of baseball (Kirsch 1989; Seymour 1956). One object of this chapter is to demonstrate that in attempting to account more adequately for social processes such as the development of baseball, one should seek to avoid these kinds of de-humanized or reductionist conceptualizations. It will be argued that it is more appropriate to view baseball as developing from a combination of intended and unintended consequences which were themselves the result of the interweaving of the actions of large numbers of people in growing networks of interdependency. There is also within conventional historical accounts a tendency to write of the 'evolution' of baseball (Foster 1995; Voigt 1966, 1987; Seymour 1956, 1960) as though this process were somehow inevitable or 'natural'. However, a properly sociological approach emphasizes that the outcomes of complex social processes –

and the development of sport is a social process of some complexity – are neither predetermined nor 'natural'.

Little, if anything, has been published about the emergence of baseball from a sociological standpoint, and it is suggested that a sociological, and more particularly a figurational, perspective can help us avoid many of the common pitfalls associated with more conventional historical accounts of the emergence of baseball as a modern sport.

Folk bat-and-ball games

Many discussions of the origins of baseball seem to be characterized by a desire to prove that the game has a longer history than the Doubleday myth permits. In so doing researchers in this area tend to produce a number of seemingly obligatory early references to the game. Baseball, we are told, was mentioned as early as 1744. As Seymour (1960: 5) points out:

> Even the name baseball was known to both English and American boys long before Doubleday supposedly hit upon it. As early as 1744 John Newberry published in London *A Little Pretty Pocket-Book*, containing a rhymed description of baseball along with a small picture illustrating the game.

References to 'baseball' appear in numerous eighteenth century sources, most notably, perhaps, in Jane Austen's (1798/1990) *Northanger Abbey* published in 1798. Although Joseph Strutt's (1801/1969) legendary book *The Sports and Pastimes of the People of England* makes no mention of baseball (or rounders), many historians have noted with interest that *The Boy's Own Book* by William Clarke, first published in London in 1828 (cited in Seymour 1956), does provide a set of rules for the game of 'rounders'. According to Seymour (1956: 378) the 'great significance of these rules' was that just six years later, Robin Carver (1834, cited in Seymour 1956) published *The Book of Sports* in the USA in which the rules were 'reproduced . . . practically verbatim changing only the title from "Rounders" to "Base, or Goal Ball"' because, Carver argues, those were 'the names generally adopted in our country'. By means of this simple title change, Seymour (1956: 379) contends, 'English rounders became American baseball'.

This explanation is far too simplistic. The development of baseball, in common with most modern sports, is not only more complex than this account would suggest but, by reducing social processes to simple, mono-causal explanations, the most interesting questions about the development of baseball are ignored. Elias (1986: 152–3) makes this point in relation to the development of football:

> In studying the development of a sport, one is often guided by the wish to establish for it a long and respectable ancestry. And, in that case, one is apt to select as relevant for its history all data about games played in the past which bear some resemblance to the present form of the particular sport whose history one is writing . . . But, by thus treating the leisure activities of the fairly distant

past as more or less identical with those of one's own time – the 'football' of the twelfth century with the football of the late nineteenth and twentieth centuries – one is prevented from placing at the centre of one's inquiry the questions of how and why playing with a large, leather ball [bat and ball with 'bases' in our scenario – DB] grew into this particular form? One is prevented from asking how and why the particular rules and conventions developed which now determine the conduct of players when they play the game and without which the game would not be 'football' [or 'baseball' – DB] in our sense of the word. Or how and why the particular forms of organization developed which provided the most immediate framework for the growth of such rules and without which they could not be maintained and controlled.

It is impossible to be as exact about the origins of baseball as, for instance, Seymour would suggest; indeed to embark on a search for such precision would be misguided. Rather, a more adequate explanation would suggest that baseball, in its 'modern' form, was derived from a number of interdependent sources and from an amalgamation of a number of different folk bat-and-ball games.

Rudimentary bat-and-ball games were played throughout much of the USA during the early decades of the nineteenth century. Folk games with slight regional variations in terms of name and regulations, such as 'Barn ball', 'Base ball', 'Cat ball', 'Goal ball', 'Round ball' and 'Town ball', were all played around this time (Foster 1995; Guttmann 1978; Henderson 1947; Kirsch 1989; Riess 1977; Seymour 1956, 1960; Voigt 1966, 1976, 1987). It is likely that these games, to varying degrees, had their origins in already existing simple bat-and-ball games played in the USA and beyond. As mentioned, several commentators have noted the strong links that these games had with rounders (Guttmann 1978; Henderson 1947; Riess 1977; Salvatore 1983; Seymour 1956), a game popular in Britain at this time. The influence that the emerging British sports forms had on the rest of the world in the eighteenth, nineteenth and early twentieth centuries is well established (see, for example, Galtung 1984; Guttmann 1994; Houlihan 1994; Maguire 1999; Waddington and Roderick 1996) and, while the primacy of rounders in this process is not certain, it does seem likely that British people, developing closer ties with the USA on a broad range of fronts, introduced the game, along with a variety of other, similar, bat-and-ball games to America. At this time, however, these bat-and-ball games remained very basic. Rules were not yet standardized or codified and, as Foster notes, 'informality prevailed' (1995: 45). Indeed, it was not until the 1830s that we see the emergence of more explicitly codified bat-and-ball games in the USA, particularly in the northeastern states; it is impossible to date the beginnings of this process more precisely. However, what we can say with some certainty is that during the 1830s, the rules for a variety of bat-and-ball games became more formalized, began to be committed to written form and that the games themselves became more organized.

Prominent among this group of imported bat-and-ball games was cricket, a sport also introduced by the British (and most particularly, the English) residing in the USA at this time. Kirsch (1989: 21) notes that 'several groups in the Albany (N.Y.)

vicinity played earlier formal matches, but the St. George Cricket Club of Manhattan, founded in 1838, claimed to be the first regular outfit governed by rules and regulations'. Those participating in cricket were largely first-generation Englishmen living in the USA. In addition, folk bat-and-ball games like town ball and cat ball, which were already popular among the urban 'naturalized' working classes in New Jersey and New York, were increasingly taken up by the middle classes. According to Kirsch (1989: 56), the 'majority of these sportsmen were prosperous . . . middle-class merchants, bankers, doctors, lawyers, clerks, and other white-collar workers'. In other words, these games had begun to undergo what Dunning (1975) has described as a process of embourgeoisement. The introduction of organized cricket, together with the increasing numbers of middle-class Americans participating in various folk bat-and-ball games, were the first indicators of the increasing standardization of the rules and regulations in these games (Kirsch 1989: 53). Developments were most marked in the northeastern states, which were concomitantly experiencing a period of relatively rapid political and cultural unification. A more rule-bound game of 'town ball', for example, became the established bat-and-ball game in the Boston and Philadelphia regions while, in New York, 'base' and 'round ball' were emerging as the most popular bat-and-ball games. Yet none of these games, in these forms, can be regarded as baseball as it is known today; rather baseball emerged in its modern form from the continuing development and refinement of each of these games over the succeeding decades.

The incipient modernization of baseball

By the 1840s, cricket was being played in various colleges and universities in the northeastern states. As in England at this time, graduates from the great American universities were influential in spreading the game as attempts were made to promote it throughout the USA. This was helped, Kirsch (1989: 24) suggests, by the 'geographical mobility and the willingness of the English immigrants to teach cricket to younger and older Americans' at this time. There was also a significant drive from those playing other bat-and-ball games to establish a single unified game that might compete with cricket for the affections of the American populace and there is little doubt that Alexander Cartwright contributed significantly by developing a game he called 'baseball'. Cartwright belonged to a New York club called the *Knickerbockers*. Members of the club found inter-club matches difficult to come by because of local discrepancies in the rules. Drawing on various existing game forms Cartwright, and a committee of men from the *Knickerbockers* club, helped develop a game which did indeed more closely resemble baseball as it is known today and committed the rules to paper. As Guttmann (1994: 72) notes, in 1845 Cartwright:

> drew up a set of rules distinctive enough from those of earlier games for us to say that the activity . . . was *baseball* and not rounders or town ball or 'cat' or any one of a number of other traditional bat-and-ball games whose origins can be traced back to medieval times [emphasis in original].

Some historians go as far as to suggest that, through this endeavour, Cartwright invented baseball (McCulloch 1995; Nemec 1990; Salvatore 1983). Nemec (1990: 62) suggests that 'Alexander Cartwright was the true inventor of baseball'. Similarly McCulloch (1995: 2), while correctly asserting, with reference to Abner Doubleday (more on this 'myth' will be outlined later), that 'no one person invented baseball', continues in somewhat contradictory fashion to promote Alexander Cartwright as 'truly the man who gave us baseball' (1995: 141). McCulloch (1995: 21) further eulogizes Cartwright by suggesting that he 'should be regarded as one of the great American innovators of all time, ranked up there with Edison, Bell and the Wright Brothers; for just as their creations became a major part of our lives, so did baseball'.

However, while acknowledging the significance of individuals and groups of individuals as catalysts for change, their involvement is more adequately viewed as that of significant 'players' in a broader figuration of relationships. As Dunning (1975: 119) has noted in relation to football:

> Essentially what such individuals did was to systematize and unify modes of playing which had already proved themselves *in the crucible of the game itself* to be appropriate for modern conditions. In other words, they were *synthesizers* rather than *innovators* in the strictest sense [emphasis in original].

As Elias has persuasively argued, the development of modern sports from their ancestral pastimes is a *social* process or, more precisely, it involves a number of interconnected social processes which Elias (1986) called sportization. The sportization process involves, among other developments, identification of strict limitations on the number of those participating on each side, strict boundaries within which the game should be played and, of course, the development of written, set rules. These features can all be said to be fundamental to a sport with 'modern' characteristics.

The fact that the development of sport, or of particular sports, is a social process does not of course mean that such developments can be explained without reference to the actions of real people. It is however important to recognize that while particular people, or groups of people, may be more or less influential in this process of development, even the most influential people do not – indeed cannot – act wholly independently of others or, to put it another way, independently of broader social processes. Nor, for that matter, is their intervention usually as dramatic as some historians are wont to portray.

Although it might be argued that Cartwright played a greater role than any other single person in the development of baseball as a modern sport, this is not akin to claiming that Cartwright was the *inventor* of baseball. In this regard, some of the work of historians in this area does not properly locate Cartwright's actions within the broader social context. For example, certain aspects of the debate that are crucial to a more adequate understanding of the developments implemented by Cartwright are often overlooked. For instance, what roles did the various members of 'his committee' play? What were the main points of debate within the committee? Who argued in favour of which particular rules and customs used in which of the antecedent games? While it is clear that Cartwright and his committee acted as a significant catalyst for change it is not satisfactory, in explanatory terms, to suggest that Cartwright should thus be labelled as the 'great inventor' of baseball.

Although Guttmann is probably correct to claim that the rules which Cartwright drew up created a game distinctive from the folk antecedents that preceded it, it is also clear that Cartwright's dependency on these earlier folk games undermines assertions, such as that by McCulloch, that Cartwright may have single-handedly invented baseball. Foster (1995), McCulloch (1995), Salvatore (1983) and Voigt (1966) all suggest that 'Cartwright's rules' were distinctive enough for historians to accept that this was 'baseball'; according to Voigt (1966: 8), 'a twentieth century observer . . . would have recognised the game'. However, Cartwright's rules produced a game that still contained many features which, by and large, would be unfamiliar to today's baseball fan. For example, under Cartwright's rules the ball had to be pitched underhand, a batter could be given out if a ball was caught after the first bounce and the first team to 21 runs won the game. All these rules would be alien to today's baseball players (Kirsch 1989: 57). Indeed, as Tyrrell (1979: 210) points out with reference to the development of baseball during the 1840s, 'baseball's early condition was chaotic'.[1] Having said this, although still at an early stage of development (Adelman 1986; Guttmann 1978; Tyrrell 1979), the first remnants of organized baseball can be traced to 1840s America. In other words, this period and this place saw the 'incipient modernization' of the game. In relation to the incipient modernization of rugby, Dunning and Sheard (1979: 65–6) have suggested that:

> When written rules were produced for the first time in the 1840s, no attempt was made to legislate for the game as a whole; several aspects continued to be subject to customary controls. Similarly although the organization of football began in this period to grow more formal, it remained for some time a purely local game; i.e. national rules were still some distance in the future.

Baseball went through a similar period of transition. Local discrepancies in the interpretation of certain laws continued. The game played in the New York area under the Cartwright laws, for instance, was still quite different from that played in the Massachusetts area, a game some simply referred to as town ball (that being the folk game to which it most directly owed its origins). But it was the game of 'baseball', as outlined by Cartwright at the *Knickerbockers* club, Manhattan, which was to diffuse most successfully during the next decade. In the late 1840s Cartwright travelled across the USA teaching his 'New York version'. His efforts were reinforced by the development of the kind of inter-city competition that Kirsch (1989: 59) suggests proved to be an effective 'means of popularizing the "New York game"'. The Massachusetts form of baseball also grew in popularity, thriving during the late 1850s, but Kirsch (1989: 56) has noted that 'it faced a formidable rival' in the form of Cartwright's 'New York City version' and that, 'modern baseball derives most immediately from the latter'.

During much of the 1850s, as in the decade before, cricket was still the most popular summer team game played in the USA (Kirsch 1989; Reiss 1999; Tyrrell 1979). However, towards the end of the decade, baseball, and in particular the 'New York' version, began to challenge cricket's ascendancy. Between 1857 and 1860 advocates of cricket and the various forms of baseball held a series of separate conventions, initially in an attempt to establish national organizations for their respective sports. The cricket conventions that were held dismissed the notion that a power base separate from the Marylebone Cricket Club (MCC) in England was necessary. The MCC had been founded in 1787 and was regarded as the most important organization for the control of first-class cricket in England. Although the game was growing in popularity among 'naturalized' Americans, the most fervent proponents of the game remained exclusively 'English' and this may explain why most people playing cricket in the USA wished to maintain links with, rather than challenge or supersede, the MCC. By extension, it also helps us to appreciate why there was a marked reluctance to 'Americanize' cricket, for many people held that such a process would mean that the 'game would cease to be cricket' (*Porter's Spirit* 9 May 1857, cited in Kirsch 1989: 30).

Since 1845, the New York *Knickerbockers* had attempted to 'establish themselves as the social arbiters of baseball, after the manner of the Marylebone Cricket Club' (Voigt 1966: 8) and, in so doing, had kept the game on strictly amateur lines. While this had the potential to become problematic as the game became increasingly popular among the American lower and middle classes (Adelman 1986; Kirsch 1989; Reiss 1999; Tyrrell 1979), 'baseball' enthusiasts attending the annual conferences had rather more pressing problems to resolve, particularly those associated with the existence of different and competing forms of the game. Advocates of the Massachusetts version of the game established the Massachusetts Association of Base Ball Players (MABBP) in 1858, as a rival to the authority of the *Knickerbockers* club. Perhaps fearful of the degradation of the New York version of baseball, the National Association of Base Ball Players (NABBP) was established in 1859, and utilized the annual conventions to promote the 'New York version'. Voigt (1966) considers that the NABBP was also established as a rival to the *Knickerbockers* club; that is to say, by representatives of 25 clubs who contested the *Knickerbockers*' right to be arbiters of the game. However, despite such internal divisions, the NABBP was certainly successful in promoting the New York game which, by the Civil War, 'was strong, growing, and known across the nation' (Kirsch 1989: 63). The promotion of baseball had been so successful that 'all of the New York City sporting weeklies regularly proclaimed baseball to be "the national game of ball" before the Civil War' (Kirsch 1989: 63). Kirsch (1989: 68) adds that the 'geography of the sport before 1861 proves this judgement to be reasonably accurate'. Adelman (1989: 289) agrees, arguing that 'while New York was the center of the sport, baseball was hardly confined to this area as teams were formed in numerous northeastern cities, a handful of Midwestern and southern ones, and by 1860 one club was established as far west as San Francisco'. Indeed, so successful was the NABBP that baseball appeared to have overtaken cricket in popularity by 1861 (Tyrrell 1979: 225).

On the basis of his review of late nineteenth-century American press reports of baseball, Furst stresses the considerable attempts made by the game's administrators to create the image of baseball as the 'national game'. Furst (1990: 2) suggests that:

> It was vital that baseball disassociate itself from the image that cricket had established in the press as the pre-eminent bat-and-ball game in America. It was argued in the press that cricket required greater physical courage and more playing skill than baseball. But as baseball matured the press sought to negate the idea that baseball was a child's game. It also sought to affirm that baseball was a 'manly game', as cricket was considered to be . . . The press also began to focus on the skill of baseball players as a means to affirm its superiority over cricket and to represent baseball as the 'National Game'.

Furst provides a good deal of empirical evidence, in the shape of numerous quotations and representations from publications of the time, to illustrate that those largely in control of much of the American press did indeed seek to promote baseball as *the* national game. In the years prior to the Civil War in America, baseball was proving more popular than cricket and developments during the war had a significant effect, directly and indirectly, on the fortunes of both sports in the USA. Cricket was to decline gradually during and after the Civil War, disappearing almost completely in the USA by the early 1870s.

What developments led to the gradual demise of cricket? Wittke (1952: 115) has argued that the demise of the sport may be explained by the 'instinctive aversion to cricket' which is held to be part of the American make-up. Besides being an example of psychological reductionism, this argument is wholly implausible. In this context it should be noted that Tyrrell (1979) has provided compelling arguments that, contrary to assertions from a variety of historians, the demise of cricket could not have been simply because baseball was a faster game; indeed the two games were very similar in speed and duration of play throughout the 1850s and 1860s and neither game form should be considered static or unchanging. Tyrrell also notes that the suggestions that the amateur stance adopted by cricket's advocates did not sit well with the vast majority of Americans is a false notion, given that baseball at this time was also steeped in a similar amateur tradition.

Guttmann (1994) and Tyrrell (1979) have argued that a major reason for the decline in the popularity of cricket was that the strongest proponents of the game in the USA were almost exclusively derived from English immigrants. This association tarnished the game's image in the eyes of the growing number of Irish-Americans and German-Americans. Furthermore, as Tyrrell (1979: 210) notes:

> Cricket proved more inflexible than baseball not simply because of its English origins, but also because the game had taken on an organized form before it reached American shores . . . When Englishmen refused to adapt the game in America, they were seeking to preserve a successful sport whose rules were already articulated.

The demise of cricket may in part have been a reflection of the increasing desire, within certain quarters, to promote post-Civil War America as a 'modern' nation. Cricket was a game regarded as symbolizing the 'past'; the 'Old World'. The events of the war dealt a fatal blow to cricket's prospects for, as Kirsch argues (1989: 85), the major proponents of cricket were removed from the sport, becoming heavily involved in military aspects of the war, whereas baseball had a significant popular base among those not old enough to serve in the military. In this respect, Voigt (1966: 12) suggests that the Civil War was a 'stimulating influence' that 'triggered a veritable baseball "mania" in eastern cities during the late 1860s'. He does not outline why, specifically, the Civil War might be considered a stimulating influence but, according to Guttmann (1994: 73), rather than hindering the diffusion of baseball, the civil war 'actually accelerated it . . . Thanks to the enforced geographical mobility of the war, soldiers and sailors from the Northeast were able to spread the good news far and wide.' An unintended consequence of the Civil War, then, was the fostering of conditions which enhanced the popularity of baseball across the USA. In 1867, two years after the war had ended, there were well over 300 baseball clubs located in 17 different states (Adelman 1989: 289). However, despite the growing popularity of the game, baseball was still only loosely organized (Tyrrell 1979) and hence we need to turn our attention to an examination of those social processes that contributed to the sportization of baseball.

The sportization of baseball

Tyrrell (1979) considers that after the Civil War, middle-class entrepreneurs saw the prospects of baseball, more so than cricket, as a moneymaking enterprise. This was largely because cricket, as we have noted, was declining in popularity in the USA. Where it was still relatively popular – in the Philadelphia region – it was played from an increasingly resilient amateur standpoint, something that middle-class entrepreneurs would have recognized as unlikely to be receptive to their commercially oriented advances. Tyrrell (1979) suggests that amateurism held little appeal to the growing numbers of people playing baseball after the Civil War; few could afford to play the game at an elite level without some form of payment. Thus it is perhaps not particularly surprising that it was baseball that became increasingly commercialized and underwent a process of de-amateurization.

Baseball teams had begun to pay their players, though not openly, prior to the Civil War (Riess 1999; Tyrrell 1979; Voigt 1966, 1976, 1987), and with games attracting growing numbers of paying spectators this trend continued. Baseball entrepreneurs increasingly sought to use the growing influence of the press to further promote 'their' game and, as Voigt (1966: 4) points out, 'the promotional myth that baseball was the "national game" had rooted itself into the culture' of American sports fans by the end of the 1860s. Reiss (1999: 12) also locates the game's rapid development as a commercialized spectacle within the context of 'such modernizing external factors as urbanization, economic prosperity, and transportation and communication innovations'. As Kirsch (1989: 16) points out, while all these processes were well underway in the USA by the 1850s, they were the preconditions for the continued rise of baseball in the 1870s. Furthermore, modern communication and transportation facilitated both inter-club and inter-city competition as well as the increasingly widespread acceptance of standardized rules. In accounting for this stage of baseball's modernization, Tyrrell (1979: 216–17) has suggested that:

> If industrialization helped to shape baseball into a faster game by restricting leisure time and promoting the work ethic, the process of industrialization certainly operated in other ways to promote commercialized baseball. Especially critical were changes in technology which helped to create the infrastructure of organized sports. A modern transportation system allowed the fans to reach the games and it also facilitated the inter-city competition on which commercial baseball in America has been built. Manufacturing industry made possible standardized equipment, while telegraph and later telephone provided a means for spreading the results of games and providing more comprehensive publicity.

However, one must be careful when analysing the impact of these wider social trends on the development of modern sports for, as Elias (1986: 151) argued, it is a common fault of many authors who claim to 'explain almost everything that occurred in the nineteenth century as a result of the Industrial Revolution'. While industrialization clearly played a significant part in the sportization of pastimes, Elias argues that this sportization process also rested, in part, on the fact that 'societies demanded of their individual members greater regularity and differentiation of conduct' and that this process was also associated with the growing length and differentiation of chains of interdependence (Elias 1986: 151). Although Elias was writing specifically in relation to the situation in England, a similar caveat is appropriate in the context of explanations of the relationship between sport, industrialization and urbanization in the United States.

This is not to deny that industrialization and urbanization, and the interrelated developments in transportation and communications technology, profoundly shaped the early development of baseball. However, it is important to avoid making sweeping, and often bland and mystifying, connections between industrialization and the modernization of sport without identifying more precisely the structure of the interdependency ties that were both enabling and constraining individuals and groups of individuals at that time. For example, and in relation to industrialization in Britain, Dunning and Sheard (1979: 66) have pointed out that 'at the "societal" level, industrialization led to a change in the balance of power between classes, more specifically to an increase in the power of the bourgeoisie – the urban-industrial middle classes – relative to the aristocracy and gentry'. The changing social dynamics that were an interrelated aspect of industrialization and urbanization processes – though quite different in the British and American contexts – contributed to baseball's growing social significance. The incipient modernization of baseball was, then, a broad-based social process.

In 1871 the first fully professional baseball league was established. The National Association of Professional Base Ball Players (NAPBBP) was created with little fuss, with few contentious changes to the rules and regulations of the former organization, the National Association of Base Ball Players (NABBP) (Voigt 1966, 1987). Baseball was, however, still only loosely organized. Playing schedules frequently proved impossible to complete, and players moved between clubs with great frequency (a process referred to as 'revolving' in the contemporary press), which some felt devalued competitions. It is perhaps not surprising, therefore, that a new body, the National Baseball League, replaced the NAPBBP in 1876. Albert G. Spalding – a prominent baseball pitcher, who had left the *Boston Red Stockings* for the *Chicago White Stockings* in 1875 – played a significant part in the development of this League, alongside William A. Hulbert who became President at Spalding's baseball club in 1876. Spalding had also recently set up his own sports goods company (Voigt 1966). Spalding and Hulbert, most noticeably, sought to unify baseball under a stronger administration. As Voigt (1966: 87) points out, 'uniformity was a major goal and was evidenced in such league decisions as employing a paid corps of umpires, adopting uniform playing schedules, standardizing the division of receipts and making players purchase and maintain standardized uniforms'. By 1879 the League managed to introduce a 'reserve rule' which effectively prohibited players from 'revolving'. These developments during the 1870s laid the foundation for the modern era of baseball (Reiss 1999; Tyrrell 1979; Voigt 1966). Of course, since then baseball, like all sports – which are, as we have stressed, dynamic social processes – has been subject to rule changes that have impacted on the game, but baseball as played in the 1880s unmistakeably had modern sporting characteristics. By the end of the decade, baseball 'had come to resemble the contest with which we are now familiar' (Voigt 1966: 208). The current Major League structure was established in 1903. Numerous attempts had been made to usurp the power of the National League without much sustainable success from the 1880s. However, in 1903 the promoters of the National League (set up in 1876) finally agreed to settle their differences with the most successful rival league, the American League, resulting in the end-of-season contest for the 'World Series' between the champion team of each league.

Baseball was, by some way, the most popular sport in the USA for the best part of 70 years, from the 1860s up to the Second World War (Voigt 1976). It is a sport that many suggest is particularly synonymous with the USA, partly perhaps as a result of the successful promotion it has received both in the past, and to this day, as the 'national sport' of the USA. Given this situation, one has to ask why, in the first decade of the twentieth century, did Albert Spalding, among others, collude in the fabrication of an 'origin myth' for the game?

The 'Doubleday myth'

Albert G. Spalding suggested in his *Baseball Guide* in 1878 that baseball owed its origins to rounders (Levine 1985: 112). However, Levine (1985: 112) suggests that, over time, Spalding 'became convinced that a game so fundamentally representative of American values had to be American in origin'. Consequently, in his baseball guide for 1905 he 'meticulously took apart, without a shred of evidence' the rounders theory (Levine 1985: 113). Undoubtedly, Spalding was an American chauvinist. His desire to promote a positive image of his country was often uppermost in his mind. That much is writ large in his 1911 publication, *America's National Game* (Spalding 1911/1992), in which he (1911/1992: 4) wrote:

> Base Ball owes its prestige as our National Game to the fact that as no other form of sport it is the exponent of American Courage, Confidence, Combativeness; American Dash, Discipline, Determination; American Energy, Eagerness, Enthusiasm; American Pluck, Persistency, Performance; American Spirit, Sagacity, Success, American Vim, Vigor, Virility.

In seeking to demonstrate that baseball was American in origin, Spalding, 'acting on no authority but his own' (Levine 1985: 113), established a commission to examine the origins of baseball.[2] A.G. Mills (the fourth president of the National Baseball League) headed the Commission, and was supported by five other prominent baseball men (Spalding 1911/1992). Seymour (1956: 370) noted that although 'rounders had been generally accepted as the ancestor of baseball',

> After the Civil War, organised teams had attained importance, and baseball evolved [sic] from a simple, primitive game into a popular show business. It had gained prestige not unmixed with American pride in having a 'national game'. Consequently, its devotees found it increasingly difficult to countenance the notion that their favorite sport was of foreign origin. Pride and patriotism required that the game be native, unsullied by English ancestry.

Yet it is important to avoid mono-causal explanations for complex social processes, for numerous other considerations were involved. Seymour (1956) himself highlights, *inter alia*, the commercial interests of those involved. Spalding's change in perspective, and his concern that the commission establish his 'American theory' for the origins of the game, cannot be solely explained in terms of his chauvinism. It was a decision, Levine suggests, also bound up in his desire to 'provide good publicity for himself and his business' (1985: 112). The promotion of baseball as America's national game, a game that unequivocally also had its origins in the USA, was seen as a useful marketing tool.

As Seymour points out, baseball had 'evolved' into a 'popular show business', and this process had a number of interrelated facets. Baseball, by this time, had long been established as the most popular spectator sport in the USA. It was also being played on a professional basis at the elite level. It became increasingly commercialized and marketed by entrepreneurs both within and outside the game. And there were those, like Albert Goodwill Spalding, who had much to gain from the declaration of baseball as the American national game. His company was already the world's biggest manufacturer of sporting goods by the time the commission reported, and he undoubtedly believed that if baseball could be 'officially' promoted as *the* national game, then demand for baseball would increase (Rader 1992: xi). The commission gathered hundreds of pages of testimonies from across the USA, although, as Levine (1985: 113) notes, even the American press at the time considered that much of what was gathered was 'pure fabrication'.

In December 1907, the Mills Commission published their report on the origins of the game. In the final report, the commission claimed that baseball was 'invented' by a late American Civil War veteran, Abner Doubleday, in 1839. However, it is now well documented that the findings of the commission were fabricated and many baseball historians refer to these conclusions as the 'Doubleday myth' (Levine 1985; Rader 1992; Salvatore 1983; Seymour 1956; Voigt, 1966, 1976, 1987). From a sociological perspective it is particularly worthy of note that the creation of myths around the origins of allegedly national pastimes is not a process unique to baseball. Similar attempts to provide individualistic and 'mythical' explanations for complex social processes have been made in relation to boxing (Sheard 1997) and rugby football (Dunning and Sheard 1979). However, as we have noted, sports are social products and it is not useful – or accurate – to see any sport simply as the creation of a single individual. Consistent with this position, it has been argued in this chapter that no one person 'invented' baseball. Rather, the development of the game was the outcome of a process of constant and continual refinement of existing rules and ways of playing traditional games, by many people, over many years.

It is germane to point out that, by the beginning of the twentieth century, the influence of the USA in world affairs, relative to Britain, was on the increase. Indeed, it is arguable that, by the time of the Mills Commission report, the power balance between the two societies had altered to such a degree that the USA had probably become the most powerful society in the world. By 1900, as Jenkins (1997: 147) points out, the USA,

> was . . . a continental empire, its cities and industries were already as large as those of the greatest European powers, and its political might was being projected overseas in the form of a new colonial empire. In a sense 'the rest of the nations' were already 'in our rear'.

The manufacture of the Doubleday myth, therefore, might be interpreted as an attempt by some within America to reject any lingering feelings of inferiority in relation to their former mother country. Several authors (Guttmann 1978; Reiss 1977; Salvatore 1983; Seymour 1956; Tyrrell 1979; Voigt 1976) have argued that the Doubleday myth was created because many baseball fans, players and entre-preneurs could not accept that 'their' national sport may have been derived from rounders. In this context, Chandler (1988: 24) suggests that 'it told Americans what they wanted to hear; America's national game was no immigrant upstart, but native-born, conceived and nourished only by peculiarly American ideals, and epitomizing peculiarly American values'. This assessment is, however, not wholly adequate. When the commission was first charged with the task of 'discovering' the origins of baseball much of the American press – and even most baseball enthusiasts – viewed rounders as its nascent form. It seems more plausible to suggest that gradually, on the back of the conclusions drawn by the Mills Commission, increasing numbers of Americans were happy to accept that baseball was indeed American in origin.

In 1939, the Doubleday myth was crystallized further in the USA with the opening of the National Baseball Hall of Fame in Cooperstown on the centenary of Doubleday's alleged 'invention' of the sport. Stephen Clark, a native Cooperstown resident whose father (partner of the sewing machine inventor Isaac Singer) had left him a substantial proportion of the $500 million fortune he had accumulated, was largely responsible for the establishment and funding of the Hall of Fame (Salvatore 1983: 67). As both Salvatore (1983) and McCulloch (1995) suggest, Clark had much to gain in terms of creating this unique tourist attraction in an otherwise quiet, isolated village. Thus the myth was created and maintained over many years, despite far more evidence suggesting alternative origins for baseball through a variety of intended and unintended consequences.

Concluding points

In summary, it is evident that several different but interconnected social developments contributed to the initial emergence of baseball as a modern sport, as well as its subsequent increase in popularity. The concept of sportization, it has been suggested, is a useful framework within which to organize the empirical data.

Baseball, like many modern sports, developed as a result of a number of planned (for example the deliberate promotion of the game as a single, codified variant of a number of already existing bat-and-ball games; copying various structural aspects of the game from cricket) and unplanned consequences (e.g. resulting from growing interdependency ties, the Civil War) over a long period of time.

The precursors of modern baseball were evident in 1840s America. In other words, the period from the 1840s witnessed the 'incipient modernization' of baseball. This was an unplanned social process, an unintended consequence of the social changes shaped by industrialization, urbanization, developments in communication processes, and the American Civil War. Continued refinement of the game took place over the next two decades and, by the 1880s, the game of baseball had taken on many of the structural characteristics found in the game played in the USA today. Driven largely by the unplanned, but rapidly developing nationalism felt by many Americans during and following the Civil War, as well as the more deliberate promotion of the game by those entrepreneurs who saw its monetary potential as a newly established sport that was ripe for alterations, baseball developed into the mass participant and spectator sport which continues to dominate the American sporting landscape of today.

Notes

1   Even Voigt seems to contradict himself in more recent work published when he suggests, in reference to developments that occurred only two decades on from Cartwright's rules, that 'old-time Knickerbockers of 1845 would hardly recognise the game as played in 1869' (1987: 21).

2   Again, as sociologists we might be well advised to be sceptical of explanations that portray human action in such individualistic, non-interdependent, terms.

References

Adelman, M. (1986) *A Sporting Time: New York City and the Rise of Modern Sport, 1820–1870*, Urbana: University of Illinois Press.

—— (1989) 'Baseball, Business and the Work Place: Gelber's Thesis Reexamined', *Journal of Social History*, 23(2), 285–301.

Austen, J. (1798/1990) *Northanger Abbey*, Oxford: Oxford University Press.

Chandler, J. (1988) *Television and National Sport: the United States and Britain*, Urbana: University of Illinois Press.

Dunning, E. (1975) 'Industrialization and the Incipient Modernization of Football', *Stadion*, 1(1), 103–39.

Dunning, E. and Sheard, K. (1979) *Barbarians, Gentlemen and Players*, Oxford: Martin Robertson.

Elias, N. (1986) 'An Essay on Sport and Violence', in N. Elias and E. Dunning (eds), *Quest For Excitement. Sport and Leisure in the Civilising Process*, Oxford: Blackwell.

Foster, M.S. (1995) 'Playing by the Rules. The Evolution of Baseball in the Nineteenth Century', *Colorado Heritage*, 57(1), 44–51.

Furst, R.T. (1990) 'Conflicting Images of Organized Baseball in the 19th Century Sport Press', *Canadian Journal of History of Sport*, 21(1), 1–15.

Galtung, J. (1984) 'Sport and International Understanding: Sport as a Carrier of Deep Culture and Structure', in I. Ilmarinen (ed.), *Sport and International Understanding*, Berlin: Springer-Verlag.

Guttmann, A. (1978) *From Ritual to Record. The Nature of Modern Sports*, New York: Columbia University Press.

—— (1994) *Games and Empires. Modern Sports and Cultural Imperialism*, New York: Columbia University Press.

Henderson, R.W. (1947) *Ball, Bat and Bishop: The Origin of Ball Games*, New York: Rockport Press.

Houlihan, B. (1994) *Sport and International Politics*, London: Harvester Wheatsheaf.

Jenkins, P. (1997) *A History of the United States*, Basingstoke: Macmillan Press.

Kirsch, G. (1989) *The Creation of American Team Sports. Baseball and Cricket, 1838–72*, Chicago: University of Illinois Press.

Levine, P. (1985) *A.G. Spalding and the Rise of Baseball. The Promise of American Sport*, New York: Oxford University Press.

McCulloch, R. (1995) *How Baseball Began*, Toronto: Warwick Publishing.

Maguire, J. (1999) *Global Sport*, Cambridge: Polity Press.

Nemec, D. (1990) *Great Baseball Feats, Facts and Firsts*, New York: Signet Publishing.

Rader, B. (1992) 'Introduction', in A.G. Spalding, *America's National Game* (re-print), Nebraska: Bison Book.

Reiss, S. (1977) 'Baseball Myths, Baseball Reality, and the Social Functions of Baseball in Progressive America', *Stadion*, 3(2), 273–311.

—— (1999) *Touching Base. Professional Baseball and American Culture in the Progressive Era*, revised edn, Urbana: University of Illinois Press.

Salvatore, V. (1983) 'The Man Who Didn't Invent Baseball', *American Heritage*, 34(4), 65–7.

Seymour, H. (1956) 'How Baseball Began', *New York Historical Society Quarterly*, 40(3), 369–85.

—— (1960) *Baseball. The Early Years*, Vol. I, New York: Oxford University Press.

Sheard, K. (1997) 'Aspects of Boxing in the Western "Civilizing Process"', *International Review of the Sociology of Sport*, 32(1), 31–57.

Spalding, A.G. (1911/1992) *America's National Game* (re-print), Nebraska: Bison Book.

Story, R. (1989) 'The Country of the Young. The Meaning of Baseball in Early American Culture', in A.L. Hall (ed.), *Cooperstown Symposium on Baseball and the American Culture*, New York: Meckler.

Strutt, J. (1801/1969) *The Sports and Pastimes of the People of England*, London: Firecrest.

Tyrrell, I. (1979) 'The Emergence of Modern Baseball c. 1850–80', in R. Cashman and M. McKernan (eds), *Sport in History. The Making of Modern Sporting History*, Queensland: University of Queensland Press.

Voigt, D. (1966) *American Baseball. From Gentleman's Sport to the Commissioner System*, Norman: University of Oklahoma Press.

—— (1976) *America Through Baseball*, Chicago: Nelson Hall.

—— (1987) *Baseball. An Illustrated History*, Pennsylvania: Pennsylvania State University Press.

Waddington, I. and Roderick, M. (1996) 'American Exceptionalism: Soccer and American Football', *The Sports Historian*, 16(2), 42–63.

Wittke, C. (1952) 'Baseball in Its Adolescence', *Ohio State Historical Quarterly*, 61(2), 111–27.

7 Game, set and match

Lawn tennis, from early origins to modern sport

Ian Cooper

This chapter traces the development of modern lawn tennis[1] from its origins in the latter part of the eighteenth century. Emphasis will be placed on the development, during the latter part of the nineteenth century, of a game-structure which was distinctively different from the folk games played in antiquity and medieval times.[2] Game-contests of classical antiquity contained a number of different features and developed in very different circumstances from modern sport. In particular they were based on a warrior ethos and traditions of honour. Elias (1986a: 126) noted 'the ethos of contenders, the standards by which they were judged, the rules of the contests and the performances themselves differed markedly in many respects from the characteristics of modern sport'. Evidence, albeit limited, does indicate that ball games possessing similar characteristics to tennis were played in the Greek and Roman Empires. However, they were held in low esteem and not deemed manly in these patriarchal societies. Similarly, winning and losing seem to have been of minor importance (Harris 1972: 80).

The development of lawn tennis and its subsequent popularity, both as a genteel garden party pastime and as a highly regulated modern sport, is located within the context of wider social processes such as the development of a modern urban-industrial nation state and changing class and gender relations. Specific reference will be made to 'sportization', a term used by Elias (1986b: 151) to explain the transformation of pastimes in English society into modern sports.

The early development of lawn tennis

References to a game possessing some similar characteristics to modern tennis can be traced back to the late 1700s. During this period the first serious attempts were made to play variations of real tennis both outdoors and on grass. Thus an early form of lawn tennis was in the process of development. Aberdare (1977: 19) cites a report by William Hickey from 1767 on a game known as Field Tennis:

> In the summer we had another club which met at the Red House in Battersea
> Fields . . . and consisted of some very respectable persons . . . The game we
> played was an invention of our own called Field Tennis, which afforded noble
> exercise . . . Our regular meetings were two days in each week . . . During

exercise we refreshed ourselves with draughts of cool tankard, and other pleasant beverages. The field, which was of sixteen acres in extent, was kept in as high order and smooth as a bowling green. Besides our regular days some of the members met every evening during the summer months to have a little Field Tennis.

This quotation indicates that the people who participated in the game were members of a private club and respectable members of society. This was also the case with the development of lawn tennis, as we shall see later.

It seems that, in addition to Field Tennis, a game known as 'long tennis' was played around 1834 and evidence indicates that a type of lawn tennis was played at Roxburghshire in 1864 and Leyton in 1868 (Heathcote 1890; Haylett and Evans 1989). Some have argued that technological innovations were important in the development of the game. For example, the lack of a suitable ball hampered the development of the game until the discovery of vulcanization by Charles Goodyear (Gillmeister 1997: 177). Schwartz (1990: 15) has noted that the ball 'had to be soft enough not to damage the grass yet have the liveliness imported to rubber, by vulcanization, a process only introduced in 1839'. Another important fact, it has been suggested, was the flat grass surface on which lawn tennis was played; in this context the invention of the lawn mower has also been deemed significant in the development of tennis.[3]

It is also conventional to credit one of two men with being the founder of tennis; which one is given the credit varies according to the sources consulted.[4] During the late 1850s, on the lawns at 8 Ampton Road, Edgbaston, Major Harry Gem and a Spaniard, J.B. Perera, experimented with new versions of the old game of real tennis. They played a form of outdoor tennis on a rectangular court using a hollow rubber ball which rebounded well, even on grass (Clerici 1976: 62). While many of the components of real tennis were discarded, the game clearly contained some characteristics of the older game and Gurney (1984: 6) has claimed that it was known as 'lawn rackets'. This would suggest that lawn tennis was adapted from real tennis. Reay (cited in Maskell 1963: 10) has argued that the game 'was, to some extent, a development of the medieval tennis'. For 12 years this game was played by Gem and his friends at Edgbaston until they moved to Leamington. Two years later, in 1872, the first lawn tennis club was founded at the Manor House Hotel in Leamington Spa.

However, it is Major Walter Clopton Wingfield who is more frequently credited with creating lawn tennis. The first record of his participation in a version of the game was in 1869 at Lansdowne House in London. Wingfield was aware of the leisure boom in Victorian society and that the lawn had become a favoured place for upper-middle class recreational activities, including the popular games of badminton and croquet.[5] In December 1873, Wingfield published a set of rules and gave a party to demonstrate and launch the new game he had 'invented'. In March 1874 he applied for a patent for 'a new and improved portable court for playing the ancient game of tennis' (Wymer 1949: 246). This was granted in July. Wingfield named this new game 'Sphairistike', a Greek word meaning 'ball game'. The game comprised elements and characteristics of a number of other popular games of the time. The United States of America Tennis Association (1984: 26) has noted that:

> From croquet and cricket, the Major borrowed the close cropped lawns which lent an air of elegance to those sports. From rackets came the scoring system, based on fifteen point games, and from badminton and court tennis came the net and the long handled rackets. The balls were a compromise between the fluffiness of the badminton shuttlecock and the hardness of the court tennis and racket balls . . . Sphairistike was Major Wingfields's attempt to capitalize on the craze for sports then sweeping England. Shrewdly attributing the wide popularity of croquet and badminton among the leisured classes to the out-door element of each and the possibility of feminine participation, the Major devised a lawn game which combined the attractive features of both games while eliminating the slow pace of croquet and the erratic flight of the badminton shuttlecock.

Whatever the claims of Gem and Wingfield to have 'invented' lawn tennis, it is clear that the development of the game can only be properly understood, as detailed later, within the context of broader social processes. However it was Wingfield who established the earliest rules and introduced the game to the upper echelons of Victorian society. As Holt (1989: 125) commented, 'Whether Gem or Wingfield deserves the credit as the founder of modern tennis is less important than the fact that Wingfield quickly saw its potential, publishing a set of rules and marketing the basic equipment in 1874'. His aim was to profit from the growing demand for outdoor games during this period.

This new game of 'sphairistike' or lawn tennis was an immediate success. It appealed to wealthy members of society and was soon being played in a jovial manner in private gardens all over the country. Well received by the press, *The Sporting Gazette* wrote: 'While admitting "sphairistike" to be a barbarous name, the writer wishes to pay passing tribute to the inventor of the game which adds another to that too limited list of pastimes in which ladies and gentlemen can join.' Similarly, *The Globe* noted that the owners of country houses 'have been at their wits end for some attraction wherewith to fill their lawns in summertime' (Haylett and Evans 1989: 11).

The game flourished and soon began to replace both badminton and croquet as the favoured summer recreational pastime of higher status groups. However, one feature of croquet aided the development of lawn tennis. The landowning classes had earlier cultivated their gardens to produce croquet lawns. For the wooden croquet ball to roll easily the lawns had to be firm and lively, also the ideal surface for lawn tennis. The indiarubber tennis ball in use at the time would not have bounced very well on soft and mossy grass. Thus lawn tennis courts can be seen, in part, as the byproduct of the croquet lawn. Haylett and Evans (1989: 12) noted: 'In a very real sense croquet had smoothed the path of its successor on the country house lawns of England . . . So lawn tennis, assisted by its own merits, made its way into popular favour with remarkable rapidity – courtesy of the game it was replacing.'

A second feature of croquet also contributed to the development of lawn tennis. Until croquet appeared in England most pastimes were relatively violent and masculine in nature and it was not customary for women or the elderly to participate in them. As Lowerson (1993: 95) has noted, 'Manly sports held one major defect for a leisure-hungry middle class; the requirement of physical fitness made them unsuitable for most over-thirty-fives and the sedentary'. However, when croquet was introduced, women competed with men more or less on equal terms. This characteristic, as well as the social opportunities the game presented to all ages and both sexes, was central to its popularity. Significantly, these features were also apparent in tennis.

Lawn tennis was, however, often not played in the precise form advocated by Wingfield. Participants recognized the similarities to other racket sports and improvised with nets, rackets and balls from other sports. Many variations arose in the rules and regulations of the game and there was no one recognized version at this time. As it was being played with nets of such varying heights and on courts of so many different shapes and sizes, sometimes it was hardly recognizable as the same game. Wymer (1949: 247) noted that those 'who tried the game laid out a court of dimensions to suit their gardens and varied the rules as they went along. The whereabouts of trees and flowerbeds played an influential part.' These variations caused more and more problems as the game flourished and grew in popularity.

Among higher status groups, the popularity of tennis began to have an adverse effect on cricket, the firmly established pastime of the upper classes. One reason for this was that cricket lawns provided an ideal surface for tennis and, as Groppel (1980: 4) noted, tennis was adopted by many cricket clubs in the 1870s. Players even dressed in the same attire as that worn in cricket. The Marylebone Cricket Club (MCC) was alarmed at the increasing popularity of the new game and there was concern at the growing tendency to play tennis on cricket lawns. In this context the MCC, already a powerful organization, attempted to take control of the game in 1875 before it could threaten the popularity of cricket. As Potter (1963: 8) pointed out, 'R.A. Fitzgerald, Marylebone's secretary, was determined that if it were to be kept in place the infant must grow up as cricket's stepchild'.[6]

One consideration that helped the MCC in its attempt to achieve early control of tennis was the fact that it had been claimed that Wingfield – who as we have seen had drawn up a set of rules and patented a 'portable court' – had not invented anything new but was a charlatan who sought to profit from his actions. Indeed, in March 1874 a letter to *The Field* magazine asked, 'Can Mr Wingfield's patent be valid if many people have already been playing the game for some years in their gardens?' (cited in Clerici 1976: 66). Clerici (1976: 66) also noted that James Lillywhite had published an advertisement in 1873 describing a similar game to the one advocated by Wingfield as, 'The New Indian Outdoor Game, more pleasant, more healthy and more fun than croquet'. There was also criticism relating to the rules of Wingfield's game and players began to alter and 'improve' on his version. The MCC, aware of this increasing acrimony between Wingfield and his opponents, suggested that they should establish the official rules for the new game (Clerici

1976; Potter 1963). This proposal was accepted by all interested parties as it had been the MCC Tennis Committee that had drawn up the rules for real tennis and Lords was still the headquarters of that game; indeed it was the same panel that established the new rules for lawn tennis in March 1875. As Potter (1963: 9) noted:

> The Marylebone Club and Fitzgerald had put the infant in shorts so as to keep him close to their apron-strings. While that may have been helpful for cricket it did little to foster lawn tennis. If Wingfield was satisfied . . . the rebels were not. If Wingfield's interest was financial as well as sentimental, lawn tennis' new stepfather had a monetary stake in the child, too.

The ongoing power struggle between the various parties seeking to control the new and expanding game of lawn tennis led to an occurrence which was to have a lasting effect on the game's future development. On 23 July 1868, the All England Croquet Club had been formed at Wimbledon, and by June 1870 had organized its first tournament. Mainly as a result of the development of lawn tennis, croquet had declined in popularity and the club began to experience financial difficulties. On 25 February 1875, a Committee meeting was held and it was agreed that, 'One ground be set apart for lawn tennis and badminton during the ensuing season . . . and the M.C.C. laws of lawn tennis be adopted' (Tingay 1977: 16).

The move was an instant success and the following year four more courts were made available for tennis. There was a growing power struggle within the confines of the Club and, after much lobbying, the name was changed to The All England Croquet and Lawn Tennis Club (AEC) in 1877. Much more significant though was the motion that:

> a public meeting be held on July 10th and following days to compete for the Championships in lawn tennis, and that a subcommittee composed of Messrs J. Marshall, H. Jones and C.G. Heathcote be appointed to draw up rules for its management.
>
> (Tingay 1977: 16)

Thus the first Wimbledon Championships were staged in July 1877 and won by Spencer Gore, a rackets player. Though the first, and subsequent, tournaments were generally acclaimed as successes they were not without controversy. There was still much wrangling between different factions over the rules and format of the game. A compromise was reached and in 1878 the AEC and the MCC met to exchange views and frame a joint code (Wymer 1949: 248). The agreed rules were predominantly the rules of the AEC and apart from a few modifications in 1883 they are still in use today.

The MCC thus relinquished control of the game to the AEC and this, initially, left the club secretary, Julian Marshall, in a very powerful position. Tennis spread even more rapidly throughout the country as individuals and associations developed the game under the rules laid down by the AEC. Courts were added to existing clubs, new clubs formed and county and regional championships instituted.

Significantly, groups started to join together to support and campaign for modifications to the rules. This led to a new power struggle between these organizations and the AEC. As the number of clubs and players increased, so too did the discontent towards Marshall at the AEC. Matters came to a head in 1883 when they challenged his authority by calling a meeting with the aim of forming a Lawn Tennis Association (LTA). It was claimed that the Wimbledon Club was no longer sufficiently representative of the country as a whole to remain the game's controlling power (Wymer 1949: 251). Marshall was sufficiently powerful to resist much of the pressure for change. He agreed to a compromise under which representatives from the various clubs would meet annually with him at the AEC to discuss their proposals and suggestions. However any proposals that were adopted at the meeting were still subject to the veto of the AEC, of which he was secretary. This authoritarian rule continued for the next four years until two critics of Marshall, H. Scrivener and G.W. Hillyard, resolved to challenge his authority again.[7] They sought the views and opinions of other club representatives and set about establishing an entirely new and representative organization.

The response was encouraging and in 1888 a general meeting of patrons and players was held at the Freemasons' Tavern in London. Here the LTA was formed in order to centralize the control of organized competitive tennis (Lowerson 1993: 108). Regulations governing the conduct of tournaments, international play and prize meetings in general were established. The AEC became a member of the LTA and Marshall resigned. However the Club did retain the right to hold 'The Championships' at Wimbledon. Marshall's strong personality earned him many friends and enemies and Haylett and Evans (1989: 15) suggested that:

> It could be said Marshall's lack of tact led to the formation of the Lawn Tennis Association. Doubtless such a body would have evolved in due course (although there is no reason why the AEC should not have grown into a world-governing body similar to the MCC), but Marshall certainly seems to have hastened the LTA's arrival.

The game soon started to be played overseas, though a detailed discussion of the globalization of tennis is beyond the remit of this chapter. However, it might be noted that the British Empire and trading networks contributed considerably to the spread of the English sporting ideal (Lowerson 1993: 25). Talbert and Old (1957: 27) noted that the game 'became popular the world over quite rapidly, largely because of its enthusiastic adoption by the British Army as a barracks exercise'.

This is evident in relation to the introduction of the game in America in 1874. While in Bermuda, Mary Outerbridge had seen officers of the English garrison playing the game with one of Wingfield's tennis sets. Before returning home she obtained a set and thus took the game back to the USA (Clerici 1976: 80ff.). Tennis rapidly grew in popularity and in 1881 the United States Lawn Tennis Association was formed. Unlike many American sports, which generally flourished within the educational system, tennis, along with golf, was associated with the American country clubs, which were established towards the end of the nineteenth century. The elite members of society tended to segregate themselves in these country clubs, which had a limited and discriminatory membership similar to the private clubs in England and other parts of Europe (Guttmann 1986: 96). Lawn tennis also developed in other countries as a game for the higher social classes (O'Farrel 1985; Timm 1981; Carlson 1988) and, significantly, tennis has remained a predominantly middle-class sport. Tennis was introduced to Brazil and India in 1875, Germany in 1876, France in 1877 and Australia and Austria in 1878 (Talbert and Old 1957).

In 1900 D.F. Davis proposed a contest between the leading players of Britain and America. However, as the game continued to spread, the Davis Cup, as the new competition was called, became open to all countries with a lawn tennis association (Trengrove 1991: 2). Tennis became an Olympic sport and featured in each of the Games from 1896 to 1924. Reinstated in 1988, the reasons behind the withdrawal of tennis and recent reinclusion of the game, particularly with regard to issues of amateurism and professionalism are potentially fruitful areas for further research.

As more and more international associations were formed there was a growing perception of a need for an overarching authority to control the administration of the game. In October 1912, the International Lawn Tennis Federation (ILTF) was founded to govern tennis throughout the world.[8] Its inaugural meeting held in March 1913, was notable for the absence of a representative from the USA. Each nation was represented by a specific number of delegates, reflecting its power and influence within world tennis at the time. With its pioneering role in the development of the game generally acknowledged, the English LTA obtained the maximum six votes and retained the status of rule-making body along with the exclusive right to stage the lawn tennis world championships, in effect, Wimbledon. However, the USA found this unacceptable and refused to join the organization. In their opinion, the Davis Cup fulfilled the function of a world championship.

In 1923, after much wrangling, the USA agreed to join the ILTF. The English LTA was forced to jettison one vote and the All England Championships were no longer known as the world championships. To satisfy the leading nations the ILTF raised the status of the tennis championships of England, France, Australia and America, which today are known as the Grand Slam Events. At the same time the LTA conceded to the ILTF the right to change and amend the rules, although it stipulated they were still to be printed in English (Gillmeister 1997: 192). Wymer (1949: 252) has argued that this was a move 'which did much to promote the adoption of the same code in every corner of the earth where the game is played'.

The development of tennis: the broader social context

In 'conventional' histories of tennis, reference is generally made to the roles of individuals, e.g. Major Harry Gem and Major Walter Clopton Wingfield, and to a lesser extent to the significance of technological developments, such as the vulcanization of rubber and invention of the lawn mower. However, while not denying the role of particular individuals or of technological innovations, the development of tennis cannot be adequately understood simply in these terms.

The development of any sport is a complex social process involving both intended and unintended outcomes of the interweaving of the actions and intentions of large numbers of people. To understand the complex networks of social relations involved in the development of sport, we have to move away from such simple explanations and ask questions about the development of sport and broader social processes. More specifically, we need to ask why lawn tennis, and indeed many other forms of modern sport, initially developed in Britain. This was the question posed by Elias (1986a: 128–9) when he wrote:

> What accounts for the fact that, mainly in the nineteenth and twentieth centuries, an English type of pastimes called 'sport' set the pattern for a world-wide leisure movement? Pastimes of this type evidently corresponded to specific leisure needs which made themselves felt in many countries during that period. Why did they emerge in England first? What characteristics in the development and structure of English society account for the development there of leisure activities with the specific characteristics which we designate as sport?

To answer these questions in relation to the development of tennis, reference will be made to a number of social processes including the emergence and expansion of clubs as an influential factor in the development of tennis; the relationship between the development of tennis and developments within the British class structure and, in particular, the relationship between tennis and social elitism and exclusiveness; and tennis and changing gender relations.

The industrial revolution and the associated urbanization of Britain, together with increased leisure time and the doctrine of Muscular Christianity, may all be seen as contributory factors in the development of modern sport. Prior to industrialization, sport largely consisted of spontaneous, unorganized activities played on a local basis. Industrialization was associated with changing work patterns, improvements in communication and transportation, urbanization and the emergence of new classes with more wealth and free time, all of which were in turn associated with the development of new attitudes towards, needs for, and patterns of leisure and recreation (Midwinter 1986; Vamplew 1988). In particular, industrialization was associated with a growth in the size and affluence of the middle classes, who sought to utilize their free time in a way which was both enjoyable and morally legitimate, given their ethics relating to work and self-improvement (Holt 1989). However, Elias (1986b: 151) noted:

> The widespread tendency to explain almost everything that occurred in the nineteenth century as a result of the Industrial Revolution makes one a little wary of explanations in these terms. No doubt industrialization and urbanization played a part in the development and diffusion of spare-time occupations with the characteristics of 'sports', but it is also possible that both industrialization and sportization were symptomatic of a deeper-lying transformation of European societies which demanded of their individual members greater

regularity and differentiation of conduct. The growing length and differentiation of chains of interdependence may have had something to do with it.

Elias was certainly correct to advocate the need to be more precise about the
relationships between the development of modern urban-industrial societies
and the development of modern sports. Indeed, he pointed to some significant
connections between changes in the structures of power in English society and the
development of pastimes into sports.

The eighteenth century saw a noticeable pacification and domestication of the
English upper classes and landowning aristocracy. There was relatively little fear of
an uprising or of rebellion from the lower orders. The threat of civil war had abated
but the memories of the violent clashes still lingered. The political climate centred
on the differences within the landowning classes, between the Whigs and Tories,
who increasingly settled their conflicts by peaceful means in accordance with
specific rules and regulations. This pacification of political conflict was associated
with pacification in other areas of social life; as Elias (1986c: 34) has put it, the
'greater sensitivity with regard to the use of violence which, reflected in the social
habitus of individuals, also found expression in the development of their pastimes'.
The wealthier, landowning sections of society were able to link the pleasures of
rural and urban life together by spending time in both the city and country. This
may help to account for the transformation of cricket, which combined rural
customs with upper-class manners, from a summer pastime into a sport during the
eighteenth century (Elias 1986c: 38). It is also reasonable to suggest that this could
be extended to include lawn tennis, in the sense that it too initially developed on
the country lawns of the gentry and also appealed to the same sections of society.

A related development was the emergence at this time of a socio-political
configuration which enabled the ruling classes to retain a significant degree of
independence from the monarchical state. As Dunning and Sheard (1979: 269–70)
noted, this enabled them:

> to resist total absorption into court society and to retain a life-style containing
> strong rural elements with a heavy emphasis on outdoor pursuits. They were
> less constrained than their continental counterparts, e.g. in France, to
> participate in highly formalized, stylized and ritualized courtly activities,
> retaining the independence to use their leisure-time as they wished. Conse-
> quently, it was outside the context of the court, namely on their country
> estates, in rural villages and in the public schools, that the more elastic, less
> rigid, stylized and ritualized antecedents of modern sport grew up.

These limitations on the power of the monarchy in England meant that
gentlemen were able to socialize in groups and form associations if they wished,
which was in marked contrast to more autocratic societies where restrictions on the
formation of associations were imposed. A consequence of this was the development
of the 'club'.[9] Many associations were formed, some of them specifically for
participation in games. Often the organization itself was as important as the

activity. Selective club membership offered social exclusiveness for members and this was particularly apparent in lawn tennis. For example the Hove Select Lawn Tennis Club, formed in 1881, provides a very clear indication of its exclusivity simply by its name. Despite the obvious seasonal nature of the game, clubs soon began to function all year round, combining exclusive social activities and entertainment. Bridge parties, dances, picnics, dinners and concerts were all part of the social life of the tennis club and generally this overshadowed competitive tennis. Indeed, the high level of social exclusion associated with tennis created a barrier to wider acceptance of the game itself and, as Holt (1989: 127) noted, those who 'ponder the relative failure of Britain to produce outstanding players would do well to remember this'.

Within the clubs tennis, as well as other sporting pastimes, was usually played according to local customs, though the need for neighbouring clubs to have uniform rules if they were to compete against each other became increasingly clear; as Elias (1986c: 38) pointed out, 'One of the distinguishing characteristics of the emergent pastimes with the character of sports was that they were regulated above the local level by means . . . of clubs'. Thus, as lawn tennis leagues and tournaments were established, initially on a local level but then on county-wide and national levels, there was a growing perceived need for agreement, not only on the rules, but also on any changes to them that were deemed necessary. Agreement on a framework of rules at this higher level of integration and of the social customs associated with a game usually led to the development of a supervisory body which was responsible for adherence to the rules and for providing referees or umpires when required. This was an aspect of the lengthening of interdependency chains as more people in different localities took up the game. Eventually this led to the formation of national associations with the responsibility for the organization and control of the sports. Subsequently there was a need for international associations to regulate international competition as modern sports began to develop throughout the world. As Elias (1986c: 39) noted:

> The higher organizational level of a regulating and supervizing club endowed the game with a measure of autonomy in relation to the players. And that autonomy grew as supervisory agencies at a higher level of integration took over the effective control of the game, as when, for instance, a London club, the MCC, took over effective control of cricket from the country clubs.

A similar situation occurred in lawn tennis and it was in this context that, as previously explained, there was a struggle for supremacy between the various associations with an interest in tennis. The MCC was initially able to take control of the game, partly because Wingfield's position was weakened by the accusation that he had not actually invented anything new and that his financial motivations made him morally suspect. As the AEC became more powerful, it was able to wrest control of tennis from the MCC but was subsequently forced to relinquish its own control of the game to the LTA, a national association. With the diffusion of tennis on a global scale the International Lawn Tennis Federation was formed, and eventually the LTA was compelled to concede its status as the rule-making body.

Tennis and the participation of women

The participation of women in sport in general was the source of great conflict and debate in the nineteenth century. This was particularly so in relation to concerns about domestic disruption, physiological make up and the extent to which codes of social etiquette would be affected by an open mingling of the sexes, which was a common occurrence on the tennis court. Incorporated into these issues were, as Lowerson (1993: 203) noted, questions of the economic independence of women, the movements for enfranchisement and the matter of private and public gender identities. It is not the aim of this study to examine the more general growth of women's participation in sport,[10] but to examine more specifically the participation of women in tennis. However, it is necessary to preface this analysis with a brief comment on women's participation in sport and exercise in the nineteenth century.

During this period women's exercise was monitored and regulated (Mangan 1989) and feminine demeanour was insisted on, particularly among the upper and middle classes. In their sporting activities, which were usually held away from public view, women were obliged to show restraint, be refined and respectable and behave in what was considered a 'ladylike' manner. With very few exceptions, men's and women's sports remained strictly segregated. In addition women's participation in sport was severely restricted by the patriarchal nature of social relations. Only those sporting activities and behaviour which were considered feminine, which did not conflict with established norms concerning gender and which legitimated the male dominated social structure were considered acceptable (McCrone 1988: 13). As Dunning (1990) noted, modern sport 'emerged as a male preserve, a fact which helps to account for the strength of male resistance to attempts by females to enter it'. Even where women were encouraged to take part in sports and games it was for entirely different reasons than that of male participation. Lowerson (1993: 208) noted that:

> The sports held safest for women to pursue had several major factors in common: they required delicate skill rather than strength, they flattered bodily appearance, were suitable zones for courtship . . . and they were initially restricted to private property . . . They operated best at the overlap between gentry and upper middle classes, and allowed men and women to compete with each other because they were treated initially as games rather than sports. Performance was often secondary to other considerations.

Women found it much easier to gain social acceptance of their participation in individual activities as opposed to team games (McCrone 1988: 154). During the nineteenth century participation in these activities took place on private lawns and centred around membership of exclusive clubs. This eliminated much of the masculinity and competitiveness associated with the development of many types of modern sport, and it was also seen to be aesthetically acceptable.

Croquet was possibly the first game in which women's participation met with approval. From its introduction and development in England during the 1850s it became established as a game for both sexes, played on the country house lawns and at private garden parties. McCrone (1988: 155) suggested that:

> The revolution in individual sports for women originated with the game of croquet . . . To women of all ages in polite society croquet provided unprecedented opportunities to combine light, elegant outdoor exercise with flirtation and romance while necessitating neither strenuous exertion nor an immediate reform of female dress or images. Croquet was more than a charming leisure activity . . . It was of considerable importance to the physical emancipation of women, for it effected a major change in the relationship of women to sport.

The game was unique in that it allowed both men and women to compete on virtually an equal basis. Equally as important, though, was that it introduced women to organized and competitive sport at the time when rules were being developed and standardized. Soon clubs were formed and competitions staged.

As previously noted, croquet helped to ensure the smooth introduction and development of lawn tennis. Although considered more energetic and exciting in comparison with croquet, tennis was also generally deemed to be a socially acceptable activity for females. There was opposition from some people who argued that the game was too taxing and tiring for ladies, that it would tarnish their beauty by making them hot and sweaty, and that women would ruin lawn tennis by introducing an element of flippancy to the game. Badminton was thought by some to be a more appropriate game for women (Gillmester 1997: 202). In general, however, tennis was considered a suitable activity for ladies, as it offered a form of mild exercise in either an informal or competitive environment (McCrone 1988: 157). Generally women tended to play doubles because it was a less energetic game.

Tennis also had the advantage of not being seen as a 'manly' sport, which may help to explain why the universities and public schools played no part in its development, unlike many other sports (Harris 1975: 155). Tennis did become a minor part of university recreation and the Oxford and Cambridge match was initiated in 1881 (Lowerson 1993: 100). However, the game was played in the early girls schools including Cheltenham College and North London Collegiate School. Often informally arranged by the girls themselves, it quickly became established as the favourite game of female students. Inter-school matches soon followed and much more than the colleges' reputation was at stake. Indeed, the participation of women in the masculine world of sport symbolized the manifest changes affecting not only women but the value systems within society more generally. In this context, Holt (1989: 126) suggested that therein 'lay its true social importance. From a gender point of view, tennis was the first truly national game.' Indeed the first secretary of the LTA, Herbert Chipp argued:

Among the manifold changes and consequent uprootings or prejudices which the latter half of this century has witnessed, nothing has been more characteristic of the new order of things than the active participation of women in its sports and pastimes . . . Lawn tennis must claim a large share of the responsibility for the introduction of this new regime . . . Although the present movement may be (and undoubtedly is) carried to excess, and the athleticism of the *fin de siecle* woman appears too pronounced, still it cannot be denied that on the whole the changes which have been brought about must ultimately prove beneficial to the race at large – at all events physically. Whether the benefit will be as great morally . . . only time can settle.

(cited in Holt 1989: 128)

Ladies first played tennis in the seclusion of the private gardens in country houses and suburban villas, and then in exclusive private clubs. Initially it was a gentle garden party game which was an aspect of upper-middle class social life during this period. Played for fun, the privacy of the suburban garden or club provided an opportunity for polite courtship. Playing tennis was viewed as a social asset providing training in graceful and charming movements. Unprecedented opportunities were available for combining light elegant outdoor exercise with flirtation and romance (McCrone 1988: 157). Similarly great importance was placed on fashion, and women dressed in a very stylish manner, especially for tennis garden parties. In 1879 a ladies magazine recommended that an outfit should consist of a 'cream merino bodice with long sleeves edged with embroidery, skirt with deep fitting, over it an old-gold silk blouse-tunic with short wide sleeves and square neck' (Cunnington and Marsfield 1969: 92, cited in Holt 1989: 127). As the primary object of tennis was to socialize, appearance was put before performance. However as Holt (1989: 128) pointed out, the 'more competitive ladies gradually liberated themselves from the athletic idiocy of their garments'. Indeed, females as well as males regularly participated in inter-club tennis matches and tournaments. Tranter (1989) provides evidence of women's enthusiasm for competitive tennis and cites a number of examples including a ladies singles tournament for members of the Stirling Lawn Tennis Club in 1880.

As the game spread a growing number of private clubs were formed, often with mixed membership. The tennis clubs were largely limited to the social elite and admitted female members on virtually the same terms as men (Lumpkin 1981: 5). This stimulated the development of elaborate rituals and rules of etiquette that guaranteed courtesy and social segregation. Lowerson (1993: 98) identified that mixed clubs:

probably had far greater importance in determining social codes than single sex bodies. The management, especially in lawn tennis might be effectively male but the real arbitrating force was often female. Style, etiquette and petty naunces were especially important where club life became the centre or part of a wider social calendar.

One of the reasons for the initial rise in popularity of tennis was that it was an unusual activity in the sense that it offered men and women the chance to play together. Mixed doubles was popular as it provided an alternative means of introduction and courtship. For many years the female mixed doubles player was seen as poor and unskilled and more concerned with flirting than playing. McCrone (1988: 162) noted:

> Garden party 'fours' were the bulwark of tennis throughout the nineteenth century, while in clubs the mixed game was the favourite type of competition with lady members who considered it interesting to spectators and players, less fatiguing than singles and more exciting than doubles.

For the reasons outlined, women's tennis at every level was not taken as seriously as the men's game. During the late 1870s, when competitions were introduced and the sport became characterized by more formal organization and the standardization of rules, the style of play was affected, and this increased the gap between male and female tennis. Indeed the Ladies Singles Championship at Wimbledon was not introduced until 1884 and they had to wait until after the men's events before commencing their tournament. The prize on offer was a silver gilt Rosewater Dish, as opposed to a cup for the men's tournament. This emphasized the relatively low regard the organizers had for the ladies game. Similarly the AEC rejected a proposal to introduce a Ladies Doubles Championship the following year on the basis that it was not conducive to competitive tennis. The mixed doubles tournament also had an inauspicious early history.[11]

Lawn tennis was, then, one of the very few nineteenth-century sports that was considered an acceptable activity in which women could participate. It was seen as a means of combining healthy exercise with pleasant social encounters. Female participation though was taken less seriously and considered far less important than the male game. However, it became established as one of the first modern sports in which women could combine with and compete against men without it seriously endangering either's status. Playing standards improved as female tennis clothing became more practical. Ladies were still required to look attractive and elegant on court though and the dominant view was that they were primarily interested in tennis because it offered a chance to flirt.

Summary

This chapter has examined the development of lawn tennis and some of the reasons for its rapid rise in popularity. It has been argued that lawn tennis developed as a result of the interweaving of a number of complex social processes. The development of tennis has been examined by reference to Elias's concept of 'sportization' and the development of clubs, and in relation to changes in class and gender relations.

Their relative independence from the monarchical state enabled English gentlemen to form clubs and adopt exclusive membership schemes. It was within these surroundings, and particularly in the mixed-sex clubs, that the sport of lawn tennis developed. Significantly, and unlike the situation in many other sporting associations, female membership was common in lawn tennis clubs which combined tennis with other social activities.

Compared with croquet, which helped pave the way for its development, lawn tennis was an energetic and exciting game. It was a desirable social game played by members of the upper and upper middle classes in the seclusion of private clubs and gardens. The principal features of lawn tennis were that, in addition to providing social opportunities, it was physically a relatively undemanding game which lacked danger; this was one of the reasons for its suitability as a mixed-sex activity for all age groups, as highlighted by the popularity of mixed doubles. The fact that it bridged the gap between upper and middle classes and was a game that could be played by people of all ages and both sexes was instrumental in its development.

These unusual features of the game were influential in its early development for, as Lowerson (1993: 103) pointed out:

> The mere invention of a pastime does not account for its considerable national popularity by the later 1870s but the ease of clubability and social selectivity do. Its adoption and regulation by the MCC in 1875 and its elevation into a 'national' championship by the AEC at Wimbledon after 1877 allowed it to cover a spectrum of participation and aspiration which suited the needs of a part of the middle classes.

Notes

1   For clarity it is necessary to establish the actual names given to various forms of the game. For around seven centuries before modern tennis evolved there was only one game called tennis. The modern game has become universally known as tennis (or lawn tennis) and the old form of tennis is now usually known as Real Tennis (UK), Court Tennis (USA) and Royal Tennis (Australia). For the purposes of this text the term 'real tennis' will be used to describe the old game and the terms 'tennis' or occasionally 'lawn tennis' will be used to refer to the modern game.

2   In general, there is a dearth of material on tennis particularly on those games possessing similar characteristics to the modern sport played from the antiquity through to medieval times. The most useful literature on this is Cooper (1996), Clerici (1976), Harris (1972) and Noel and Clarke (1991).

3   The lawn mower was invented around the middle of the nineteenth century by Alexander Shanks and Thomas Green.

4   In rugby William Webb Ellis is often credited as being the founder of the game but there is good reason to believe this is a myth (see Dunning and Sheard 1979: 60ff. and Dunning and Curry in this volume, Chapter 3). However with lawn tennis there is adequate evidence to demonstrate that Major Gem and Major Wingfield, while not as such 'inventing' the game, were instrumental in codifying the rules of an early modern version of it.

5   It seems that badminton was developed by expatriate British residents in India and evolved from the children's game of 'battledore and shuttlecock'. It was first played in England around 1870 on the Duke of Beauford's estate in Badminton, Gloucestershire. Croquet was introduced in England during the 1850s and was adapted from the French game 'maille'.

6   The MCC pavilion at Lords, which was rebuilt following a fire in 1825, contains a real tennis court for use by members.

7   Scrivener was president of the Oxford University LTA and had been in charge of arranging the annual match with Cambridge. The dates clashed with Wimbledon and led to an argument. Scrivener found an ally in George Hillyard who had a grudge against the AEC and they planned to form an LTA in which the AEC would have a powerful, but not overriding, voice. Marshall rejected this but as they had the support of over a hundred representatives from all over the country they went ahead with their plan. Hillyard's resentment towards the AEC centred on its refusal to give up the privilege of holding the Ladies Championships, which had been extremely profitable. Indeed, the reigning champion, Blanche Bingley was married to Hillyard.

8   The founder members of the ILTF were Australia, Austria, Belgium, British Isles, Denmark, France, Germany, Holland, Russia, South Africa, Sweden and Switzerland.

9   For the relatively new sporting pastimes, including lawn tennis, a few enthusiasts would see or read about a game, acquire the necessary equipment and handbook, play it informally until joined by friends, then hold a 'public' meeting to form a club. A largely self-appointed committee would emerge, premises and grounds leased and a limited membership opened. There would be an entrance fee and subscription, largely determined by estimated running costs. Lowerson (1993) provides a detailed study of sporting clubs during this period.

10   For detailed sociological discussions see, for instance Hargreaves (1985, 1994) and Dunning (1986, 1990).

11   In 1899 a ladies doubles non-championship event was included but this was withdrawn after 1907. It was not until 1913 that the AEC restored the ladies doubles on an official basis. The AEC rejected a mixed competition in 1887 and it was not introduced until 1900 but even then on an unofficial basis. In 1913 this too became a recognized championship but the stigma of frivolity was difficult to erase.

References

Aberdare, M. (1977) *The Royal and Ancient Game of Tennis*, London: Wimbledon Lawn Tennis Museum.

Carlson, R. (1988) 'The Socialization of Elite Tennis Players in Sweden', *Sociology of Sport Journal*, 5(2), 242–56.

Clerici, G. (1976) *Tennis*, London: Octopus.

Cooper, I. (1996) 'Game, Set & Match: A Developmental Study of Tennis with Particular Reference to Lawn Tennis', unpublished MA thesis, University of Leicester.

Dunning, E. (1986) 'Sport as a Male Preserve: Notes on the Social Sources of Masculine Identity and Transformation', *Theory, Culture & Society*, 3(1), 79–90.

—— (1990), 'Women and Sport: Sport and Gender in a Patriarchal Society', paper presented to the World Congress of Sociology, Barcelona.

Dunning, E. and Sheard, K. (1979) *Barbarians, Gentlemen & Players*, Oxford: Martin Robertson.

Elias, N. (1986a) 'Sport as a Sociological Problem', in N. Elias and E. Dunning, *Quest for Excitement*, Oxford: Blackwell, pp. 126–49.

—— (1986b) 'An Essay on Sport and Violence', in N. Elias and E. Dunning, *Quest for Excitement*, Oxford: Blackwell, pp. 150–74.

—— (1986c) 'Introduction', in N. Elias and E. Dunning, *Quest for Excitement*, Oxford: Blackwell, pp. 19–62.

Gillmeister, H. (1997) *Tennis: A Cultural History*, Leicester: Leicester University Press.

Groppel, J.L. (1980) *Principles of Tennis*, Illinois: Stripes Publishing Co.

120   Ian Cooper

Gurney, G.N. (1984) *Tennis, Squash and Badminton Bygones*, Aylesbury: Shire Publications.
Guttmann, A. (1986) *Sports Spectators*, New York: Columbia University Press.
Hargreaves, J.A. (1985) '"Playing Like Gentlemen While Behaving Like Ladies": Contradictory Features of the Formative Years of Women's Sport', *The British Journal of Sports History*, 2(1) 40–51.
—— (1994) *Sporting Females: Critical Issues in the History and Sociology of Sport*, London: Routledge.
Harris, H.A. (1972) *Sport in Ancient Greece and Rome*, London: Thames and Hudson.
—— (1975) *Sport in Britain: Its Origins and Development*, London: Stanley Paul.
Haylett, J. and Evans, R. (1989) *The Illustrated Encyclopedia of World Tennis*, Hampshire: Automobile Association.
Heathcote, C.G. (1890) *Sports and Pastimes: Tennis*, London: Longmans, Green & Co.
Holt, R. (1989) *Sport and the British: A Modern History*, Oxford: Oxford University Press.
Lowerson, J. (1993) *Sport and the English Middle Classes 1870–1914*, Manchester: Manchester University Press.
Lumpkin, A. (1981) *Women's Tennis: A Historical Documentary of the Players and their Game*, New York: Whitson Publishing.
McCrone, K.E. (1988) *Sport and the Physical Emancipation of English Women 1870–1914*, London: Routledge.
Mangan, J.A. (1989) 'The Social Construction of Victorian Femininity: Emancipation, Education and Exercise', *International Journal of the History of Sport*, 6(1), 1–9.
Maskell, D. (1963) *Start Lawn Tennis with Dan Maskell*, London: George Allen & Unwin Ltd.
Midwinter, E. (1986) *Fair Game: Myth and Reality in Sport*, London: George Allen & Unwin.
Noel, E.B. and Clark, J.O.M. (1991) *A History of Tennis*, London: Duckworth.
O'Farrel, V. (1985) 'The Unasked Questions in Australian Tennis', *Sporting Traditions*, 1(2), 67–86.
Potter, E.C. (1963) *Kings of the Court: The Story of Lawn Tennis*, New York: A.S. Barnes & Co.
Schwartz, G.H. (1990) *The Art of Tennis 1874–1940*, California: Wood River Publishing.
Talbert, W.F. and Old, B.S. (1957) *The Game of Doubles in Tennis*, London: Gollancz Ltd.
Timm, W. (1981) 'The Social Structure and Development of Tennis in the Federal Republic of Germany', *International Review of Sport Sociology*. 13(16), 23–41.
Tingay, L. (1977) *100 Years of Wimbledon*, Middlesex: Guinness Superlatives Ltd.
Tranter, N.L. (1989) 'Organized Sport and the Middle Class Woman in Nineteenth Century Scotland', *The International Journal of the History of Sport*, 6(1) 31–48.
Trengrove, A. (1991) *The Story of the Davis Cup*, London: Stanley Paul.
United States of America Tennis Association (1984) *Tennis: A Professional Guide*, New York: Kodansha International U.S.A. Ltd.
Vamplew, W. (1988) 'Sport and Industrialization: An Economic Interpretation of the Changes in Popular Sport in Nineteenth Century England', in J. Mangan (ed.), *Pleasure, Profit and Proselytism: British Culture and Sport at Home and Abroad 1700–1914*, London: Routledge.
Wymer, N. (1949) *Sport in England*, London: George G. Harrap.

8 The influence of state formation processes on the early development of motor racing

Alex Twitchen

Introduction

Although the British played a central role in the development of many modern sports, they cannot lay claim to having instigated or nurtured the early development of motor racing. Instead it was in France, during the late nineteenth and early twentieth centuries, that the initial creation and popularization of motor racing took place. Not only, for example, were the majority of important early races organized and regulated by the Automobile Club de France (ACF), but these races were also dominated by French racing cars and French racing drivers. However while the French might have dominated the early history of motor racing, the British did make an important and lasting contribution to the development of the sport. This was achieved by successfully organizing the 1903 Gordon-Bennett cup race, the first significant motor race to take place in the British Isles. What was notable about this race, and in sharp contrast to the Paris to Madrid race which had taken place just a few weeks earlier, was that the Gordon-Bennett cup race took place without the loss of any competitor or spectator lives. While the Paris–Madrid race was abandoned after the first day, and the very existence of motor racing as a publicly acceptable sport was being seriously questioned throughout much of Europe, the safe organization of the Gordon-Bennett cup race, as Montgomery (2000) suggests, saved motor racing from the possibilities of being banished into extinction during the very infancy of its development.

Based on these observations the aims of this chapter are twofold. First, I will seek to explain more adequately than motoring historians have hitherto done, why motor racing initially developed in France and not in Britain. Second, I will examine how the hostility and widespread disapproval at first shown towards motor racing in Britain unintentionally enabled the sport to survive the calamitous loss of life suffered on the first leg of the Paris to Madrid race in 1903. In both cases my arguments will be focused around the extent to which the early history of motor racing can be connected to the outcome of long-term, unplanned, state formation processes that produced a stark contrast in the political, economic and cultural opportunities experienced by the upper classes of France and Britain. In this regard the analysis in this chapter will revolve around ideas that, as Dunning (1999) has pointed out, lie at the very centre of Elias's theory of civilizing processes.

The influence of legislation on the development of motoring and motor racing

In 1865 the British Parliament, dominated by 'country gentlemen' (Richardson 1977: 11), passed a law that restricted the speed of steam powered road locomotives to 4 miles per hour (mph) in open country and 2 mph in towns. Furthermore, someone carrying a red flag was required to precede these large and cumbersome vehicles at a distance of at least 60 yards. Although such speed limits were relaxed to 12 mph in 1896, national legislation regulating the permissible speed at which motor cars could be driven would prove to be a significant impediment to the development of motor racing in the British Isles. This was simply because any form of motoring competition that used the public highways could result in competitors being prosecuted for exceeding the speed limit.[1] Only through an Act of Parliament could the speed limits imposed on those using the British public highways be lawfully suspended to allow motor racing events to take place.

In France, by way of contrast, such national legislation was absent and the task of organizing motor races was made considerably easier by not having to seek legislation that made the public highways available for racing competitions. Furthermore, as Laux (1976) points out, the public highways in France tended to be of a better standard than those found in Britain. This was largely a consequence of the high standard of engineers graduating from the École des Ponts et Chaussées who were largely responsible for building French roads, and a Highways Act of 1836 which enabled local French governments to collect taxes to pay for the maintenance of public highways. In Britain the turnpike trusts[2] that served to maintain the most important highways had generally become insolvent as the expansion of the railway network ensured that in the nineteenth century travel by rail, and not by road, became the principal mode of inter-town transportation (Richardson 1977: 4–5). Unable to fund appropriate maintenance, the standard of the main highways in Britain was considerably poorer at the end of the nineteenth century than those in France, thus making them less amenable to staging competitive races between motorized vehicles (Plowden 1971: 23).

Despite such variations in the standard of roads between France and Britain, the passing of legislation in Britain regulating the speed at which it was permissible to travel, and the relative absence of such legislation in France, is widely recognized by motoring historians to have been a fundamental factor in accounting for the initial development of motor racing in France and not Britain. Yet motoring historians have generally failed to explain why such legislative differences existed in the first place and, as such, their accounts can only begin to provide a partial and incomplete explanation of the social processes which led to the development of motor racing. Instead, what I propose is an analysis that associates the more stringent use of Parliamentary legislation in Britain with the continuing political power of the landed upper classes whose habitus largely prejudiced them against the introduction of the motor car. In France a politically powerful landed upper class of equivalent status was largely eradicated by the development of an absolutist monarchy that uprooted the French nobility from the country and transformed them into an urban class of courtiers. Consequently the failure of the British monarchy to establish an absolutist form of rule, along the lines of that achieved by Louis XIV, is pivotal to an explanation of why the habitus and political power of the British landed upper classes instigated a culture of hostility and disapproval towards the motor car that was largely absent in France. To further these arguments Elias's seminal study of the French court has much to offer as a principal source of inspiration and analysis.

The court of Louis XIV

In his examination of the processes that enabled Louis XIV to develop an absolutist form of monarchical rule, Elias (1983) clearly illustrates the consequences that such processes had for the character and personality structure of the French nobility. According to Elias the court of Louis XIV initiated a civilizing transformation in the personality structure of the French nobility because this particular pattern of human interdependencies demanded that individuals develop a greater degree of rational calculation in the art of dealing with other people and a stricter form of emotional self-discipline. Advancement into more powerful and prestigious positions within the court became largely contingent on the ability to display these personality traits. Court life also promoted a more complex form of ceremonial etiquette and custom that likewise encouraged a greater level of refinement in the manners and behaviour of court members. Consequently the structure of life at the court, with all its etiquette, intrigues, alliances and insecurities, initiated a civilizing transformation in the personality structure of the French nobility as they learnt to acquire and practise the refined skills of courtly behaviour.

But the development of an absolutist monarchy, which required almost perma-nent residency of many nobles at the Palace of Versailles, also diluted the status and power of those members of the nobility who retained their residence in the country. As Elias (1983: 206) explains, the process of state formation in France during the eighteenth century was characterized by the 'magnet' of the urban court becoming extremely powerful. Because the court became the only mechanism through which the nobility could have access to economic opportunities and social prestige, attendance became compulsory for anyone who aspired to be seen as, and to assume the identity of, a noble. In such circumstances, maintaining a primary place of residence in the country became, for many members of the French nobility, an unrealistic ambition as access to greater political and economic power lay solely in becoming an integral member of the monarch's court. The centralization of economic and political power within the confines of Versailles therefore deeply affected the structure of the French upper classes. It detached and isolated the provincial nobility from the apparatus of the state and consolidated power within the urban nobility who, as Elias (1983) noted, perceived the provincial nobility as being relatively less civilized rustics or backswoodsmen.

It might also be argued in this connection that as a greater proportion of the French nobility took up residence in Versailles, their habitus was also transformed by the urban culture of the court. Furthermore the power and influence of the court ensured that the links between town and country were gradually eroded, thus increasingly divorcing the urban nobility from any direct and material affiliation or attachment to rural culture. The extent of this process might be seen in the development of a romantic nostalgia for 'country life' that, in the words of Elias (1983: 215), represented a 'symbol of lost innocence, spontaneous simplicity and naturalness' over the 'greater constraints and hierarchical pressures' of the urban court. Residence at the urban court therefore left its stamp on large tracts of the French nobility by moulding their habitus towards the demands of urban culture and creating a nostalgia for what was perceived to be the less complex environment of life in the country. As Elias (1983: 230) noted, the culture of the urban court became 'flesh and blood' for its members; no longer was it a costume that could be thrown off by living in the country.

The emergence of an absolute monarchy, and the widespread estrangement of the French nobility from the country which occurred during the eighteenth century, continued to manifest itself within the structure of French society throughout the nineteenth century. There was not, for example, any significant return to living in the country, and the French nobility mostly remained resident in Paris, embodying as a consequence a habitus that was influenced by their isolation from rural culture. At the end of the nineteenth century, therefore, the outcome of long-term, unplanned, state formation processes meant that the balance of political and economic power within the noble class of French society favoured the urban nobility whose affiliations and attachment to rural culture and country life had long been broken. For the urban nobility of France, country life only remained within their imagination as part of a romantic nostalgia for a way of life that they perceived to be less complex. In Britain however the structure and balances of power within the upper classes were very different.

The British state formation process

In contrast to the experiences of the French nobility, significant sections of the British aristocracy and gentry were still, by the late nineteenth century, embedded within the culture of country life. This arose since the processes associated with the formation of the British state never uprooted or separated the landowning sections of the British upper classes from the country in a way similar to that evidenced in France. As Elias (1986) explained, successive British monarchs never compelled the landowning classes of Britain to leave their estates, because the monarchy was never powerful enough to make the urban court the centre from which the country was governed. In Britain, political power was shared between the monarch and the upper strata of British society through the establishment of a parliamentary system of government that did not exert the same kind of residential pressures on the upper classes as did the development of an absolutist monarchy in France. As a consequence of what Elias (1986) termed the parliamentarization of political power, the landed aristocracy and gentry of Britain managed to avoid being subsumed and assimilated into an autocratic monarchy that would transform their status into a clearly defined class of urban courtiers.

Yet what is important for understanding the early development of motor racing in France and not in Britain is the extent to which parliamentarization, and the balance of political power within Britain, enabled the landed upper classes to remain largely resident in their country estates. The British monarchy's failure to establish an absolutist form of rule, therefore, never compelled the majority of the British upper classes to live permanently in London or, indeed, wherever else the monarch's court resided. Furthermore, residence in their country estates enabled the landed classes of Britain to demonstrate their relative independence and autonomy from the monarch's power. However, this is not to say that the landed upper classes remained solely a provincial or rural class. As Elias (1986: 38) noted, the 'London Season', a time when members of the British upper classes would reside in their London houses, became an important institution that linked town and country and facilitated the influence of rural interests within the urban institutions of government. The tradition of the 'London Season' subsequently helped to ensure that the landed upper classes of Britain would never become entirely immune or distinct from urban culture, but equally they were never to become as incorporated into urban culture as their French counterparts.

The outcome of long-term, unplanned, state formation processes can be seen to have created some fundamental differences between the French and British upper classes at the turn of the nineteenth century. These, it may be argued, lay primarily in the extent to which the British landed upper classes, whose habitus was mostly shaped and influenced by the traditions and characteristics of rural culture, were still able to wield significant political power. In France, by contrast, the provincial nobility were politically far weaker than the urban nobility. An appreciation of these differences helps us to understand more adequately why the motor car and motor racing were more stringently legislated against in Britain than in France, and why the upper classes of France tended to embrace motoring more fervently than did their British counterparts.

The early development of the motor car and motor racing

In his reminiscences, John Scott-Montague MP recalls an incident at the Houses of Parliament which illustrates the hostility and opposition to the motor car in Britain among the rural upper classes. In the summer of 1899 Montague took his Daimler motor car to the House of Commons but was initially refused entry and permission to park his motor car. Claiming his right for free entry and exit to the House, Montague was allowed by the Speaker of the House to park his motor car alongside the other members' horse drawn carriages. Montague recalls (cited in Nicholson 1962: 79) that the incident was widely reported and that: 'when I returned to the House some of the "horsey" Members were inclined to be angry with me, and made various rude remarks as to stinking, rattling, dangerous vehicles, and intimated that no gentlemen would drive a motor car.'

Montague's identification that it was the 'horsey' members of the House who were most angry with him serves to illustrate that hostility and opposition to the motor car was most fervent among the landed aristocracy and gentry who viewed it with suspicion and as an unwelcome intrusion into their traditional way of life. As Dewer-Mclintock (1962) has argued, at the beginning of the twentieth century most of Britain's wealthiest and influential people, and not least members of Parliament, regarded the horse as an indispensable animal for the purposes of tilling the land and travelling the countryside. To them the motor car threatened the status of the horse and represented the progress of a 'machine culture' that had no part to play in the more 'natural' ways of rural culture. The motor car was, after all, a potent symbol of industrialization, urbanization and mechanization; developmental processes which jarred acutely against the traditions and characteristics of rural culture. In Britain, and given that the balance of power within the upper classes was still, at the end of the nineteenth century, tilted in favour of the landed classes, the motor car was widely perceived as a dangerous and noisy intrusion into a way of life that was traditionally supported by the politically powerful landed aristocracy.

It might therefore be reasonably speculated that, as the British state formation process served to maintain the power of the landed aristocracy and gentry, the emergence of the motor car was unlikely to be embraced with any great enthusiasm in Britain. The motor car represented urban-industrial culture, it signified the emergent power of the industrial and urban bourgeoisie and, whatever the realities of people's fears about the dangers of motoring, these fears were heavily laden and influenced by sections of the British upper classes who were deeply rooted and attached to rural culture. As Plowden (1971: 35–40) argues, the conflict between early motorists and others was an 'urban/rural one' in which it was 'rural opinion' that helped to support police campaigns to enforce speed limits and prosecute those who the police could prove had exceeded the speed limit.

In France, by contrast, it appears that the French nobility more fervently embraced the motor car. As James Laux (1976) suggests in his outstanding study of the early French motoring industry, it was 'wealthy Parisian aristocrats' who became fascinated by the motor car in the late nineteenth century, viewing it as the 'perfect means of self-advertisement' for the fashionable. Circumstances – we might call them figurations and power balances – were, then, very different in the two nation-states. In France the motor car became established as a plaything among the rich and privileged, it became an object of conspicuous consumption and the hostility to the motor car that was shown by many sections of the British upper classes was not nearly so evident among their French counterparts. In this respect the trajectory of the French and British state formation processes helps us to understand the contrast noted in *The Engineer* journal which reported in 1899 (cited in Laux 1976: 73) that:

> The French people do not love horses as we do on this side of the Channel; . . . the average Briton does not care for locomotion on the highway other than that which is provided by his own legs or that of a horse.

The uprooting and estrangement of the French nobility from the country and the dilution of a politically powerful rural class that this produced may well help to explain these attitudinal differences. The severing of the ties between town and country and the consolidation of political power by the urban nobility meant that one of the most politically and socially influential sections of French society was not so deeply attached to either rural culture or the horse as were the British, or indeed the German, upper classes.[3] Indeed, Laux suggests that for Parisian aristocrats the purchase of a motor car was an ideal way to advertise their status and power. Consequently, in France, the balance of political power meant that the passing of national legislation constraining the development of the motor car was unlikely. For similar reasons a sustainable and growing market for motor cars first developed in France. Yet interest in the motor car among the wealthy elites would not, on its own, enable the motor car industry to expand greatly. Rather, the stimulus for this came through motor racing which also enabled manufacturers to alert a wider audience to the merits of their motor cars relative to those of their commercial rivals. It was for these reasons that the sport of motor racing received its most important source of momentum and development.

The early motor races

The first recorded competition between self-propelled vehicles took place on 19 July 1894 with a reliability trial between Paris and Rouen. The event was organized by the French newspaper *Le Petit Journal* and the first prize of 5,000 francs was awarded to the vehicle that best combined the virtues of safety, ease of handling and economy. A steam powered vehicle built by a company owned by the aristocratic Count de Dion finished the trial in the quickest time, but first prize was awarded jointly to motor cars powered by internal combustion engines from two other French manufacturers, *Panhard et Levassor* and *Peugeot* (Cimarosti 1990). A year later a group of Paris-based newspapers organized a Paris–Bordeaux–Paris competition in which first prize was awarded to whoever could finish the distance in the shortest time. Frenchman Emille Levassor won the race driving a motor car made by his own company. The Automobile Club de France (ACF) was formed out of the organizing committee for this race and the club soon began to assume an unrivalled position as the organizational and regulatory authority for motor racing competitions across Europe.

In 1896 the ACF organized its first major race from Paris to Marseilles and back to Paris. This event covered a distance of just over 1,000 miles and appears to have attracted much more interest among the public than the two previous competitions. As *The Autocar* (3 October 1896) commented:

> Two years ago the interest of the trials was mainly confined to engineers, and to the comparatively limited section of the public who had come to see the enormous possibilities of the autocar. Then the race between Paris and Bordeaux awakened a spirit of curiosity among the public generally, and this year the curiosity has developed into a lively interest in the doings of the mechanical vehicle.

It was this opportunity to awaken public interest in the motor car that provided the rationale behind the organization of the first major motor races, for manufacturers were gripped by a belief that racing could promote the virtues of the motor car to a wider public. Consequently the races were not organized solely as sporting competitions but were, instead, imbued with the commercial expediency of creating a viable market for the motor car. As *The Autocar* (24 October 1896) commented, the Paris–Marseilles race gave a 'formidable stimulus to the autocar movement', while the pioneering English racing driver Charles Jarrott (1906: 226–9) held that motor racing had been an 'invaluable' method of demonstrating how the motor car was a 'great and marvellous invention' which had brought about an 'extraordinary change in everyday life'. Moreover racing, he argued, was 'responsible for nearly all of this'.

Motor racing events were not only intended to popularize and advertise the virtues of motor cars generally, but also gave manufacturers an opportunity to extract a competitive advantage over their rivals by demonstrating the relative capabilities of their machines. While being seen to compete in motor racing events was important, winning races also endowed a significant commercial benefit on the successful manufacturer. As *The Automotor Journal* (30 May 1903) commented:

> Every car successfully competing in a great Continental race provides the most paying form of advertisement for the firm that built it . . . The public seems to be determined to buy from firms that win the races, and no motor car builders can afford to neglect races as long as races are held.

The earliest motor races were thus created and organized not so much for the competition and sense of excitement that competitors could experience, but because competition helped to stimulate public interest in the motor car. As Laux (1976) suggests, such was the importance attached to motor racing events that the sporting aspects of the motor car initially overshadowed all its other functions. With the French, of all European upper classes, seemingly the most enthused by the possibilities of the motor car, the French market became the most developed and important for motor car manufacturers. The organization of races that began and finished in Paris not only helped to create this market but also to develop it further.

Although motoring historians have previously identified how restrictive legislation was a principal impediment to the development of motor racing in Britain, and how motor racing developed in France as a means of publicizing the motor car, few have grappled with explaining the broader social context in which these conditions existed. What I have argued here, albeit in a preliminary sketch, is that an examination of state formation processes can account for differences in the habitus of individuals from different societies. In the case of motor racing, the strong association of the British upper classes to rural culture and the political power they were able to wield, mitigated against the development of motor racing through the enactment of repressive legislation. By contrast the absence of such a politically powerful rural upper class in France meant that circumstances were far more favourable for the development of the motor car and motor racing. The greater urbanization of the French nobility, through the establishment of an absolutist monarchy, created a habitus that did not provoke prejudices against the motor car in a way comparable to the prejudices expressed by many sections of the British upper classes. Moreover, the French upper classes were positively disposed towards the motor car as an expression of conspicuous consumption. However, motor racing still owes a debt to the sense of disapproval that was generally shown by the British upper classes to the sport at the turn of the nineteenth century.

The 'saving' of motor racing

However much the dangers of motoring and motor racing may have been exaggerated by their opponents, there can be no doubt that dangers did exist. Whilst Emille Levassor had won the 1895 Paris to Bordeaux race at an average speed of 15 mph, by 1903 the French driver Gabriel, in a French built Mors, was able to cover the same route at an average speed of 65 mph (Rose 1909). In the space of less than a decade very significant advances had taken place in the performance and potential speed of racing cars. While it could be expected that racing drivers would develop and practise a form of civilized self-restraint in exercizing the potential speed of their racing cars (Elias 1995), accidents could be expected to occur and, as the speeds increased, the consequences of these accidents became potentially more serious. Moreover, and given increasing concerns being expressed about the dangers of motoring and motor racing, accidents involving injuries and fatalities could be expected to receive intense scrutiny by the media.

In 1901 the ACF organized another 'Town to Town' race, this time from Paris to Berlin and back. During the race there were a number of relatively minor accidents and, more seriously, a small boy was knocked down and killed by a competing car. These accidents were widely reported and appear to have initiated a strong backlash in France against motor racing. The view of the newspaper *La Petite Republicaine* (cited in Rhodes 1969) is worth recounting as being indicative of the resistance to motor racing that was beginning to develop. It stated that:

> a veritable act of folly has been perpetrated since yesterday morning on the main roads between Paris and Berlin . . . at this moment seventy one dangerous madmen are driving over open country at speeds of express trains. These maniacs who crouch over the wheels of their mechanical carriages at fifty miles per hour knock down human beings, cyclists, cattle, anything in their path.

The source of this resistance in France, as the title of the newspaper might suggest, was not among the French nobility but from French socialists who closely associated the motor car with wealthy Bonapartist right wingers. Accordingly some French local departments with left wing majorities had placed speed limits on local roads or banned motor racing events altogether (as the Prefect of the Seine department had done in 1900). In the aftermath of the Paris–Berlin race the French Prime Minister announced that no more racing permits would be issued for events in France, a decision which led *The Autocar* (6 July 1901) to speculate that the Paris–Berlin race would be the last great race of any magnitude, since 'the regrettable accidents . . . had moved the French authorities to propose something very like panic legislation'. *The Autocar* (1 February 1902) later suggested, however, that the French Prime Minister's decision had been a politically motivated move made in order to appease socialists, thus ensuring that their votes would not be alienated in a forthcoming general election.

This backlash meant that, at the end of 1901, the prospects for the organization of motor racing events in France looked bleak. However, the French motoring industry was the most developed in the world and had quickly become both an economically important industry to the French state, as well as a significant source of French national pride. Motor racing, as already noted, was also considered an essential tool to the continued development of the motor car market. As the now Marquis de Dion is reported to have argued, 'a great yearly test is indispensable for the automobile industry. The livelihoods of 25,000 workers depend on that test' (cited in Villard 1972). Lobbying by the ACF was subsequently successful in persuading the French government to issue a permit for a race from Paris to Madrid that was planned for the late spring of 1903.

The Paris–Madrid race

The Paris–Madrid race started from Versailles at 3.45 am on 24 May 1903 with 160 cars setting off at intervals of one minute. The cars were divided into three classes: large cars, weighing over 650 kilos; light cars, weighing between 400 and 650 kilos; and voiturettes, weighing between 250 and 400 kilos. They headed along Route Nationale 10 for the town of Bordeaux that would mark the end of the first day's competition. The race had been heavily publicized in the French press and a number of claims had been made as to the performance potential of the racing cars taking part; so much so that at Versailles alone an estimated 100,000 people gathered to watch the start of the race, and between one and three million spectators were thought to have lined the route to Bordeaux (Rhodes 1969). However, this public enthusiasm was to cause chaos at the beginning of the race. As the British racing driver Selwyn Edge (1934: 129–30) reminisces:

> There was a dense block of people on the road in front, and how the racing cars were going to get through was more than anyone knew. No official could explain, and the handful of soldiers who were supposed to clear the road for the start were so hopelessly inadequate to cope with the crowd that they made no attempt to do so and disorder and chaos reigned supreme. On seeing what was taking place, I had grave misgivings for the safety of the race . . . if the start were a sample of the organisation which was to follow, it would be a miracle if the race passed off without many serious accidents.

Selwyn Edge was right. On the road to Bordeaux several accidents occurred resulting, according to the report of the race in *The Autocar* (30 May 1903), in the deaths of two drivers, two riding mechanics, two female spectators and two soldiers. A number of other serious injuries were sustained by competitors and spectators. In the immediate aftermath of these events, the French Minister of the Interior ordered the race to be abandoned at Bordeaux, and the cars transported back to Paris on trains.

During their extensive reports of the race, both *The Autocar* (30 May 1903) and *The Automotor Journal* (30 May 1903) were unequivocal in their verdicts that the calamitous events on the road to Bordeaux would signal the end of motor racing on the public roads of France. It is, however, worth noting some of the reasons put forward within the reports to explain why so many serious and fatal accidents had occurred. *The Autocar*, for example, was firstly critical of what it referred to as the 'defective organization' of the race, and especially that an insufficient number of policemen and soldiers had been deployed to control and restrict spectators from going onto the road. Furthermore, poor organization had meant that no attempts had been made to prepare the road in order to minimize the dust clouds generated by the cars which, in the view of *The Autocar*, 'accounted for at least one-half of the accidents – possibly an even greater proportion'. With no restriction on the number of entrants, the problem of blinding dust clouds was exacerbated by the volume of traffic. In addition to the poor organization, *The Autocar* also identified the significant improvements in the performance potential of racing cars that had been made in the relatively short space of time as a further contributing factor. This, combined with inexperienced spectators, who, according to *The Autocar*, had 'no sort of idea of what sixty or seventy miles an hour really meant', magnified the risks to a level previously unencountered. Lastly *The Autocar* noted that while a proclamation intending to clear the road of other road users had been issued, it seems to have been ignored and, on the day of the race, competitors came into conflict with a variety of non-race vehicles. As *The Autocar* reported:

> On some parts of the road . . . long trains of wagons piled up with wood . . . spread out in such a way [that] it was highly dangerous for the [racing] cars to squeeze through them. We refer to this state of things as a part explanation of the lamentable series of accidents which really appear to have finally put a stop to autocar racing in this country [France].

If the tragedies of the Paris–Madrid race cast gloom and doubt over the future of motor racing on the open roads of France, in Britain they were met with a profound sense of consternation, especially since the next major motor race, planned for the summer of 1903, was to be the Gordon-Bennett cup race in Ireland. Questions were subsequently asked in the British Parliament as to what precautions were being taken to safeguard spectators and competitors from injury and King Edward VII, even though he was a noted motoring enthusiast, expressed fears about the safety of individuals attending the race in Ireland (Plowden 1971). Indeed following the accidents during the Paris–Madrid race the King's private secretary, Lord Knollys, wrote to the Prime Minister expressing King Edward's opinion that the forthcoming race in Ireland should not be allowed to continue.

The running of the Gordon-Bennett cup race in Ireland in the aftermath of the fatalities and serious injuries sustained in the Paris–Madrid race represented a critical stage in the development of motor racing. Further fatalities may have compounded the fears expressed across Europe that both motor racing and motoring in general were too dangerous. The organizers of the race were therefore highly sensitive to the need to conduct the race in conditions which minimized, as far as possible, the risks of motor racing. As we shall see, the precautions put in place did indeed help to ensure that no serious or fatal injuries were sustained and this did much to rebuild the public's confidence in the safety of motor racing and the motor car.

The Gordon-Bennett cup race of 1903

The Gordon-Bennett cup series was instigated by an American newspaper magnate, James Gordon-Bennett, who wished to stimulate the expansion of the motoring industry outside France. Gordon-Bennett turned to the undoubted expertise of the ACF to help organize the first race in 1900. In accordance with his desires, the race was devised along a format which promoted international competition. Only two cars per country were allowed to participate, and each had to be designed and built in that country, as well as being entered on behalf of their National Automobile Club rather than by the manufacturers who built them.

France won the first event in 1900 and retained the cup in 1901. The 1902 race also seemed destined to produce a French victory but with 30 miles to go before the finish at Innsbruck, the leading French car broke down. This gave Selwyn Edge, driving a British entered Napier, a victory that was celebrated by *The Automotor Journal* (5 July 1902) for being achieved despite 'repressive legislation' and the paralysing influences of hostility shown towards the motor car in Britain. Edge's victory also entitled the Automobile Club of Great Britain and Ireland (ACGBI) to organize the race in 1903.

Given the legislation and general antipathy towards motoring and motor racing in Britain, finding a suitable venue to hold the cup race proved problematic. Furthermore, whereas the first three races had started in Paris and could traverse a route across continental Europe, Britain's geography mitigated against such a 'point to point' route. After much lobbying, two connected circuits of closed public roads were chosen in southern Ireland and a special Act of Parliament, the *Light Loco-motives (Ireland) Bill*, enabled the roads to be closed and the speed limits on these sections of the British public highways to be suspended for the duration of the race.

Given the fears about serious and fatal injuries occurring on the Gordon-Bennett cup race the ACGBI and the motoring media in Britain did much to publicize the extensive nature of the safety precautions being taken for the race. First, choosing a circuit of closed public roads would make guarding the course much easier than a 'point to point' route. As *The Autocar* (30 May 1903) indicated:

> some 7000 police officers will guard the Gordon-Bennett route ... they
> will have strict instructions to keep people out of harm's way; in fact, it is

doubtful whether some of the spectators will get a view of the race at all. It is only a question of putting them far enough off the course for them to be perfectly safe.

Second, only 12 cars would start the race and this should, in the view of *The Autocar*, greatly reduce the problem of blinding dust clouds. Third, the populated areas of the course were to be 'neutralized' and the racing cars would only be allowed to proceed through them at 'very slow speeds'. *The Times* (26 May 1903) also noted that on the Gordon-Bennett circuit, '£1500 has been spent on removing gulleys and sharp bridges, and all the corners will be treated to prevent dust being raised'. The same report in *The Times* also explained that an advantage of the circuit format meant that the racing drivers would come to know the course in detail and this should prevent accidents occurring as a consequence of not knowing what obstacles or corners lay ahead. As Richardson (1977: 121) also indicates, such was the level of organization and desire to minimize the dangers of the race that 'villagers were ordered to stay in their homes and the whole weight of the police force thrown into the task of ensuring that the race took place in conditions of perfect safety'.

The precautions and measures taken in the process of organizing the Gordon-Bennett cup race in Ireland, measures which were described by *The Automotor Journal* (6 June 1903) as being 'extra and elaborate', were without doubt heavily influenced by the resistance towards motoring and motor racing in Britain and by the fatalities and serious injuries sustained during the Paris–Madrid race. Serious or fatal injuries sustained during the race in Ireland would have given more ammunition to the anti-motoring lobby in Britain and elsewhere in Europe. In Britain any casualties during the race would have influenced the contents of the *Identification Bill*[4] imminently to be passed through Parliament. Certainly more restrictive and punitive measures would have been written into the Bill, which represented the most comprehensive legislation concerning motor cars ever introduced in Britain.

The comprehensiveness of the measures put in place to prevent injuries and minimize the risks of motor racing during the organization of the Gordon-Bennett cup race can be seen as related to the British state formation process and the influence this had on the balance of political power within Britain. Such was the political power of the landed upper classes and their close association with rural culture, that their attitudes towards the motor car were laden with fears which symbolized the oppositions between urban and rural culture, between progress and tradition, between industrial wealth and landed wealth and between the car and horse. To appease the hostility to the motor car demonstrated in Britain, the Gordon-Bennett cup race had to be organized in such a way as to ensure the safety of spectators and competitors. What *The Automotor Journal* (11 July 1903) heralded as the 'perfect arrangements' which demonstrated how a 'great road race' could be managed in the British Isles without causing 'any fatal or even serious accidents taking place', saved motor racing and motoring from constricting and stultifying legislation that would have further impeded the development of the sport and the more widespread acceptance of the motor car.

As Elias (1995) has pointed out, a continuous process of learning and adjustment is required by individuals to exploit fully the benefits of new technologies (which the motor car clearly represented). Elias himself (1995: 20) specifically indicated that the abandoning of the Paris–Madrid race signified a threshold moment in the process of learning how to utilize safely the considerable benefits that the motor car could bring to the mobility of a modern society. All those connected with organizing motor races and promoting the motor car had to learn the lessons of the Paris–Madrid race. Yet in Britain the task of learning how to hold motor races safely was shot through with prejudices and hostilities that reflected the social and cultural tensions between rural and urban classes. Safely organizing the Gordon-Bennett cup race was thus not just about learning how to organize a motor racing event without endangering lives – understanding for example the extent of the safety precautions that needed to be put in place – but it amounted to a wider competition between those who wished to develop and promote the motor car and those who wished to restrain its development. The Gordon-Bennett cup race therefore marked a watershed in the history of motor racing. If, during the race, accidents causing serious and fatal injuries had occurred, motor racing would probably have been condemned as a sport where the risks of injury were not to be tolerated by the public, and the development of the motor car in general could have been seriously restricted. That the race was successfully organized did much to allay the criticisms of motor racing and helped to rebuild the confidence among the public towards motor racing as an acceptably safe sport as well as towards the motor car as a safe method of travel.

Conclusions

In this chapter I have sought to explain why motor racing initially developed in France. The principle thread of my argument has been that the French state formation process diluted the status and political power of the provincial nobility and instead consolidated power within the urban nobility which then, in the late nineteenth century, ensured that there was not the same kind of pressure to legislate against the motor car as that evident in Britain. Furthermore the greater urbanization of the French nobility also helped to promote their attraction to the possibilities of the motor car. In Britain the process of state formation maintained the power of the landed upper classes and structured their habitus towards an ongoing and continued attachment to the character and values of rural culture. In what Setright (1981) describes as a deeply committed 'horse drawn society', mechanized forms of travel and sport were initially viewed as a heresy among large sections of the British population. Yet, paradoxically, such hostility led to the first major motor race to take place in the British Isles being organized with such attention to minimizing the risks of motor racing, that the sport was saved from potential extinction.

In this chapter, I have sought to draw on Elias's theory of civilizing processes, a central aspect of which is concerned with the ways in which power relationships and the habitus of individuals are shaped by the unplanned outcome of long-term state formation processes. In pursuing this argument I have attempted to demonstrate that the value and analytical purchase of Elias's work is not limited only to those sports in which debates about the control and regulation of violence have featured explicitly in the sport's history (e.g. boxing, football, rugby). What I hope this chapter illustrates in this respect is that a figurational approach is not more or less confined to the analysis of violence and violence control, as some critics have suggested (Stokvis 1992), but that an imaginative and creative engagement opens up possibilities for understanding many other aspects of the development of sport.

Notes

1 The presence of legal limits did not prevent organized time trials and competitions taking place on public roads. *The Autocar* (13 July 1901) carries a report for example of a time trial held at Dashwood Hill in Buckinghamshire (part of the A40 between London and Oxford). But, as *The Autocar* report stated, the publication of results for competing cars that had exceeded the speed limit of 12 mph were withheld in the fear that this information could be used to prosecute competitors.
2 Turnpike Trusts managed the principal roads of Britain. Tolls were levied and in 1838 about 17 per cent of Britain's roads were turnpiked (Clapham 1967).
3 As Laux (1976) notes, even though two Germans, Nicholas Otto and Gottlieb Daimler, are credited with having invented the internal combustion engine, the German motor car industry lagged well behind that of the French. Laux speculates that this may be due to the structure of German society where, as in Britain, the aristocracy primarily resided in country estates. This likewise shaped their habitus towards what Laux describes as the 'cult of the horse'. Indeed Laux reports Kaiser Wilhelm II stating that he would never set foot in a motor car while 'there is a warm horse left in the stable'.
4 This Bill was called the *Identification Bill* because a principal part of its contents lay in legally ensuring that motor cars were registered to individuals, and that a registration plate enabling the police to identify owners of motor cars was displayed on the vehicle.

References

Cimarosti, A. (1990) *The Complete History of Grand Prix Motor Racing*, London: MRP Ltd.
Clapham, J.H. (1967) *An Economic History of Modern Britain: The Early Railway Age 1820–1850*, Cambridge: Cambridge University Press.
Dewer-Mclintock, J. (1962) *Royal Motoring*, Chatham: W&J Mackay.
Dunning, E. (1999) *Sport Matters: Sociological Studies of Sport, Violence and Civilization*, London: Routledge.
Edge, S. (1934) *My Motoring Reminiscences*, London: G.T. Foulis and Co.
Elias, N. (1983) *The Court Society*, New York: Pantheon Books.
—— (1986) 'Introduction', in N. Elias and E. Dunning, *Quest for Excitement: Sport and Leisure in the Civilizing Process*, Oxford: Blackwell.
—— (1995) 'Technization and Civilization', *Theory, Culture and Society*, 12(3), 7–42.
Jarrott, C. (1906) *Ten Years of Motor and Motor Racing*, London: E. Grant Richards.
Laux, J. (1976) *In First Gear: The French Automobile Industry to 1914*, Liverpool: Liverpool University Press.

Montgomery, B. (2000) *The 1903 Irish Gordon Bennett: The Race that Saved Motor Sport*, Witney: Bookmarque Publishing.

Nicholson, T.R. (1962) *The Motor Book: An Anthology 1895–1914*, London: Methuen and Co Ltd.

Plowden, W. (1971) *The Motor Car and Politics: 1896–1970*, London: The Bodley Head.

Rhodes, A. (1969) *Louis Renault*, London: Cassell.

Richardson, K. (1977) *The British Motor Industry: 1896–1939*, London: Macmillan Press.

Rose, G. (1909) *A Record of Motor Racing*, London: RAC.

Setright, L.J.K. (1981) *The Pirelli History of Motor Sport*, London: Frederick Muller Limited.

Stokvis, R. (1992) 'Sports and Civilization: Is Violence the Central Problem?', in E. Dunning and C. Rojek (eds), *Sport and Leisure in the Civilizing Process: Critique and Counter-critique*, Basingstoke: Macmillan.

Villard, H.S. (1972) *The Great Road Races 1894–1914*, London: Arthur Baker Ltd.

9 Clay shooting
Civilization in the line of fire

Stuart Smith

The central purpose of this chapter is to examine aspects of the development of clay pigeon shooting in Britain within the broader socio-political context of firearms legislation. The development of clay pigeon shooting in Britain, and some of the recent changes in the socio-political context in which it continues to develop, involves an apparent paradox. On the one hand, the gradual replacement of live targets – caught or bred for use in competitions – by inanimate and ultimately clay targets, represents a civilizing development in the sense that Norbert Elias (1994 [1939]) used this term. In this regard, the development of clay pigeon shooting is similar to the development of birdwatching (Sheard 1999), not least in that they both reduce the possibility of anyone – or anything – getting seriously hurt. On the other hand, and notwithstanding these civilizing processes, many of those currently involved in shotgun sports in Britain (shotgun owners) feel that large sections of the general population regard them as a potentially dangerous group. Opposition to shooting is most apparent in single-issue groups such as the Gun Control Network.[1] Sports shooters, clay pigeon enthusiasts among them, see participation becoming increasingly difficult due to more proactive policing and ever more restrictive legislation, nominally based on concerns to limit the availability of firearms and their criminal use.

More specifically, the purposes of this chapter are twofold. First, I shall provide a figurational analysis of aspects of the development of clay pigeon shooting in Britain. Second, I shall provide an analysis of aspects of the changing socio-political context in Britain over the same period. In the conclusion these two analyses merge to demonstrate that the paradox referred to above is more apparent than real and that the future for sports shooting is uncertain.

The development of clay pigeon shooting in Britain

Descended from various game hunting antecedents, clay pigeon shooting began to emerge as a modern sports-like activity towards the end of the nineteenth century. Hunting game by shooting it in flight dates from the development of the flintlock in the seventeenth century, but long before the introduction of clay pigeons, some people had begun to rationalize their sports hunting. No longer were they required to trek through woodland in search of their game – although many continued to do so – for their quarry could be brought to them, placed on the ground and covered with a shooter's top hat. Shooters would then pick up the hat covering the bird, place the hat on their head, mount the gun and fire as the bird flew away. Some involved in shooting formed 'Top Hat Clubs' for this purpose (Cradock 1993: 36).

Later, pigeons would be caught or specially bred for shooting. 'Trappers' would, on command, pull a piece of string that released the birds from boxes (known as traps) at a chosen location. From about 1830 clubs were formed in most major European countries and in the latter years of that century, competitions using live game as targets were held regularly. There were large wagers made by the wealthy on the outcome of these contests and the contests themselves offered relatively significant prizes, such as a shotgun by Messrs Purdey of London (Lynch 1993: 143). While organized game shoots (where, typically, 'beaters' drive game out of woodland, towards a line of shooters; such shoots do not involve any kind of formal competition) continue in Britain to this day, the live bird trap competitions became less popular here prior to the First World War and were made illegal in 1921. Live bird trap competitions are still held regularly in some southern European countries where they remain popular. The 1993 Live Bird World Championship was held in Malaga, Spain; it attracted 735 competitors and the prize money for just one of the six events was £12,000 (1 million pesetas) (Lynch 1993).

If shooting live targets in competition has a long history, so too does the use of inanimate moving targets. In England, King Henry VIII's archers practised shooting at moving targets using a 'popinjay'.[2] As early as the 1780s muskets were used to shoot at a disc dangling by two rings threaded over a cord strung between two poles 30 feet high and 40 yards apart. The disc was moved along the static cord by means of a man running 'smartly away' from this contraption, holding a string that was attached directly to the disc (Cradock 1993: 35). In the early 1800s 'active' retainers (servants) threw potatoes and small turnips into the air for target practice. In London in the 1880s, some British gunmakers set up shooting schools where clients could have their bespoke guns fitted (tailored to their physical build and shooting style), and practise their shooting. These schools, such as Holland & Holland's, began by using live game targets and gradually moved to using a range of artificial targets such as wooden blocks and spinning propellers (Cradock 1993: 36–9).

As wealthy Victorians began to holiday in Scotland, in the wake of several visits by the Queen and Prince Albert, they enjoyed hunting, fishing and shooting (at both live and artificial targets). Initially glass balls were used as targets but transparent glass was soon replaced with coloured glass balls filled with dust, flour or feathers (Boothroyd 1996). In 1890, the Inanimate Bird Shooting Association (IBSA) was formed. Glass balls were subsequently replaced by clay targets. The original Ligowsky patent clay target was invented by an American, George Ligowsky (Cradock 1993: 38) but was also 'made by Georg Egerstorff in Germany' (*Clay Shooting*, February 2001: 57). Both were imported to Britain where the American clay targets, along with mechanical launching devices, were advertised as early as 1912 (Rawlingson 2001a). Yet the trajectory of the glass balls could not be made to resemble a bird in flight, whereas the newer clay targets, shaped like a very small 'Frisbee', could. The association changed its name to the Clay Pigeon Shooting Association (CPSA) in 1920, a year before live bird trap competitions became illegal (Boakes 2001). The Welsh Clay Pigeon Association was formed in 1928 (Osborne 2002), followed by the Scottish Clay Pigeon Association in 1929 (Wright 2002).

The early decades of the twentieth century saw the introduction of various 'trap' disciplines into Britain from America, some of which took root in an unmodified form while others were modified locally. Each of the trap disciplines has its own specific layout or configuration of targets, each has codified rules and most come under the auspices of the CPSA or its Welsh or Scottish equivalent. Other codified disciplines such as 'English Sporting' and, much later, 'Compact' or 'Sportrap' were developed in Britain and, in common with many other disciplines, the terminology used harks back to the live bird competitions of earlier days or game hunting. Targets are routinely referred to as 'birds', they are 'killed' rather than 'hit' and the command to 'release' the clay pigeon from the electrically powered launching device – still known as a 'trap' – remains 'Pull!' (a custom derived directly from earlier live bird trap contests). In English Sporting the traps are often set so that the target re-creates the flight or behaviour of particular birds or animals. A target fired towards and above the shooter is referred to as a 'driven pheasant', others as a 'springing teal', 'driven grouse', 'crossing pigeon', 'dropping duck' and a specially designed target that rolls along the ground at speed as a 'bolting rabbit'. Some newer disciplines also developed in Britain over the second half of the twentieth century and others have been developed in continental Europe. The discipline of 'FITASC', named after the French federation which controls it (*Federation Internationale de Tir aux Armes Sportive de Chasse*), involves using a gun which must remain completely un-mounted (the stock held below the shoulder) until the bird comes into view and 'Helice' (formerly known as ZZ) involves shooting specially designed propeller targets which fly away erratically and have to be 'downed' before they reach a certain distance.

The development of a variety of clay pigeon disciplines has been mirrored, in part at least, by developments in shotgun design and specification. Most of the major developments in basic shotgun technology were in place in the nineteenth century. The first reliable pump action shotgun was in use before 1900 and the first reliable semi-automatic was a Belgian Browning, available in 1902[3] (Rawlingson 2001b: 20). Up until 1915, when British clay pigeon shooting was in its infancy, there were no guns specifically designed for clay shooting on sale domestically, although they were not uncommon in America. Models for live bird competition shooting were, however, still available and guns with names like 'Demon' and 'Formidable' were 'guaranteed for their "long range" and "hard shooting". Low recoil? – That was for wimps' (Rawlingson 2001a: 63–4). In the inter-war years the sport developed further as the number of disciplines expanded and the gun and accessory trade recognized the potential of the market. By the mid-1930s, specialist clay pigeon guns were available for between £15 and £30, but this meant the sport remained the province of the relatively prosperous, for a small family saloon car cost £100 at the time (Rawlingson 2001a). It was not until the 1960s, when cheaper gun imports from Spain and elsewhere arrived on the British market, that clay pigeon shooting started to come within the reach of wider sections of British society. Continued technical innovations have meant that the development of a variety of clay pigeon disciplines has been accompanied by the production of corresponding types of shotgun with specifications that make them much less suitable for traditional game shooting.

Thus the development of clay pigeon shooting can be seen as a civilizing development in the sense that Norbert Elias (1994 [1939]) used the term but – and Elias is often misunderstood on this point – civilizing processes should not be seen as either uniform or unilinear. Many of those who shoot clay pigeons also shoot live game, but many do not. The proportions are difficult to judge, but estimates in the specialist press are that around 50 per cent of the readership of *Clay Shooting* magazine also shoot game (January 2001: 98) and 70 per cent of the readership of *Sporting Gun* magazine shoot clays as well as game (March 2001: 113). It would appear from the occasional letters in the shooting press calling for the CPSA to drop the word 'pigeon' from its name, that some of those who do not shoot game are uneasy about killing even a *symbolic* pigeon. This would follow a trend where the Welsh Association became the Welsh Clay Target Association (WCTA) in 1986 (Osborne 2002) and the Scottish Association changed its name to the Scottish Clay Target Association (SCTA) in 1991 (Wright 2002). This leaves only England and Ireland where the term 'pigeon' is retained. A similar tendency can be seen in the way in which shotgun manufacturers now name, or rather number, particular models. Long gone are names like 'Demon' and 'Formidable'. Today most models have nondescript numbers, like the 425 (Browning) or the MX8 (Perazzi). Although there are exceptions, the 686 Silver Pigeon (Beretta) being one of them, even shotguns designed for game shooting tend to have a model number, such as No. 2, No. 4 or 53 (AYA) or, when they are named, given titles such as 'Lowlander' and 'Highlander' (McNab), which have little connection with hunting or power.

Clay pigeon shooting has also undergone a sportization process; a process whereby pastimes develop codified rules, mechanisms to enforce them and a governing body, or bodies, responsible for their maintenance and amendment. Such rules serve several purposes. There are rules that are intended to limit the possibility of participants being injured or killed. These lay down limitations on violence in contact (and non-contact) sports and/or prescribe safety procedures. In shooting competitions, for example, guns may only be loaded when the competitor is on the shooting stand and the barrels of the gun facing down range. At all other times, two barrelled guns must be carried empty and 'broken'. Formal competitions have an appointed safety officer and all other officials, from scorers to the referee, have a safety remit. Another purpose of codified rules is, insofar as it is possible, to create equality of competition (e.g. rules which limit the number of players in a team). In clay shooting, this process was evident from the earliest days. Live bird trap competitions meant that each shooter could be presented with an identical number of targets, rather than being dependent on the vagaries of the field. The adoption of inanimate targets further standardizes competition in that shooters can now be presented with targets that have virtually identical trajectories. English Skeet is shot on an identical layout as prescribed by the rules, no matter which ground a shooter visits. Targets are standardized for distance, height, direction and speed, so that shooters should always face an identical range of targets, released in an identical order. In other trap disciplines, the target trajectories are also standardized within fine limits. The standard trajectory for Olympic Trap targets has been set at 76 metres plus or minus just 1 metre (Pearce 2001). In English Sporting, the shooting order of the squad is rotated between stands so that every competitor will take their turn at shooting first (considered to be a slight disadvantage). When a competitor is to be the first to shoot, the official will release a pair of birds at that stand, so that the first competitor can observe them. However, that competitor is not allowed to observe those targets from the shooting position itself, but must do so from behind or to the side of it. In this way, all competitors have a prior and identical preview of the first release. Large sections of the rulebooks in many shooting disciplines are concerned with artificially creating equality through standardizing the conditions under which competitors shoot and the targets they face.

Another, linked, purpose of sporting rules is to control a process Elias (1998a) referred to as technization. Elias argued that, as technology develops (e.g. the introduction of the motor car), new forms of self control are 'demanded' of people. In the sporting context, rules are introduced both to enable improvements in sporting performance via these new technologies, but also to constrain the impact of such innovations. Motor racing formulae provide clear examples of this purpose, as do rules in other sports that prescribe or proscribe equipment. Virtually all clay pigeon disciplines limit the calibre of shotgun to 12 bore (gauge), even though larger 10 or 8 bore guns are available. The rules of most disciplines also limit the number of attempts to kill a particular 'bird' to one or two (although some pump action shotguns can fire up to ten rounds consecutively and some semi-automatics up to seven). So called 'spreader loads' – cartridges that deliver a more widely spread shot pattern – are illegal in most clay disciplines (Yardley 2001: 250).

In these ways, the development of clay pigeon shooting in Britain can be seen as part of a broader civilizing process as live targets were gradually replaced by inanimate objects. Some participants have even become uneasy about shooting at objects that merely represent live animals. It reflects, too, many aspects of the linked process of sportization, involving the development of rules to ensure standardization, the control of technization and attempts to minimize injury and create equality of competition. As in other sports, these changes have been associated with the development of a governing body to maintain and amend rules, administer the sport and serve as a focus for international links. However, in the case of clay shooting, a variety of governing bodies have been established with responsibility for different disciplines.

The socio-political context of development

The development of what might be called the 'British shooting figuration', of which clay shooters form a part, is characterized by power struggles between a growing number of competing interest groups. Each of these groups seeks to influence the future through its access to economic, coercive or knowledge resources. Governing bodies, interest groups and individuals have access to economic resources, but their ability to organize themselves effectively will be a determining factor in the influence they ultimately wield (Elias and Scotson 1965; Elias 1998b). All will be involved in efforts to monopolize the provision of knowledge; that is, to persuade others that their version of social reality is valid. Some groups, like the state, have access, ultimately, to the use of coercive force.

The importance and influence of those groups involved in the development of clay pigeon shooting in Britain have varied over time. Central players, however, have been politicians (in various alliances), a number of arms of the state (such as the police, Home Office, HM Customs and Excise, the War Office, the Irish Office), interest groups within those arms of government (e.g. the Association of Chief Police Officers (ACPO)) and elements of the media. More recently special interest groups seeking the abolition of private gun ownership or the prohibition of game shooting have come to the fore. The interest of the British public more generally waxes and wanes over time. In this part of the chapter, I wish to trace the power struggles within the British shooting figuration, the impact of such struggles on the development of firearms legislation in Britain, and the consequences of these legal developments for sports shooters.

There have been many Acts of Parliament over the years dealing with aspects of gun ownership. While a number of them introduced only minor changes, more significant developments, and most of the current legislation's more restrictive features, have a relatively short history. The 1870 Gun Licences Act, with some exceptions, required that any person carrying a firearm outside their home should have a licence. According to Greenwood (1972), however, raising revenue was the major purpose of the Act; the licence was available from any Post Office on payment of a fee. Prior to the Firearms Act of 1920 there was no legal prohibition on any adult, providing they did not have a criminal history, carrying firearms.

In 1918, the Committee on the Control of Firearms, chaired by Sir Ernest Blackwell, produced an unpublished report – known as the Blackwell report – which resulted in the introduction of the 1920 Firearms Act. The Committee itself was a secret committee whose existence only came to light when documents were declassified under the 50-year rule. It was composed of career civil servants, representatives of the police, Prison Service, War Office, Irish Office and HM Customs, but took no evidence from any outside organization. The declared aim of the 1920 Firearms Act – to disarm criminals – is, however, open to doubt. First, the Act imposed even more stringent restrictions on the possession of firearms and greater penalties for offences in Ireland, in the context of rebellion against British rule.[4] Second, it was introduced at a time of mass unemployment, of continuing labour unrest on the mainland and when many firearms from the First World War were in general circulation. There was a distinct fear among the political elite that radicalized labour, including ex-servicemen from the recent war, were bent on their own Bolshevik revolution. If the only motivation for the 1920 Act was to 'disarm criminals' then it might be supposed that its focus would have been on handguns for, at the time, these were the favoured weapon of the criminal. But the Act required handguns and *rifles* to be licensed and made no reference to shotguns. The reason for this may have been that shotguns are of little use in the context of an armed insurrection, when pitched against rifles and machine guns. This is underscored by the Home Office's recent evidence to the Select Committee on Home Affairs, where they describe the 1920 Act as being, 'intended to control those types of firearms likely to be used by terrorists and revolutionaries' (Home Office 2000: 11). It seems, then, that the first important piece of British firearms legislation resulted from the fear of widespread revolutionary violence and that one significant, unintended consequence of this Act was to establish the present two-tier system of gun controls in Britain.

While the possession of shotguns continued to be unregulated, subject to the purchase of a licence from any Post Office, the 1920 Firearms Act marked a sea change in firearms legislation in Britain and laid the foundations for many of the currently existing controls. The Act meant that the holding of firearms (pistols and rifles etc.) ceased to be a right and became a privilege, by making the possession of a Firearms Certificate (FAC) compulsory. Applicants had to satisfy their Chief Constable that they were suitable people to be entrusted with a weapon and that they had 'good reason' for requiring one.[5] Each firearm held was registered on the certificate and a variation of the certificate was required for any new acquisition or disposal. Limits were also set on the amounts of ammunition that could be held and purchased at any one time. The Act created new offences, with whole categories of people being regarded as guilty unless exemptions were granted at the discretion of the police – thus shifting the burden of proof to the applicant. The basis on which FACs were granted had the effect of giving Chief Constables sweeping powers. In assessing an application to hold a firearm, Chief Constables may pursue any enquiries they deem necessary and take account of any information they deem relevant, including gossip and rumour.

There were minor pieces of firearms legislation passed in the 1930s, which were consolidated in the Firearms Act of 1937. These Acts, *inter alia*, introduced a total prohibition on fully automatic weapons and the first form of shotgun control since 1870. Shotguns with barrels of less than 20 inches were re-classified as firearms and a FAC would, thereafter, be required for any such weapon.

In 1965, the Murder (Abolition of Death Penalty) Act suspended capital punishment for murder for a period of five years, in effect, throughout Britain. It was an Act passed without public support at the time, as well as in the decades that followed, and probably lacks majority support among the British public even now. Around the same time as the death penalty was suspended, there were several well publicized criminal cases involving the use of guns, some of them sawn-off shotguns. In response to public fears, the government introduced the 1965 Firearms Act, which increased the penalties for the criminal misuse of firearms, restricted the carrying of firearms in public and created the offence of 'armed trespass'. Although there were calls to do so, the Act did not significantly regulate possession of shotguns by adults any further.[6]

Two years later, in 1967, three police officers were shot and killed in Shepherds Bush, London. This incident involved the use of pistols and led to a press and public clamour for the reintroduction of the death penalty. The then Home Secretary responded by introducing (in the 1967 Criminal Justice Act) further controls on the possession of shotguns which, he believed, could be purchased too easily, an idea he had rejected just three months earlier. As has often been the case in Britain, the then government's response to a perceived danger from illegal firearms was to tighten controls on those held legally and, in this case – as in 1965 – to focus on a different category of weapon from that used in the initial incident. Since the 1967 Act was in many ways a highly contentious piece of legislation, the subsequent public debate focused on other issues and the new restrictions on shotguns (to be the subject of a certification procedure) went almost unchallenged.

The 1968 Firearms Act consolidated earlier legislation under a single Act, retaining existing restrictions on shotguns and introducing further restrictions, some of which were similar and some of which were different from those imposed on other firearms. The Act re-classified long barrelled 'pump action' shotguns, making them subject to the FAC procedure. Shotgun ammunition remained uncontrolled but a Shot Gun Certificate (SGC) was required for the possession of any number of shotguns with a barrel length of more than 24 inches. One of the distinguishing features of the SGC was that applications would be granted by Chief Constables if they were satisfied that the applicant was not a person prohibited from possessing a shotgun (e.g. by being of unsound mind or with a criminal record etc.) and was not a danger to public safety. The question of an applicant having a 'good reason' for possessing a shotgun did not at that time arise.

There were indications that the government viewed the introduction of SGCs as the first stage in an ever more restrictive programme and there is a widespread belief in the current shooting community that, for some considerable time, the secret/parallel agenda of the Home Office and police has been to reduce the number of legally held shotguns. Such an agenda may, alternatively, be seen as the state consolidating its monopoly of violence by progressively disarming its citizens. This agenda, if it existed, appears to have re-surfaced in 1972 when a report commissioned by the Home Office was produced by the McKay Committee, but never published (Greenwood 2000: 7)[7]. In 1973 the Home Office produced a Green Paper (a consultative document) that was believed to have been a much watered-down version of the never-published report. The Green Paper concluded that a reduction in the numbers of firearms of all categories held in private hands was a 'desirable' end in itself (Greenwood 2000: 7–8). Fees for the renewal and granting of certificates rose steeply and many shooters regarded them as punitive. Many in the sports-shooting community believed that the Home Office and police sought to put every possible difficulty in the way of gun owning members of the public. However, despite the Green Paper, firearms legislation remained largely unchanged until the late 1980s.

In August 1987 Michael Ryan killed 17 people, including himself and his mother, in the town of Hungerford, England. An unemployed labourer, Ryan walked around the town with a semi-automatic rifle and a semi-automatic pistol (both held legally), shooting indiscriminately. As Ryan illegally held other firearms few legislative measures, it seems, would have prevented this incident, but this did not stand in the way of a huge public demand, and extensive media campaigning, for new legislation. While the sports-shooting community seem to recognize that there is a problem with firearms being involved in crime in this country, they perceive that problem as residing with the illegal possession of weapons in the hands of criminals, rather than those held by sports shooters. Yet in the wake of events in Hungerford and the public outpouring of grief, anger and revulsion that followed, the arguments of sports shooters went largely unheard.

Hungerford became the catalyst for the Firearms (Amendment) Act 1988. An official report, conducted by the Chief Constable of Thames Valley Police and made available only to members of Parliament (Greenwood 2000), concluded that nothing in the firearms legislation that existed at the time had contributed to the massacre and that no specific legislation could have prevented the incident. It nevertheless also recommended that legislation be tightened *since the public was in the mood to accept it* and some of the measures that the police had thought desirable, including some initially floated in the 1973 Green Paper, were resurrected and became law. There is, therefore, little doubt that the Home Office and police used that climate of public fear to press for legislation that would not otherwise have been enacted. The 1988 Act banned the private ownership of semi-automatic rifles and paid only a fraction of the real value of confiscated arms as compensation (Greenwood 2000); semi-automatic shotguns with a capacity of more than two rounds became the subject of a FAC; each separate shotgun had to be listed on the SGC; variations were required for each acquisition or disposal; regulations for the secure storage of shotguns were introduced and ammunition for shotguns could only be purchased on production of a SGC. In future SGCs would only be granted or renewed if the Chief Constable was satisfied – in addition to the criteria already in place – that the applicant had a 'good reason' for requiring one. There is a subtle, but important, difference in this aspect of the legislation as it affects firearms and shotguns. In order to reject an application for a SGC on these grounds, the Chief Constable has to demonstrate or be satisfied that the applicant does *not* have a good reason, rather than requiring the applicant to demonstrate that they do. Thus legally for SGCs, the burden of proof remains with the police.

Nine years after Hungerford, in March 1996, Thomas Hamilton entered the gymnasium of a primary school in Dunblane, Scotland, armed with four pistols and hundreds of rounds of ammunition. A quarter of an hour later he had shot dead a teacher and 16 children and wounded another ten children and three adults before shooting himself dead. A national reaction of grief and anger that, almost inevitably, bordered on hysteria, resulted. Since Hamilton's firearms had been legally held there were immediate calls for the total ban on all kinds of guns in private hands. The then Conservative government set up an inquiry, headed by Lord Cullen, but before that report was delivered Anne Pearson of the Snowdrop Petition – a campaign group that included bereaved parents from Dunblane – gave a highly emotional speech, again calling for a ban on private ownership of all guns, at the opposition Labour Party's conference. This speech, Greenwood (2000: 104) argues:

Shifted the ground entirely from the original agreed approach of calmness and rationality to making the issue a Party Political football in the light of the coming election. It is clear that Labour politicians in particular, but also some Conservative politicians, saw the issue as a vote winner or vote loser. From that moment on, rational political action became increasingly less possible.

In the emotionally charged atmosphere of the time, thinking tended to be more 'involved' than 'detached' (Elias 1998c) as some organizations sought to promote their version of social reality, almost irrespective of the evidence. That fact may be reflected in the quality of some of the submissions to the Cullen Inquiry. By way of example, the Labour Party's evidence contained the following statement: 'the number of offences of burglary and theft in which weapons (generally presumed to be licensed) were stolen, though broadly stable, is unacceptably high' (The Labour Party 1996). While the trend was, indeed, broadly stable, that stability was maintained by a steep rise in the theft of 'air weapons', the vast majority of which would not be subject to licensing controls, and a corresponding decline in the theft of shotguns and other types of firearms. No figures were produced to indicate those stolen items that were subsequently recovered or discarded since many are stolen in the course of thefts of other property. Data were produced and others ignored, it seems, which promoted the legislation that the public appeared to desire, despite the fact it would almost certainly not prevent a similar incident occurring in future, only one committed with legally held weapons.

Elias can help us understand the emotionally charged atmosphere that occurred in the wake of these incidents and its effects on the way people and organizations argued their case(s). It is true that much of Elias's work is concerned with how and why people in Western Europe came to control their emotions more routinely over the long term. In his work *The Court Society* for example, he demonstrates how in the court of Louis XIV the conditions of internal competition between courtiers there made behavioural restraints imperative. Every move, every gesture, had delicate connotations of meaning for others and so life at court involved 'a curbing of the affects in favour of calculated and finely shaded behaviour in dealing with people' (1969: 111) and outbursts of emotion were to be avoided at all costs. Although behaviour at court was towards the extreme of a continuum at that time, over the long term more generally, more restrained patterns of behaviour diffused through societies and higher social echelons tended to develop yet more controlled patterns of behaviour, in part as a way of distinguishing themselves from others. The changing standards of people's behaviour over the long term is, Elias argues, interdependently connected to the process of state formation as the central authorities in jurisdictions in Western Europe tended to acquire and consolidate their monopolies on the use of violence and the right to levy taxation. The relative internal pacification of a jurisdiction by a central authority required, enabled and depended on these changes in people's personality structure, where people more routinely controlled their emotions, such as their aggressive impulses. In modern societies this has moved to the point where, for example, people no longer wish to indulge in or witness violent acts in ways that gave pleasure to their forebears in the Middle Ages (Elias 1994 [1939]) and those who do, are viewed as pathological.

However, in some other respects Elias sees emotion playing a greater part in people's lives in modern societies. As violence is pushed more and more behind the scenes in these societies and more rarely intrudes into the everyday lives of their citizens, as social relations in them become more calculable and predictable, so people tend to become more and more concerned about, and more exercised by, that violence which remains. When Elias talks of the advance of people's threshold of repugnance at violence (1994 [1939]), he is clearly talking of an emotional response to violence. Over time, people in general find themselves repulsed by acts which are, in fact, less and less violent and their repugnance at acts of similar levels of violence tends to intensify over time. Given the events in Dunblane, where a number of members of a socially valued group (children) were killed, it is hardly surprising that the emotional response to this violence bordered on the hysterical.

The Cullen Report (1996), when delivered, studiously avoided apportioning blame and stopped short of calling for a ban on any further classes of firearm. However, one of its major findings was that Thomas Hamilton had been investigated by the police in relation to serious charges on more than one occasion and, by implication, should have had his FAC revoked, or at least not renewed. This would not, of course, have guaranteed that Hamilton had no access to firearms, in the sense that no licensing system or weapons ban can *guarantee* anything.

The then Conservative government went further than the Cullen Report and proposed a ban on larger calibre handguns, while the Labour opposition, upping the ante in the run-up to the election, adopted a policy of a total ban on all handguns. The Conservative government passed the 1997 Firearms (Amendment) Act and later that year, the newly elected Labour government passed the 1997 Firearms (Amendment No 2) Act. Between them, the Acts banned pistol shooting as a sport in Britain, a sport in which British competitors had had some success at the Olympics. Neither of the 1997 Acts, however, has had the effect of reducing the number of offences involving – now totally banned – handguns, which has continued to rise (Frost 2001).

Currently in the United Kingdom, there are calls for the prohibition of (legal) gun ownership. Among those making this call is the Gun Control Network (2002) whose mission is: 'Working towards a gun free environment'. There are also calls for the prohibition of game shooting from People for the Ethical Treatment of Animals (2002) and the League Against Cruel Sports (2002), or for yet more controls on legally held sports guns. This is the case even though ACPO accept that something like 96 per cent of firearms-related crime involves weapons that have *never* been legally licensed and that the remaining 4 per cent includes a proportion of firearms stolen from their legal owners (oral evidence to the Home Affairs Select Committee 2000). Estimates of the numbers of illegally held firearms in circulation in Britain are necessarily vague and range from less than 2 million to some 4 million. Some of these weapons will be held illegally by (otherwise) law-abiding citizens; in 'amnesties' in the 1960s, where the public could hand firearms to the police with 'no questions asked', 1,250,000 weapons of all descriptions and almost 1 million rounds of ammunition were surrendered (Greenwood 1972: 235–6). Yet with firearms much more readily available in many parts of continental Europe – where shotguns are sold in supermarkets – than they are in Britain (Greenwood 2000), the illegal importation of firearms and replica firearms reactivated at home or abroad clearly provides far more common routes through which firearms enter the criminal arsenal than does the theft of legally held weapons. Consequently campaigns, driven largely by the desire to reduce gun-related crime, often have a misplaced focus on the sports-shooter community.

Since the events in Dunblane, those organizations that administer various forms of shooting have taken steps to defend their sports by coming together under the umbrella body, the British Sports Shooting Council (BSSC). Most support the Countryside Alliance (an organization formed to defend country sports) and their campaign on behalf of shooting entitled 'Foresight'. Despite such steps, press coverage could be described as mixed with some informed comment in the broadsheets but rather more sensationalist coverage in the tabloids, linking almost any discussion of firearms to Thomas Hamilton and Dunblane.[8] Consequently many gun owners feel 'persecuted' by the public, press and police. In practice, some Chief Constables are demanding that applicants for a SGC actively demonstrate that they have a 'good reason' for owning a shotgun (and sometimes a 'good reason' for owning each shotgun), a condition that goes beyond the terms of the 1988 Act, where the burden of proof clearly remains with the police. The British Association for Shooting and Conservation (BASC), an organization that grew out of wildfowling and represents game shooters, published advice for resisting these unlawful demands on its website (2000).

It is easy to understand how sections of the media have their own agenda, and it is clear that the tabloid press particularly see 'scare' stories as a means of selling newspapers. But it is through reference to Elias's (1987) work on the sources of power in interdependencies, and the concept of civilizing processes (1994 [1939]), that we can seek to understand why these kinds of gun-related stories find such fertile ground among the general population, politicians and police. In modern societies access to physical power and the capacity to engage in physical violence remain an important source of power, but one that has increasingly been pushed behind the scenes of everyday life (Elias 1987). Dunning has argued that part of men's positive power ratio in relation to women is derived from the fact that, on average, they are bigger and stronger than women, but he also notes that, 'modern weapons technology has the potential for offsetting and perhaps removing altogether the in-built fighting advantages of men' (1994: 165). Dunning makes this point in the context of male–female power balances but the argument has more general relevance; that is to say, whether male or female, those without access to modern weapons, such as shotguns, are forced to cede a potentially very unequal power balance to those who do.

Second, the development of longer chains of interdependence in more modern societies is itself interdependently linked with changes in people's personality structure. Modern life depends on a level of internal pacification where people feel relatively confident in using planning and foresight in their dealings with others.

Modern societies would not be possible if we could not reasonably expect, in a general way, that people could and would routinely control their 'spontaneous libidinal, affective and emotional impulses' (Elias 1986: 41). In this context, people are forced to rely on measures by the state, and also on the routine control of their impulses, drives and emotions on the part of gun owners. Given the present system of gun control, the British experience is that the general public can, in almost all cases, rely on such self-control. However, two major tragic incidents have reminded the public of the fragility of the state's monopoly over violence. The knowledge that legislation could not have prevented one of those incidents, and that the second was possibly avoidable, does not assuage public anxiety and leaves many sympathetic to ever tighter legal restrictions. For many in the British public, it seems that 'guns are guns' and little significance is attached to the distinction between legally held sports guns and illegal semi- or fully automatic weapons in the hands of criminals.

The power struggle between competing interest groups involved in sports shooting in Britain is complex and multifaceted. Single-issue groups working for the prohibition of (legal) gun ownership, and those which seek to prohibit all forms of game shooting, lobby politicians and give evidence to Select Committees (whose members have their own interests), as do some of the sport's various governing bodies. However, both the prohibitionist lobby and the governing bodies have recognized that public opinion has become an increasingly important battle-ground in terms of promoting or preventing further legislation, for recent British history has shown on a number of occasions that public opinion has encouraged politicians to enact legislation that has not, ultimately, had the effect that the public appeared to desire. Furthermore, experience has also shown that such legislation is unlikely to be repealed.

For several reasons then, the power struggle between the prohibitionist lobby and the shooting community over the future of shooting sports is an unequal one. First, those who support the prohibition of (legal) gun ownership or of game shooting realize they are in a 'win once' situation. They can campaign indefinitely, they can 'lose' the debate many times, but only require 'success' on one occasion. Once legislation has been enacted, it is unlikely to be repealed even though, as experience shows, it would not prevent the 'homicidal use of [illegally held] automatic weapons in our inner cities' (Select Committee on Home Affairs 2000 – author's insertion). Second, these groups exist for no other reason than to promote their message of prohibition and have organized themselves for that purpose. Both in the context of a community study (Elias and Scotson 1965), and in work on game models (Elias 1998c), it is clear that the degree to which a particular interest group can organize themselves is an important determinant in the influence they wield in any figuration. Sports shooting, on the other hand, is administered by a plethora of diverse organizations, as an article in the specialist shooting press illustrates:

> I sometimes amuse myself by imagining how one might explain how the sport of clay pigeon shooting is administered to a Martian. It would take hours to go through the alphabet soup – CPSA, WCTSA, SCTA, BICTSF etc. – and

that's without even attempting to unravel the complex political background of Irish shooting affairs. . . [or] international administration.

(Rawlingson 2001c: 102)

In the sense that it exists in some other countries (e.g. the US), there is no effective 'gun lobby' in Britain, as the multiple agencies have overlapping functions and responsibilities. It is only recently that many of the diverse bodies involved in shooting have come together under a new umbrella organization, the British Sports Shooting Council (BSSC). The organization claims to be a 'unified voice for shooting in Great Britain', but it does not have a large secretariat or a regional structure and while it seeks to be a conduit between sports shooting and government, it 'does not seek to usurp the work or contacts of its individual members' (2002). In other words, sports shooters are still not speaking with a single voice.

Third, for the reasons outlined earlier, large sections of the British population are likely to be sympathetic to the prohibitionists' appeals and regard shooters as a potentially dangerous group. Those who shoot are all too aware of the feelings of large sections of the general population and feel the long-term trend is moving against them. Many, too, seem aware that, irrespective of the logic of their case, the future of their sport will ultimately depend on how non-shooters *feel* about gun ownership. An article in the shooting press expressed just that view:

I am sure you have all been in the uncomfortable position of having to defend our sport to outsiders, the strained silence when you reveal you own a gun. The same urban majority that would ban [fox] hunting would also take our shotguns away from us. It would be dressed up with all kinds of spin about public safety, but at the heart of it would be a simple sentiment; we do not like what you do and we will stop you doing it – because we can.

(Rawlingson 2001d: 98)

There is no real evidence of an urban/rural divide in respect of foxhunting in modern Britain's geographically mobile population, but the broader point may be more sustainable. Many in shooting circles see the progressive restrictions and prohibitions placed on sports shooting as being the result, in part, of prohibitionists, politicians and press responding to, and in some cases feeding, public fears for their own ends. They would see the character of the debates and the resultant legislation that followed events both in Hungerford and Dunblane as strong evidence to support that view. It would seem that despite the trend in shooting towards more civilized forms of the sport, public anxiety and the trend towards the state's monopoly of violence will mean more state regulation, if not ultimately an outright ban.

Notes

1   The Gun Control Network seeks to prohibit the private ownership of all guns. People for the Ethical Treatment of Animals and the League Against Cruel Sports both seek the prohibition of all forms of game shooting and the former seeks the prohibition of all forms of fishing.

2   A popinjay was a 30 foot high pole with a 6 foot diameter revolving ring at its top. Targets such as live pigeons or even bunches of feathers were tied to the ring with cord and fluttered as it revolved.
3   A semi automatic shotgun utilizes either the force of the recoil or the gases produced by the first shot to eject the spent cartridge case and load the second shot and so on.
4   Firearms legislation has for many years been different in Ireland and, subsequently, Northern Ireland because of the particular problems there. This discussion, therefore, deals with legislation as it applies to England and Wales and, with minor differences, to Scotland.
5   A Chief Constable is the Police Officer responsible for all aspects of policing in an area, normally based on a single county or a grouping of counties.
6   The barrel length below which a shotgun came into FAC procedures increased from 20 to 24 inches. Virtually all shotguns have barrels longer than 24 inches and therefore remained outside that legislation.
7   Sir John McKay was then HM Inspector of Constabulary for England and Wales and the committee members were drawn exclusively from the police, the Home Office and the Scottish Office.
8   The *Daily Telegraph* (17 July 2001: 5), for instance, covered a report by the Centre for Defence Studies at King's College, London that had been commissioned by the Countryside Alliance, which concluded that policies targeting sporting and farming communities were misplaced. Conversely, The *Sunday Mirror* (3 March 2002: 31), a national tabloid, included a picture of Thomas Hamilton alongside an article on youth participation in sport shooting (permissible only on private land when supervised by an adult over 21 years of age).

References

Boakes, P. (2001). 'History of the CPSA', online, e-mail:info@cpsa.co.uk (8 January 2001).

Boothroyd, H. (1996) 'Exploding Balls', *Clay Shooting* (February), 22–4, Hants: Brunton Business Publications.

British Association for Shooting and Conservation (2000) 'Legal Advice', online, available http: http//www.basc.org.uk (10 April 2000).

British Sports Shooting Council (2002) Online, available http: http//www.bssc.org.uk (23 June 2002).

Clay Shooting (2001) 'History Under the Hammer' (February), 56–7, Hants: Brunton Business Publications.

Cradock, C. (1993) 'A History of the Sport', in M. Barnes (ed.), *The Complete Clay Shot*, Newton Abbot: David & Charles.

Cullen Report (1996) *Inquiry into Events at Dunblane*, London: The Stationery Office.

Dunning, E. (1994) 'Sport as a Male Preserve: Notes on the Social Sources of Masculine Identity and its Transformations', in S. Birrell and C. Cole (eds), *Women, Sport and Culture*, Champaign, IL: Human Kinetics.

Elias, N. (1969) *The Court Society*, Oxford: Blackwell.

—— (1986) 'Introduction', in N. Elias and E. Dunning (eds), *Quest for Excitement*, Oxford: Blackwell.

—— (1987) 'Retreat of Sociologists into the Present', *Theory, Culture and Society* 4, 223–47.

—— (1994 [1939]) *The Civilizing Process*, Oxford: Blackwell.

—— (1998a) 'Technization and Civilisation', in J. Goudsblom and S. Mennell (eds), *The Norbert Elias Reader*, Oxford: Blackwell.

—— (1998b) 'Game Models', in S. Mennell and J. Goudsblom (eds), *Norbert Elias on Civilization, Power and Knowledge*, London: University of Chicago Press.

—— (1998c) 'Involvement and Detachment', in S. Mennell and J. Goudsblom (eds), *Norbert Elias on Civilization, Power and Knowledge*, London: University of Chicago Press.

Elias, N. and Scotson, J. (1965) *The Established and the Outsiders*, London: Frank Cass.

Frost, D. (2001) 'Firearms and Crime', *Sporting Gun* (March), 76, London: IPC Media.

Greenwood, C. (1972) *Firearms Control*, London: Routledge & Kegan Paul.

—— (2000) 'Memorandum by Mr. Colin Greenwood', Select Committee on Home Affairs, *Second Report on Controls over Firearms*, Appendices to the Minutes of Evidence, Appendix 8, London: The Stationery Office.

Gun Control Network (2002) Online, available http: http://www.gun-control-network. org (28 June 2002).

Home Office (2000) 'Memorandum by the Home Office', Select Committee on Home Affairs, *Second Report on Control over Firearms*, Appendices to the Minutes of Evidence, Appendix 1, London: The Stationery Office.

Labour Party (1996) 'Control of Guns, Evidence to the Cullen Inquiry May 1996', *The Cullen Report: Inquiry into Events in Dunblane*, Appendix 4, London: The Stationery Office.

League Against Cruel Sports (2002) Online, available http: http//www.league.uk.com (23 June 2002).

Lynch, P. (1993) 'ZZ Target Shooting', in M. Barnes (ed.), *The Complete Clay Shot*, Newton Abbot: David & Charles.

Osborne, J. (2002) 'WCTA', online, e-mail: wctsajonc@themail.co.uk (7 June 2002).

Pearce, R. (2001) 'Rule Changes', *Clay Shooting* (February), 35, Hants: Brunton Business Publications.

People for the Ethical Treatment of Animals (2002) Online, available http: http://www. peta-online.org (23 June 2002).

Rawlingson, R. (2001a) 'Shooting History: Days Gone By', *Clay Shooting* (January), 63–4, Hants: Brunton Business Publications.

—— (2001b) 'Gun Test', *Clay Shooting* (December), 98, Hants: Brunton Business Publications.

—— (2001c) 'On Report', *Clay Shooting* (November), 102, Hants: Brunton Business Publications.

—— (2001d) 'On Report', *Clay Shooting* (January), 98, Hants: Brunton Business Publications.

Select Committee on Home Affairs (2000) *Second Report on Controls over Firearms*, London: The Stationery Office.

Sheard, K. (1999) 'A Twitch in Time Saves Nine: Birdwatching, Sport, and Civilizing Processes', *Sociology of Sport Journal*, 16(3), 181–205.

Sporting Gun (2001) March, 113, London: IPC Media.

Wright, R. (2002) 'SCTA', online, e-mail: scta.secretary@talk21.com (11 June 2002).

Yardley, M. (2001) *The Shotgun: A Shooting Instructor's Handbook*, London: The Sportsman's Press.

10 The development of sport in Japan

Martial arts and baseball

Koichi Kiku

Introduction

The object of this chapter is to use Elias's theory of the civilizing process to examine the development of martial arts and western sports in Japan. Explanations of the development of Japanese sports have usually emphasized the differences between the development of western sports and Japanese sports, and have also often emphasized the mysticism, collectivism and formalism which some writers have held to be characteristic of traditional Japanese culture. Many explanations have also drawn on Ruth Benedict's characterization of Japanese culture as a regulated 'shame culture', compared with western 'guilt culture', while the *Bushido* spirit has been held to provide the essential background or cultural character of Japanese sports.

While *Bushi* or the *Bushido* spirit, which was established by the samurai (*Bushi* being another term for samurai), was certainly apparent in Japanese sports in the past, it has been affected by several developments, including the lengthening of chains of interdependency and the processes of state formation in modern Japan. This changing figuration unintentionally resulted in a movement towards the civilizing of Japanese sports and, in this regard, there are similarities between the sportization processes in England, as described by Elias (1986a) (and by other authors in this volume) and sportization processes in Japan.

In this chapter I will focus in particular on the 'Honorific Individualism' which defined the spiritual character of the samurai class and which originated in the medieval period (Ikegami 1995). I will seek to clarify how the spiritual character of the samurai was related to the sportization and civilizing of Japanese sports and, in so doing, I will document the historical continuity from the *Edo* era to the *Meiji* era, which is often seen as the beginning of Japanese modernization. In this regard, I will examine, first, the development of judo to illustrate how the old martial arts, *Bujutsu* or *Bugei*, as played before the Meiji era, have been modernized through 'the invention of *Budo*' as a new concept, and second, the development of baseball as representative of how western sports have been modernized through 'the invention of tradition' in the name of Budo. This chapter examines civilizing processes common to both developments, with particular emphasis on the control of violence and emotion. Finally I will consider, from the viewpoint of the sociology of knowledge, why the Bushido spirit as an ideology has been regarded as having de-civilizing tendencies when, on the contrary, it contributed very much to the sportization process, in an Eliasian sense, in modern Japan.

Western prejudice against Japanese sports

Western people generally appear to regard the culture of small Asian countries and perhaps particularly Japan, located in the Far East, as 'specialized' and to view it as a mysterious, almost incomprehensible phenomenon. This view of Japanese culture in particular was perhaps influenced by such things as the '*Kamikaze*-suicide pilots' and 'group honourable death' as practised by the Japanese military in the Second World War. The significance of such activities has been exaggerated by the mass media in the West, perhaps as a means of showing what is often taken to be the basic 'difference' between western and non-western cultures, with the implication that non-western is 'de-civilized' while the culture of the West is 'civilized'. Of course, this view, which contrasts a 'civilized' culture with one that is 'uncivilized', is quite different from Norbert Elias's concept of civilization. Elias pointed out that there is

> in the social development of the human species no zero-point of civilization, no point of which one can say, it was here that absolute barbarity came to an end, here that civilized life among humans began. A civilizing process, in other words, is a social process without absolute beginning.
>
> (Elias 1986b: 46)

Elias's 'civilizing process' refers to an interrelated set of processes which encompass the degree of internal pacification in a society; that is, the refinement of customs, the degree of self-restraint and reflexivity involved in social relations, and the experiences of growing up in a society (Elias 1969, translated into Japanese 1977: 1–56).

Journalists and researchers frequently suggest that the modernization of sport in Japan differs from the global standard due to certain specific factors. For example, Whiting (1977, 1989/1990) has drawn on the work of Benedict (1967) to suggest that the pattern of Japanese culture can be described as a culture of 'shame' as opposed to Western cultures of 'guilt'. Whiting suggests that the collectivistic principles of Japan are quite distinct from the principles of the modern West, most particularly in that they militate against individual rationality and emphasize allegiance, in the sphere of production, to the boss and co-worker. He consistently contrasts western individuality with collective Japanese group practices. In this context he refers to the strong influence of the Bushido spirit that is still apparent in Japanese society and he insists that Japanese baseball, which is the most popular sport in Japan, demonstrates this type of mental character and style of activity. Whiting argues that Japanese baseball players are governed by Bushido to follow values of allegiance, self-discipline, respect for nature, frugality and modesty. This mind-set, he argues, influences the whole of Japan and sometimes appears anti-modernizing and in stark contrast with modern global standards. Such ideas are widely accepted, even by the Japanese themselves, and the acceptance of such ideas serves to justify negative views of Japanese practices (Whiting 1977: 14–16).

In this context it is clear that the individualism that is a characteristic of much of the modern world is much less developed in Japan and, in this sense, it may be said that Japan is 'falling behind'. Following the Second World War intense historical reflection of the role of Bushido spirit led to a masochistic acceptance of the 'mistake' of pre-war Japanese culture. Similarly post-war sports culture in Japan became dominated by such masochistic beliefs.[1] But such cultural adaptations have not removed the notion of inferiority; these new, different cultural styles are also often regarded as 'negative' (Tatano 1997: 129–49). Thus western people still retain prejudice because, on one hand there continues to be a perception of, and an emphasis on, the peculiarity of non-western cultural forms, and on the other hand, the 'mistake' of pre-war Japan has been replaced by masochistically accepting and emphasizing the peculiarity of Japanese culture and the Bushido spirit. There exists an 'ideological' acceptance of peculiarity by the Japanese themselves who attempt to modernize the sports of post-war Japan without being influenced too strongly by the spirit and ideology of such traditional cultural forms.

For example, many Japanese sports researchers have argued that the Bushido spirit is quite different from the spirit of modern sport. The modernization of Japan began during the Meiji era and is often called '*Wakon Yosai*' (Kado 1975: 139–74; Kinoshita 1976: 97–120; Kusaka 1985: 23–44; Sugawara 1984: 136–45). The use of this term in relation to sport implies that modern Japanese sportspeople have accepted the skills and rules of modern sport on the surface while, as players, retaining an anti-modern mind-set. According to this interpretation, the development of Japanese sport has been based on the Bushido spirit and therefore it cannot properly be considered modern sport. However, was the development of martial arts and other sports in Japan really very different from the social processes involved in the 'sportization process' that Elias has documented in relation to western sports? In the next section, we examine the sportization of martial arts in Japan.

Changes in the samurai class pre-sportization in Japan

According to Elias, the English sportization process developed in the eighteenth century (Elias 1986a: 126–49), in association with the cessation of the cycle of violence of earlier periods and a change in the direction of greater civilization of the habitus of the nobility and gentry in England, who began to develop less violent forms of entertainment and leisure activities under the name of 'sports' (Dunning 1999: 107). The background to this is that after the English Civil War in the seventeenth century, the nobles and gentry limited the power of the sovereign and developed parliamentary procedures which involved non-violent ways of resolving disputes. The sportization of pastimes and the associated changes in social habitus developed concomitantly. Taki, a Japanese researcher, followed Elias in relating the origin of modern sports to the development of non-violent means of resolving political conflict in Britain. These increasing controls on the use of violence were extended to other areas of social life and were shown typically in the physical cultural phenomenon which is today called 'sport' (Taki 1995: 32–5).

In France, the situation was rather different. Elias (1986b: 35) argued that, in relation to civilizing processes in France, the role of the court was central:

> It was there that the character of a civilizing process as a spurt, not simply towards greater restraint, but also towards a more differentiated, sublimatory pattern of conduct and sentiment, showed itself to the full. Learning the highly specific skills of a courtier, acquiring a courtier's social habitus, was an indispensable condition of social survival and success in the context of court life. It demanded a characteristic patterning of the whole person, of movement no less than of outlook and sentiment, in accordance with models and standards which marked off courtiers from the people of other groups.

In the French medieval period, before the establishment of court society, the social position of the knights was relatively secure; they used violence freely and were not subject to pressure to control their violent attitudes and behaviour either from above or from below. However, when the knights and the gentry were brought together at court, the contrasts between these groups gradually lessened and the search for distinguishing characteristics, related to their competition for position at court in order to attain the favours of the king, generated increasing varieties of ceremonialization in relation to bodily controls, manners and attitudes. As Elias (1983: 90–1) noted:

> The position a person held in the court hierarchy was . . . extremely unstable. The actual esteem he had achieved forced him to aspire to improve his official rank. Any such improvement necessarily meant a demotion of others, so that such aspirations unleashed the only kind of conflict – apart from warlike deeds in the king's service – which was still open to the court nobility, the struggle for position within the court hierarchy.

These power struggles within French court society were an aspect of a figuration in which growing emphasis was placed on emotional control and on what was coming to be considered as good manners. However Dunning points out that the influence of the French court society on sportization was less than that of the nobility and gentry in England, because the English nobility and gentry were much more powerful than their counterparts in the French court, who did not have a power base that was independent of the monarch, as was the case in England (Dunning 1999: 114). In this regard, the trend towards the reduction in violence that was increasingly becoming part of the social habitus of the English nobility and gentry was also increasingly reflected in the sports and leisure life of the gentry, who also played a vital role in the sportization process through their establishment of relatively autonomous sporting clubs.

How did the situations in England and France compare and contrast with the figurations of which the soldier samurai classes were a part? To what types of attitudes and spirit did this Japanese figuration give rise? And how did this influence the development of Japanese martial arts? More particularly, how did activities which originally had strong military connections persist in modern times? How were the original military connections lost and how were sports like judo and karate disseminated around the world?

In terms of their political-military dominance and their relationship with the central authority, it is possible to identify three broad periods in the development of the samurai classes. The first of these was the *Kamakura* period (1190–1333), during which the samurai were the dominant group within a semi-centralized government. The samurai classes established hegemony over the *Kuge* (that is, the aristocracy of pre-modern Japan) in which the leader of the samurai became the commander-in-chief. During the *Sengoku* period (the latter part of the fifteenth century to the sixteenth century), the relatively centralized power system collapsed and the Sengoku *daimyo* (Japanese feudal lords) governed each district independently. During the *Tokugawa* period (*Edo* period) (1603–1867) there was a process of pacification and consolidation into a 'neo-feudal state' in which the military functions of the samurai became increasingly nominal and symbolic. The changing situation of the samurai class during these three periods is shown in Table 10.1 (Ikegami 1995: 333).

The increase of the samurai's power as landowners in the *Kamakura* era of medieval Japan was attained by extending the land owned by the *Shogun* or the

Table 10.1 The reorganization of the samurai

Items	Time periods		
	Kamakura (1190–1333)	*Warring states (late 15th–16th century)*	*Tokugawa* (1603–1867)
State formation	First samurai semi-central government	Transitional period of regional state-making by warlords	Pacification and consolidation into 'neo-feudal state'
Class relationships	Samurai as military specialists gaining hegemony over the aristocracy	Aristocracy in total decline; increasing resistance by villagers	Collective victory of the samurai; demilitarization
Vassalage characteristics	Personal relationship; relative autonomy of vassals	Transition to hierarchical vassalage: 'high exits'	Hierarchical bureaucratic vassalage: 'low exits'
Military characteristics	One-on-one combat of mounted samurai in private armies	Technological and organizational military revolution	Military function of samurai nominal and symbolic
Honour culture	Honour based on pride in violence and autonomy	Military practice of honour culture glorified	Honour remains critical as class identity, but is 'refocused'

Source: Table revised from Ikegami (1995: 333).

Shikken who was the commander-in-chief. When his power was at its height, he was able to bring both the emperor and the nobility under control. In this context, from a relatively early period, the power of the king and nobility in Japan became nominal compared with the situation of the monarchy in France and England; in Japan, it was the samurai class that owned a great deal of land and held real political power. However, the samurai submitted themselves to the control of stronger regional power-holders in order to secure their own control over land. This situation led to a general domestication of violence from an early period and the model of *Bugei* and *Bujutsu* (that is, the original martial arts with strict codes of manners) that continued until the *Tokugawa-Edo* period, became part of the samurai culture. 'The subsequent domestication of the Tokugawa samurai – and of their honour culture – was possible because Japanese state formation in the early modern period took this course of development' (Ikegami 1995: 337). In this context, as Ikegami (1995: 352–3) has noted:

> Japanese honorific individualism [in the samurai class] emerged as a form of 'possessive individualism', a conviction about the self that grew up among the members of the landed elites, who acquired a firm sense of self-possession paralleling their pride in the ownership of land.

In this respect, the samurai came to occupy a position broadly similar to that of the nobility and gentry in England in the seventeenth century. While on one hand, this figuration was characterized by a high degree of interdependency between the samurai leader and his subject class (similar to the court society in France), on the other hand, dependence was based on and maintained by military power; that is, by violence. Consequently, the culture of honour evolved such that it became understood that honour was something for which, ultimately, a man could die (Ikegami 1995: 354).

From the Kamakura period to the Sengoku, the physical culture of the samurai class came to be characterized by relatively de-civilized forms of violence. In the Tokugawa period which followed, characterized by the dissolution and reorganization of the relationship between sovereign and subject, the internal centralization of power and long period of national isolation, the physical culture of the samurai class gradually changed to more civilized *Bugei* and *Bujutsu*. Put another way, as the military functions of the samurai became nominal and symbolic, so the soldier's view of honour in violence, which had previously been a particularly overt symbol of the samurai class, increasingly became concealed. From the organizational structure of vassalic bureaucracy to various edicts and legal procedures, from the requisite etiquette for formal interactions among the samurai to the visible signs of status differentials, every Japanese institution in the early modern period expressed the implicit assumptions of the neo-feudal state (Meyer and Rowan 1977: 340–63). However even at this stage, there were some cases in which the self-control of violence, as a means of distinguishing oneself from others, as described by Elias in the French court, led to more intensive struggles for status *within* Japanese samurai society. In this regard, the demonstration of non-violent mannerisms had *negative* connotations within the samurai class and would serve to undermine hereditary status. Yet in the context of the bureaucratized state, the demonstration of non-violent manners was an indication of social standing, and violence inflicted on the classes of farmers, artisans and merchants was frowned upon. As Ikegami (1995: 355–6) notes:

> The medieval form of samurai honor culture was fundamentally threatened by the formation of the Tokugawa state. The social foundation of the individual's sense of sovereign honor was swept away as the result of new institutional constraints stemming from Tokugawa state formation. The *bafuku* state's formation not only altered the political details of the samurai's life but also defined in fundamental terms a man's anticipation of his life's course, his chances for upward mobility, and, perhaps most important, his opportunities to enjoy stimulating or exciting life experiences. Not only was there no possibility of adventure in a future war, but the newly emerging institutional constraints forced the samurai to recognize that the range of possibilities was circumscribed already through his status at the time of birth. The criteria of honor were provided in objective form as hierarchical status categories attached to visible symbols in ceremonial distinctions and dress codes.

It might be argued that the degree of self-control over violent impulses in Japanese culture between the seventeenth century and mid-nineteenth century was lower than in Britain and France. But we can say that, from the medieval period through the Tokugawa-Edo period of pre-modern times, the figurational dynamics of the specific context led to a gradual advancement of, and growing respect for, self-control in the performance of bellicose behaviour and/or expressive violence. Through long-term changes in the samurai class figuration, *Bujutsu*, which included violent action to wound and kill, was 'de-violenced' leading to the formation of the original model of martial arts, 'Budo', around 1920. In the next section, I will discuss the role of the samurai or Bushido spirit in reducing levels of violence in *Bujutsu* and *Bugei*, which led to the original model of martial arts that appeared in the Tokugawa-Edo period.

The pre-sportization process and the Bushido spirit in Japan

Bushido, the spiritual philosophy behind *Budo*, originally emerged in response to the evolving social position of the warriors (that is, '*Bushi*' or samurai) in the seventeenth century as the Tokugawa shogunate pacified the country and consolidated its rule. Shogunal policy dictated a shift from a martial arts lifestyle, in which the goal was combat-readiness and warfare, to new bureaucratic roles in the shogunal administration. There were four strictly regimented classes in the Tokugawa-Edo era: warriors (samurai), farmers, craftsmen and merchants. The samurai were the highest class and were strictly demarcated from the other three. For the samurai it was necessary to exhibit their cultural differences in order to maintain their social position relative to the other three classes. As noted, although the development of manners under the Tokugawa shogunate system did not significantly improve the position of the samurai class, it was fundamental to the maintenance and stability of the samurai's social position. The physical culture of the samurai class was described by Confucian scholars Hayashi Razan and Yamago Soko in the seventeenth century and became known as both a physical and an ethical model called 'shido' (Sogawa 2000: 42–3). The word *Bushido* is, then, a combination of the terms *Bushi* and *Shido*, but the concept of Bushido is somewhat different from Shido.

Some have argued that Bushido was originally seen as a kind of aesthetic of death, where fear of death was suppressed to give a physical impression of a self-controlled, cultured style (Naramoto 1975: 86–93). Therefore *Hara-kiri*, or ritual suicide, has an aesthetic value that demonstrates honour and obedience to the master. This is an important point, demonstrating that under Bushido even an act of suicide could be incorporated into a system of physical culture, resulting in the custom gaining precedence over the physical act itself (Yoro 1996: 139). Though apparently paradoxical, this can be viewed in the same way that the refinement of manners described by Elias in the *Civilizing Process* acted to restrain 'natural' bodily functions as the modernized body developed.

In recent years, the discourse of 'Budo', including the Bushido spirit, has been shown in books of military arts written in the Tokugawa-Edo Period in Japan (see e.g. *Gorin Syo* by Musashi Miyamoto, and *Heiho Kaden Syo* by Yagyu Munenori). Some have argued that this connection between the Bushido spirit and martial arts is because, in order to appeal to people, especially foreigners, Budo should be seen as being based neither on a post-modernistic belief that an unstable 'independence' and 'self' were born in the modern west, nor on too great an admiration for the Orientalism from which it is derived. The paradigm that is the discourse of 'Budo' has, on the one hand, a cultural base that aims to demonstrate a condition of 'naturalness' and, on the other, the aim to demonstrate a denial of the artificial. This is important to bring an image of harmony and combination of a natural and artificial culture (Inoue 2000: 126).

A common feature of Bushido (the spiritual philosophy which affirmed a kind of aesthetic death) and Shido (the physical and ethical portrayal model described earlier) is that both involve a sense of self-control (Sogawa 2000: 42–3). In its extreme, a fear of death was seen to be overcome, but at a more mundane level it served to produce values whereby desire and pain were subjects of self-control. For instance the physical agony experienced by Japanese *Ichiko* students as part of their baseball practice in the Meiji period is sometimes justified under the Bushido philosophy (discussed in more detail later). Furthermore, it formed the basis for the foundation of the 'obedient body', which Foucault argues is the necessary basis for the foundation of modern society (Foucault 1975, translated into Japanese 1977: 141–74).

The increasing webs of interdependent relationships – that is the figuration – promoted change to 'Katsuninken'[2] wherein people actively seek to raise levels of self-control. Although the sword that was used to wound and kill was necessary for the samurai, its military function gradually declined after the mid-seventeenth century leading to the development of *Kenjutsu* (Japanese fencing, now called

Kendo) (Tatano 1997: 186). This allowed the samurai to continue using the sword in training, though not to kill. In the late-eighteenth century, competition and training using bamboo swords began. This was the origin of modern kendo, perhaps the first martial art in which a sportization process occurred. This process of violence reduction is said to have extended to many kinds of *Bujutsu* such as *Kenjutsu Sojutsu* (Japanese fencing using a spear), *Jujutsu* (the original form of judo), which promoted the physical skill needed for close combat conducted on the ground, and *Suijutsu* (traditional Japanese swimming) (Tatano 1997: 186–7). The case of judo is discussed in greater detail later.

Thus it can be seen that the physical theories of Bushido have an affinity with the 'mind-set' required as an antecedent to the sportization process. Bushido has also provided an ideology for the acceptance of modern sports. So, in Japan, both the sportization of Budo, and the Budo-ization of foreign sports were achieved under the common framework of the Bushido spirit. Thus the modernization of sports in Japan, and the civilizing processes related to this development, could not have happened without the Bushido spirit which appeared in the Tokugawa-Edo Period (Kiku 2002: 45).

The acceptance of western sports and the abolition and reorganization of the samurai class: the case of baseball

The social class system of warriors, farmers, craftsmen and merchants that had underpinned the rank of samurai was abolished in the Meiji period (starting in 1868) as a move towards political equality began. *Horoku*, the salary that had formerly supported the samurai class financially, was cancelled and thus the samurai class's privileged status was formally abolished. The political system of the Meiji period effectively shifted the samurai class into the middle and lower classes in local communities through the diminishing of what Elias would call class contrasts. This caused a 'revolution' between the ruling and ruled classes in Japanese society. But by making the Emperor, who had become merely a political figurehead, appear like a feudal general characterized by a brave, manly image akin to that of samurai leaders, they created a new validation of, and prestige for the samurai image, 'Bujin' (Takahashi 1999: 291–330).

These are complex and somewhat contradictory processes. The dissolution of the samurai class, combined with the ingenious use of samurai imagery, meant that the loss of privilege and the decline of the samurai's honour culture, led to the diminishing of contrasts between the upper, middle and lower classes. Concurrently, the samurai image came to distinguish not only the samurai from other classes but also the different strata within the samurai class itself. As a result, although the upper samurai class in the Tokugawa Edo period were abolished in an economic sense, they attempted to distinguish themselves through their children who, on entering public service under the new Meiji government, would keep the traditions of honorific individualism which, in addition to property, had previously differentiated this group from the middle and lower samurai classes. According to Sonoda (1990: 103):

In 1881, the ex-samurai and their families made up 5.3 percent of the total population. This small group occupied 68,556 of a total of 168,594 official posts, or 40.7 percent. Moreover, the higher the official post, the higher the rate of occupation by former samurai . . . In 1885, among 93 high-ranking officials above the bureau heads of the central government, we find 4 members of the peerage, 88 ex-samurai, and one commoner.

In the early Meiji period, many children of the ex-samurai class, especially the middle and upper class, entered the elite *Dai-ichi* junior high school (initially called *Ichiko*, it later became known as *Dai-ichi* high school). Due to the broader structural changes which made the status of the ex-samurai unstable and insecure, parents hoped to attain positions in public officialdom for their children (Sonoda *et al.* 1995: 335–42). Complicating the social situation were the contradictory pressures. On the one hand, the former samurai class were required to prove their own ability as individuals in a competitive, meritocratic society. At the same time, however, they experienced relative status enhancement via the trend of emphasizing pride in the upper samurai class and their concept of honour (as personified by the Emperor). The prominent physical activity within this cultural figuration was 'baseball', a western sport brought to the country by American employees and Japanese who had studied in the USA.

Japanese baseball had been played by a part of the elite who had studied in the USA and schools other than *Ichiko*. However, baseball involved aspects – such as catching a hard ball with bare hands, intentionally hitting the ball at opponents, and wearing 'immodest' forms of dress – which some considered violent and uncivilized. In relation to the situation within the schools, the samurai, dispirited by their change of status in society more generally, maintained that their children were higher in status than their teachers. In this respect there were clear parallels with the situation in the English public schools in the early nineteenth century (see Dunning and Sheard 1979) and there were also similarities in the way in which this problem was resolved in the two countries. From the 1890s Hirotsugu Kinoshita, the principal proponent of *Ichiko* and regarded as the Japanese Thomas Arnold, encouraged the reformation of schooling in the style of the British public schools and promoted school sport based on the ideology of student self-rule. Consequently, with player safety improved through, for example, the use of gloves, baseball gradually developed and followed the formal rules as determined in the USA. Players tried to demonstrate their ability and character both within the game and beyond it; success in the game proved that their practice was productive while practice itself emphasized self-control and endurance, based on the principles of Bushido (Kiku 1993: 84–122). This tied in with the direct opportunity to promote the international position of Japan after the Meiji period; in a time of rapid change following a long period of national isolation, Japan increasingly opened up to foreign influence. Though it was mimetic it was symbolic of the character of pre-modernized Japan. Furthermore the biggest factor aiding the promotion of the baseball figuration was the mass media, which contributed to the formation of a modern nation state and a closer relationship with western sports.

For example, in 1896 the baseball club of *Ichiko* faced an amateur club of Americans who lived in Yokohama and won by a large margin of 23–9. The victory was extensively reported in the contemporary press who presented the story in highly nationalistic terms (*Asahi Shinbun*, 7 June 1896). After that, the press reported a tour of the USA by Waseda University in 1905 and a tour to Hawaii by Keio University in 1908. The universities had also invited American university clubs, semi-professional clubs and sometimes even professional major league teams to Japan, and conducted international exchanges through baseball. About a hundred such exchanges occurred in the 30 years from 1905 to 1936 (Kiku 1993: 113–14).

Waseda, Keio and other universities played a key role in developing active international baseball exchanges and helped change the centre of baseball from the national college, *Ichiko* school to private universities. This meant that the educational locus of baseball transferred from *Ichiko* and the children of the upper samurai class, to private schools and the children of the lower and middle samurai classes and the children of common people.[3] Parallel to the transfer of class responsibility, the mass media generated interest in baseball through reporting a greater quantity of baseball news.

Even in this context, the Bushido spirit and the discourse of Budo were maintained by ex-samurai because, as previously noted, the spirit was an ideology that supported the reduction of violence in *Bugei* and *Bujutsu* during the Tokugawa-Edo period, and formed the foundation of the Japanese sportization; that is, the Japanization of baseball from its western origins. However, the mass-media reporting of games against non-Japanese teams led to a growing antagonism from foreigners to delays in the modernization of Japan. Such misgivings caused a de-civilizing trend as players sought to use violent actions in order to win matches. 'Yakyu Gaidoku Ronso' (or the debate about baseball's harm) featured heavily in the press of 1912, as intellectuals and people who were worried about the state of schooling in Japan expressed concern at the tendency towards the Budo-ization of Japanese baseball, which was thought to have introduced violence and partisan rivalry between factions within schools, and to have eroded the civilized attitude of players, as evidenced, for example, by their loss of self-control. In fact, despite requests from enthusiastic fans, the baseball game between Waseda and Keio known as *Sokeisen* was cancelled for 20 years from 1906 due to violence between opposition supporters.

Thus the Japanization of baseball was disseminated to the general public through advances in the mass media and in the context of diminishing contrasts between social classes. The emphasis on civilized self-control, which characterized the Bushido spirit, was regarded as a symbolic tool which enabled the modern state of Japan to catch up with foreign countries (especially the USA) through the cultural commonality of sports. At the same time, increasing varieties of behaviour within Japanese society led to an increase in violence aimed at victory for victory's sake and nationalistic, anti-foreign sentiment. The development of Japanese sports as a specific variety of sports has subsequently become more generally ideologized as a symbolic de-civilizing process in pre-Second World War Japan, even though the characteristics that defined a sport as 'Japanese' had been emphasized as traditional 'Budo' and 'Bushido spirit' from Japanese ancient times. From the 1930s to the Second World War, the meaning of the spirit of 'Budo', which had formerly been associated with the development of self-control of violence in the sportization process, took on the very opposite meaning; that is to say, the meaning of Bushido spirit was reinvented and the very same word became used in relation to some of the more violent aspects of baseball in Japan. Domestic and international sports researchers' agreement on the peculiar characterization of Japanese sport, noted in my introductory remarks, may stem from this. In the next section I will discuss the case of judo and examine how the Japanese sportization process advanced after the Meiji period.

The sportization process of *Bujutsu* and the formation of Budo: the case of judo

As we saw in the case of baseball, some western sports underwent a process of Japanization. However, '*Bugei*' such as *Kenjutsu* and *Gekiken* (later, kendo), *Jujutsu* (later, judo), *Kyujyutsu* (later, kyudo) or other martial arts called 'Bujutsu' were regarded as 'old', or of a 'lower status', in the context of the extreme Europeanism or 'westernization' that characterized the early Meiji period (although this extreme Europeanism was not a constant force). However in 1877 a *Kenjutsu* group named '*Battotai*', which belonged to the government army, was victorious in action during the *Seinan* war of rebellion by the ex-samurai class. This victory raised the status of traditional *Bujutsu* and the activity became increasingly utilized by the police (especially the metropolitan police department in the capital, Tokyo) as part of their enforcement of a state monopolization of violence. Ironically *Bugei* and *Bujutsu*, which themselves had been transformed from the wounding and killing activities of the samurai class into a relatively civilized activity for training, became regarded more as a practical tool for suppressing competing forces. This process saw the re-introduction and re-emphasizing of the more violent aspects practised in former times (Yuasa 2001: 304–30).

However *Bujutsu* still did not conform to westernized notions of appropriate physical activity and criticisms were made that *Bujutsu* did more harm than good to people's health (Kimura 1975: 46–52). Though, in the shorter term, this idea provided symbolic support for the abolition of the samurai class which had supported *Bujutsu* up to the Meiji period, it gave an opportunity to form a figuration to restart *Bugei* in new varieties, by reforming the ex-samurai class in the longer term interests of the Meiji. That is to say, these figurational dynamics, as in the case of baseball, formed the basis of an oppositional movement. What appeared in this reformation was 'Budo', a major part in the process being played by Jigoro Kano, the originator of Kodokan-Judo. Kano played an important part in both the change of name from *Jujutsu* to *Judo* and also in the sportization of *Jujutsu* from *Bujutsu*. Subsequently the activity became, in the words of Kano, 'Most suitable for current society' (Kodokan 1988: 102). The main aspects of Kano's conversion of civilized *Jujutsu* to judo were as follows (Inoue 1998: 229):

1   He selected and systematized the most effective *Waza* (techniques) of the older schools of *Jujutsu*.
2   He introduced the ranking system (*Dan-Kyu Sei*) to encourage trainees.
3   He established the rules concerning contests and refereeing.
4   He made *Kodokan*, which was a kind of private governing body for Judo, an incorporated foundation in 1909, thus improving the organization's efficiency and influence.
5   He advocated the moral and educational value of learning judo, maintaining that judo served to cultivate people with the ability to make a contribution to modern society.
6   He successfully raised awareness of judo in the world through his lecturing and publishing activities.
7   He sought the 'globalization' of judo and tried to propagate and promote it abroad.
8   He accepted female pupils and fostered the growth of women's judo.

Since the Meiji period many of judo's rules have changed as the sport has internationalized. We can see evidence of a civilizing process in this respect through such changes as the prohibition of dangerous techniques, the more stringent punishment of foul moves, the more strict enforcement of etiquette, the introduction of subdivisions of Waza enabling a greater variety of (and less violent) ways of concluding bouts, and an increasingly objective role for the referee (Morishita and Murayama 1973: 199–235). Among the most significant rule changes have been the following:

1   Two games were required to win the match, judged on Nage-waza (throwing technique) and Katame-waza (the collective name for ground work techniques). Dangerous techniques such as Atemi-waza (technique for striking vital parts including the sexual organs) and Kansetsu-waza (techniques for dislocating joints) attacking fingers, toes and ankle were removed from the sport in 1899.
2   Improvements in judo clothing in 1907 led to a change from Ko-waza (minor throwing technique) such as Ashi-waza (foot and leg technique) to Oo-waza (major throwing technique) such as Koshi-waza (hip throw technique).
3   In 1925 the time fighters were allowed to transfer from Nage-waza to Katame-waza was restricted to quicken the pace of matches.
4   In 1930 different classifications of players were introduced into national championships; for example general and special, early-prime, late-prime, early-adult and late-adult.
5   In 1940 'winning on decision' or 'on points' or through penal regulation (in the case of a fighter leaving the mat) was introduced.
6   In 1951 the game area, the range of mat named *tatami*, became more standardized. Regulations were revised with regard to: (a) the duration of the match; (b) the system of having three referees; (c) the process of winning through advantage or injury; (d) the further subdivision of valid Waza (e.g.

'Ippon', 'Waza Ari', and 'Yuko'); and (e) the time necessary to complete a 'Waza Ari' hold-down was reduced to 25 seconds.

7   In 1957 weight divisions were introduced for junior and high school students.

8   In 1961 a classification of foul play was introduced: Shido (for a slight infringement), Chui (for a serious infringement), and Keikoku (for a grave infringement). Fighters cited three times for Chui would lose the bout. This connected the penal regulations with the validity of Waza as a standard of winning or losing by points.

9   In 1963 the regulations relating to the spatial limits of the contest were revised. The playing area was strictly defined as a 9 m square area with a 1 m surrounding border.

10   After 1965 dangerous Waza were increasingly prohibited and the progress of matches was speeded up through the encouragement of positive 'play'. The enforcement of regulations became more strict in general.

The sportization of martial arts such as judo seems to follow a smooth and somewhat uninterrupted civilizing process, smoother perhaps than the processes that western sports such as baseball underwent in Japan. Jigoro Kano has argued that the sport's patronage by Prime Ministers, various Ministers and many elite graduates of Tokyo University was significant in enabling him to direct this process, though the ex-samurai upper classes sought to distance themselves from the newer forms of these activities. The installation of the *Dan-Kyu* system (of grading participants) gave the lower, non-ex-samurai classes the opportunity for social mobility through judo and this acted as a further source of motivation for participants. Figure 10.1 shows the number of new 'disciples' entering the sport from 1882 when Kodokan-Judo was established, up to the Taisho period. We can see that, despite some fluctuations, the overall number increased steadily (Inoue 2000: 77). Judo's civilizing process gradually gained general acceptance and new attitudes to training and the reduction in violence became more prevalent.

The character-forming aspects of judo, and the suitability of this character within a modern nation, were emphasized as significant benefits to be derived by participants. After about 1910, the notion that the ultimate purpose of training was 'a complete self and help for the world' developed. The similarity of this ethos to the national government's request for new, talented personnel to be nurtured for the nation's benefit aided judo's development as the sport was seen to contribute significantly to the kind of personality or character that the nation 'needed'. When Japan militarized after the 1930s, the term 'Budo' was increasingly used in the discourse surrounding judo and character formation. As mentioned before, martial arts such as judo in modern Japan had been formed in the long history of sportization processes from the former *Bujutsu* and *Bugei*. The name 'Budo', created around 1920, was chosen in preference to the old *Jujutsu*, as it combined an emphasis on the tradition of denial from *Bugei* and *Bujutsu* with Kano's emphasis on 'rationality' and 'modern nature', as manifested through a respect for self-control and a reduction in violence. Therefore Budo such as judo were not viewed merely as martial arts compatible with the demands of a modern society, but as a physical

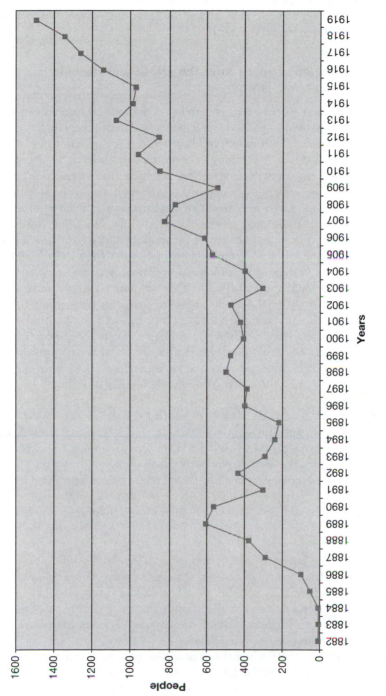

Figure 10.1 The number of entry disciples per year for Kodokan-Judo (1882–1920) (data revised from Iboue 2000: 77)

culture symbolizing the racial identity of the Japanese grounded in older traditions, yet not resistant to the modernization of the society. Thus we can say that Budo was 'the invention of modernity', and at the same time, it was 'the invention of tradition' (Hobsbawm and Ranger 1983).

The Budo-ization of sports after the 1930s and Bushido ideology in post-war Japan

Japanese sports and martial arts in modern Japan progressed through the sportization process together, influencing and supplementing each other through the concept of 'Budo'. As a result, both sport forms kept refining the self-control and codes of behaviour that had been developing since pre-modern times in *Bugei* and *Bujutsu*. Concomitantly, the strengthening feelings of nationalism increased the emphasis on victory for victory's sake, as opposed to an emphasis on the style in which participants competed. In other words, martial arts such as 'Budo' retained a close relationship with traditional Japanese values while also being linked to the maintenance of the cultural identity of the modern nation. The development of Japanese sports, and their acceptance in preference to their western counterparts, was based on the Bushido spirit, which appeared not just to have derived from, but to *be* the traditional spirit of 'Budo'. This was related to the formation and strengthening of national consciousness in countries throughout the world, augmented by the increasing frequency of international competition and more intense international rivalry. Thus, it might be suggested, the sportization process of Japanese sports, which involved both martial arts and western sports, established a clear distinction between Japanese and Japanized sports, and raised the modern national consciousness through increased varieties of sport forms.

> As the 19th century drew to its close, the volatile aspects of the Japanese samurai ethos were stirred up by a spreading sense of national crisis. At the end of the Tokugawa period, when Japan was forced to confront the direct military threat posed by the Western powers, the 'sleeping samurai spirit was awakened'. ... This new locus was the nationalistic image of the Japanese state, which, conveniently combined with fresh incentives for individual economic aspirations, could serve as the focal point for visions of glory and honour.
> (Ikegami 1995: 361–2)

Moreover the Japanese sportization process involved a subtle balance that promoted the development of civilized self-control and codes of behaviour on the one hand, and the increasing value placed on victory that led to a heightening of violence on the other. Such a subtle balance may be specific to this figuration in which members of a 'backward' nation were consciously trying to emulate, or catch up with, the 'modern' states of the West.

So, in the early 1930s when the militaristic trend began to gain strength – a development unprecedented in Japanese history – the balance between sportization and Budo was destroyed. Budo gained strength and gradually became superior.

Budo, it was argued, reflected development, but the process of development was secondary to extreme nationalism and militarism. In the eyes of the world, from the Manchurian Incident in 1931 to the China–Japanese war (1937–45) and to the Pacific War (1941–5), Budo was connected to the Japanese principle of historical notions centred on the Emperor. Budo became a 'national sport' and it became part of the ideology used to mobilize the nation for war (Inoue 1998: 233). Western sports accepted by Japan were Japanized to the extreme by the Bushido spirit contained within Budo, with particular emphasis placed on tradition 'from the ancient time' of Japan. For example, in baseball in the Pacific War the call of 'out' or 'safe' was made in English, but these calls were changed to their Japanese equivalents, '*Yoshi*' and '*Dame*'. The demonstration of self-control and of certain types of manners were transformed into codes of behaviour peculiar to the Japanese at that time, and distinct from the behaviour evident in ancient times.

Thus, in accordance with the development of the Budo ideology, the continuity of the sportization process shown in Judo's case was severed, and only the traditional part that connected with violent actions for military purposes was emphasized. The civilized side, such as development of self-control and manners, was used as the 're-invention' of the tradition which promoted Japanese militarism. Then the standard of action resulting from this 're-invention' of tradition became the standard by which the Japanese sought to reform western sports in Japan.

From this perspective it is easy to understand why some writers have emphasized the role of Budo and Bushido in post-war Japan as being simply connected with nationalism. However as this chapter has argued, Budo and Bushido have played a much more important part in the long-term development of sport in Japan, particularly in relation to civilizing processes in Japanese sport. From this perspective, a reconsideration of the history of Japanese sports and martial arts from the view of figurational sociology offers a more adequate explanation than do the more mystical explanations generally offered by western sociologists.

Notes

1   By 'masochistic acceptance' I refer to the tendency of Japanese researchers, especially when studying Japanese sport, to emphasize the way in which Japanese sports are seen to 'lag behind' their western counterparts, and the extremely 'negative' regard in which Bushido spirit is held (Tatano 1997: 130). It is therefore easy for Japanese people to be receptive to the kinds of image Whiting and other foreign writers portray.
2   'Katsuninken' is defined as an attitude whereby people regard a sword as a tool not to kill the opponent, but to promote respect for each other, uplifting their mentality.
3   In the Japanese school system of the Meiji era, national schools were more prestigious than their private counterparts because of the Japanese government's national education policy of selecting elite students. As a result, Japanese private schools attracted many poorer students, as did private universities.

References

Benedict, R. (1967) *The Chrysanthemum and the Sword*, Boston: Houghton Mifflin (trans. M. Hasegawa, 1972, *Kiku to Katana*, Tokyo: Syakai Shiso Sha).

Dunning, E. (1999) 'Violence and the Civilization of Sports', *iichiko* 52: 105–27 (trans. K. Higuchi, 1999, *Boryoku to Sports no Bunmeika*).

Dunning, E. and Sheard, K. (1979) *Barbarians, Gentlemen and Players*, Oxford: Martin Robertson.

Elias, N. (1969) *Uber den Prozeß der Zivilisation*, Bern and Munich: Francke (trans. K. Akai et al., 1977, *Bunmeika no Katei: Jo*, Tokyo: Hosei Daigaku Shyuppan Kyoku).

—— (1983) *The Court Society*, Oxford: Basil Blackwell.

—— (1986a) 'The Genesis of Sport as a Sociological Problem', in N. Elias and E. Dunning, *Quest for Excitement*, Oxford: Basil Blackwell.

—— (1986b) 'Introduction', in N. Elias and E. Dunning, *Quest for Excitement*, Oxford: Basil Blackwell.

Foucault, M. (1975) *Surveiller et Punir-Naissance de la Prison*, Paris: Galliard (trans. H. Tamura, 1977, *Kangoku no Tanjo*, Tokyo: Shincho Sya).

Hobsbawm, E. and Ranger, T. (eds) (1983) *The Invention of Tradition*, Cambridge: Cambridge University Press.

Ikegami, E. (1995) *The Taming of the Samurai*, Cambridge: Harvard University Press.

Inoue, S. (1998) 'Sports and the Martial Arts in the Making of Modern Japan', in Japan Society of Sport Sociology (eds), *Sports and the Transformation of Contemporary Society*, Kyoto: Sekai Shiso Sha, pp. 225–35 (in Japanese, 'Kindai Nippon ni okeru Sports to Budo', Nippon Sports Syakaigakkai (hen), *Hen'yo suru Gendai Syakai to Sports*).

—— (2000) *Sociology of Sports and Arts*, Kyoto: Sekai Shiso-Sha.

Kado, O. (1975) 'Social Change and Physical Education', in R. Sugawara (ed.), *Introduction to the Sociology of Physical Education*, Tokyo: Taishukan, pp. 139–74 (in Japanese, 'Shakai Hendo to Taiiku' in Sugawara Rei (ed.), *Taiiku Shakaigaku Nyumon*).

Kiku, K. (1993) *The Historical Sociology of 'Modern Professional Sports'* (in Japanese, *'Kindai Puro-Sports' no Rekishi Syakaigaku*), Tokyo: Fumaido Shuppan.

—— (2002) 'Bushido and Modernization of Sports in the Viewpoint of the Body Theory: The Approach for the Problem of Modern Sports', *Annual Report in Sports Studies in Nara*, 6, 41–50 (in Japanese, 'Shintai ron kara mita Bushido to Sports no Kindaika: kindai sports no mondaisei heno approach', *Nara Taiiku Gakkai Kenkyu Nenpo*).

Kimura, K. (1975) *The Formation of Modern Physical Education in Japan* (in Japanese, *Nippon Kindai Taiiku Shiso no Keisei*), Tokyo: Kyorin Shoin.

Kinoshita, S. (1976) *The History of Sport in Modern Japan* (in Japanese, *Sports no Kindai Nihonshi*), Tokyo: Kyorin Shoin.

Kodokan (1988) *The Code of Kano Jigoro*, Vol. 2 (in Japanese, *Kano Jigoro Taikei – Dai 2 Kan –*), Tokyo: Hon no Tomo Sha.

Kusaka, Y. (1985) 'A Cultural-sociological Study on the Principles of Bushi and Bushido in Baseball during Japan's Meiji period', *Sociological Journal of Physical Education and Sport*, 4, 23–44. (in Japanese, 'Meijiki ni okeru "Bushi"teki "Bushido"teki YakyuShinjo ni kansuru Bunka Syakaigaku teki Kenkyu', *Taiiku-Sports Shakaigaku Kenkyû*).

Meyer, M. and Rowan, B. (1977) 'Internationalized Organizations: Formal Structure as Myth and Ceremony', *American Journal of Sociology*, 83, 340–63.

Morishita, I. and Murayama, T. (1973) *The Rules of Judo Match* (in Japanese, *Judo Shiai Shinpan Kitei*), Kyoto: Gakugei Syuppan Sha.

Naramoto, T. (1975) *The Genealogy of Bushido* (in Japanese, *Bushido no Keifu*), Tokyo: Chuo Koron Sha.

Sogawa T. (2000) 'Budo and Education', *Monthly Journal of Physical Education*, 48(1), 42–43 (in Japanese, 'Budo to Kyoiku', *Taiiku ka Kyoiku*).

Sonoda, H. (1990) 'The Decline of the Japanese Warrior Class', *Japan Review*, 1, 73–111.

Sonoda, H., Hamana, A. and Hirota, T. (1995) *Historical-sociological Study on the Samurai Class* (in Japanese, *Sizoku no Rekishi Syakaigaku teki Kenkyu*), Nagoya: Nagoya daigaku syuppankai.

Sugawara, R. (1984) *The Sociology of Physical Education and Sport* (in Japanese, *Taiiku to Sports no Syakaigaku*), Tokyo: Fumaido Shuppan.

Takahashi, M. (1999) *The Formation of Samurai and the Creation of Image of Samurai* (in Japanese, *Bushi no Seiritsu, Bushizo no Sosyutsu*), Tokyo: Tokyo Daigaku Syuppan Kai.

Taki, K. (1995) *Thinking about Sports* (in Japanese, *Sports wo Kangaeru*), Tokyo: Chikuma Shobô.

Tatano, H. (1997) *Theories and Surveys of Sport Sociology* (in Japanese, *Sports Syakaigaku no Rironto Chosa*), Tokyo: Fumaido Shuppan.

Whiting, R. (1977) *The Chrysanthemum and the Bat*, Tokyo: The Simul Press.

—— (1989) *You Gotta Have Wa*, London: Macmillan (trans. M. Tamaki, 1990, *Wa wo motte Nippon to nasu*, Tokyo: Kadokawa Shoten).

Yoro, T. (1996) *A History of Japanese Views of the Body* (in Japanese, *Nihonjin no Shintaikan no Rekishi*), Kyoto: Hozokan.

Yuasa, A. (2001) *Reading the Traditional Books of Budo* (in Japanese, *Budo Densyo wo Yomu*), Tokyo: Baseball Magazine Sha.

11 After Olga

Developments in women's artistic gymnastics following the 1972 'Olga Korbut phenomenon'

Tansin Benn and Barry Benn

Over thirty years after the Munich Olympics of 1972, the name of Olga Korbut still tops the list when we enter debate with our university student-teachers about key influential people in the world of gymnastics. She did not win the coveted all-around championship title that year, which went to Ludmilla Tourisheva, but she won gold on beam and floor, which was an outstanding performance for someone who had travelled as a reserve on the Soviet team (Wright 1980: 137). More significantly, Olga became a 'superstar' through her charismatic personality, skill, daring, originality, courage, emotion and fallibility. The audience loved her child-like qualities and her breathtaking routines, smiles and tears, beamed around the world by the media, transformed women's artistic gymnastics. As Moran (1978: 2) wrote: 'The world of gymnastics must acknowledge her enormous contribution to the sport for it is possible that we will never see the like again.' Olga Korbut's success led both to accolades and to controversies. She was exploited internationally by the Soviets for political reasons while, in the sport, coaches and judges were divided on the risky, original skills she produced. Tensions arose between those wanting to ensure the sport retained a safe, mature, artistic dimension and those who welcomed the excitement of adventurous new risky acrobatic skills that challenged previous boundaries of human potential.

Perceived as risky and innovative at the time, Olga's routines 30 years on would score only a fraction of the 'high nines' gained at the 1972 Olympics because what then captured the world as exciting and daring is now commonplace. Boundaries of expectation in terms of human achievement have been in a constant process of change. This chapter traces some of the many influences that have contributed to such advances in the sport.

The world governing body for all forms of gymnastics is the Federation International de Gymnastique (FIG), which was founded in 1881.[1] Women's artistic gymnastics (WAG) started in its current form at the 1952 Helsinki Olympics, with Soviet gymnasts, such as Olga Korbut, dominating the sport until 1984. There were other stars as well, particularly from former Eastern bloc countries, such as Vera Caslavska from Czechoslovakia (1968 Olympics) and the Romanian, Nadia Commaneci (1976). Since then, there has been little significant change in world rankings. The countries in which the sport and its stars enjoyed high social and cultural status, for example Russia, Romania, Belarus, Ukraine and China, still lead the way (Lyberg 1999; Atkinson 2001).

However, in other respects, the global scene is changing. In competition statistics the largest world championships event was in Tianjin, China, in 1999, in which 260 gymnasts from 72 countries competed. This was far more competitors than had ever previously competed in a world championship; between 1987 and 1999, the number of competitors ranged from 88 to 201.[2] At the lower levels of gymnastics, however, concern was already being expressed about the declining interest and numbers of gymnasts participating in the sport, indicating that the pool nurturing tomorrow's elite was shrinking. While little is known about the precise causes of this trend, Yutaki Shirashi, a member of the FIG Scientific Commission, speaking at the 1999 FIG Medico Technical Symposium in China, suggested that the declining numbers taking part in the sport were related to the fact that: 'competitive gymnastics is generally believed by most people to be too "difficult" and "dangerous"' (FIG Medical Symposium 1999: 93).

With regard to the problem of difficulty, Shirashi reasoned that, compared with sports such as soccer, it takes too much time in gymnastics to make significant progress while gymnastics also has demanding strength and flexibility requirements at early stages before success can be seen or measured. In relation to the problem of danger he noted that 'one small mistake can incite trauma and complicated fracture' (ibid.: 95). The media hype surrounding such accidents stresses the risk and resulting misery which, in turn, sets up a panic, particularly as performers appear so young and vulnerable. However, while the difficulty and the associated risks of gymnastics are perceived by some to have increased, it is also the case that there have been in other respects improvements in safety; as Juan Webber, President of the Apparatus commission, suggested at the same symposium: 'Over the past thirty years, tremendous progress . . . has been made in improving safety for athletes' (ibid.: 5). For those familiar with the work of Elias (2000), and with the work on civilizing processes in sport in particular (see e.g. Chapter 2 by Sheard and Chapter 9 by Smith in this collection) this paradox will be recognized as more apparent than real. While we will touch on these issues throughout the chapter, our intention here is not to address the role of civilizing processes specifically, but to use a broader figurational perspective to help understand the accelerated development of women's gymnastics since the 1970s.

Through historical and sociological investigation it is possible to identify key players in the figurations that have shaped developments within women's artistic gymnastics since the early 1970s. At a global level, developments are largely directed by international representatives elected every four years on to the various committees and commissions of the FIG. Consultative commissions have specific responsibilities for advising and contributing to development and currently include medical, scientific and disciplinary commissions and an athletes' commission. There are also internal commissions with responsibilities for financial and executive matters, media and communications, development statutes, competitions and apparatus. Technical matters related to coaching and judging, including the quadrennial production of the Code of Points, the book of competition rules and regulations, are the responsibility of the Women's Technical Committee (WTC) of the FIG. In turn, the decisions of the FIG are interpreted and applied within each affiliated association. For example, within British gymnastics, a Women's Technical Committee (WTC) applies and adapts international directives for coaches, judges and gymnasts within the UK.

Processes of standardization, globalization, scientization, medicalization, politicization, commercialization, bureaucratization and technicization have all been observable in the development of women's artistic gymnastics since 1972, resulting in an increasingly complex sport, influenced by multiple networks of 'mutually oriented and dependent people' (Elias 2000). Gymnasts, coaches and judges form the hub of the competitive gymnastics figuration but these people are influenced by many others (for example, gymnasts' parents, governing body officials, sports medicine practitioners, sports scientists, journalists, apparatus manufacturers and spectators). In this chapter, processes of technicization will provide the main framework for examining recent developments and, in this connection, we will use evidence from changes in apparatus and coaching. By 'technicization' we refer to advances in material technology applied to the development of apparatus and training aids, and the development of training methods which have led to increasing technical complexity of the skills performed within the sport. These central aspects of technicization have recently been highlighted by the President of the FIG (Grandi 2000: 5):

> Modern sports have reached an extraordinary level in terms of presentation and performance. There are many reasons for this, some of which include the following:
> – Progress in training methods as well as in scientific, biomechanical and psycho-educational developments;
> – Technology invested in apparatus and their didactic use during training.
> In short, sports are clearly following the course of a technologically developing civilisation that is advancing ever more rapidly towards new discoveries.

The following discussion will focus on apparatus designers and coaches, their interdependence and their influence on progress in gymnasts' performance levels. As will be shown, central to this trend is the attempt to balance a concern with safety issues with the quest of innovating athletes, coaches and equipment designers for more exciting performances.

Developments in technology, apparatus and the sport

Women's artistic gymnastics involves girls and women performing routines on four pieces of apparatus: the floor, vault, beam and asymmetric bars. When Olga Korbut amazed the world in 1972 her skills heralded a challenge to judges, coaches and fellow gymnasts, particularly in the West. The potential of gymnasts to perform increasingly complex skills has been influenced by the technical developments made by entrepreneurs in the apparatus design field. In order to break new ground in terms of skill progression, apparatus designers are reciprocally dependent on innovative gymnasts and coaches with the vision and ability to experiment. The questions of who leads, who follows, who is commissioned to design and who is sanctioned by whom to provide approved apparatus, are all important to the debate about advancing standards of performance, but Elias stressed that central in any understanding of such complex social processes is not simply the actions of individuals and groups, but the relationships between the respective parties. Since 1972, it has been within the FIG that such tensions and struggles have been played out between elected international representatives. Publicly accessible FIG Bulletins[3] record debates among influential groups of people with regard to the development of the sport in safe but 'exciting' directions. The risks associated with this 'quest for excitement' (Elias and Dunning 1986) were summed up by Hardy Fink (Chairman of the Men's Technical Committee) in 1999, as follows:

> our goal must be to allow gymnasts to progress, but to provide safe conditions for that progress. Unfortunately, progress in gymnastics and safety in gymnastics tend to be mutually exclusive. As they progress, gymnasts must generate and sustain ever greater forces; their greater rotational speeds are associated with higher shear forces; the increasing complexity of skills requires more critical precision and timing; and all of this requires increased numbers of repetitions to assure mastery. Each of these factors increases the possibility of error and the susceptibility to injury.
>
> (FIG Medical Symposium 1999: 103)

FIG members representing the medical, apparatus, and technical commissions have mutual interests but distinctive perspectives when seeking to influence developments within the sport. Such tensions, involving both cooperation and conflict, have led to changes in apparatus dimensions, sizes, stipulations and usage at world and Olympic championship levels. Changes have been made in the interests of achieving new performance levels in the sport and, increasingly, of overt safety for the gymnast. This is clearly demonstrated in the introduction of the radical vaulting table in 2001, which will be discussed in greater detail later.

Members elected to serve on the FIG have controlled the sport of gymnastics formally on a global scale for over 50 years. Previously, in the 1948 London Olympics, chaos followed from the 'bring your own apparatus' regulations that resulted in multiple sets of apparatus, and swapping, which made a farce of concepts such as fairness and safe preparation for international competition. It was clear that standardization of apparatus was essential to the future of international competition; indeed it might be argued that, prior to this level of standardization, gymnastics cannot be termed a modern sport in a sociologically meaningful sense (Guttmann 1978; Dunning and Sheard 1979). At the FIG Congress of 1949 in Stockholm, a new format for Olympic and World gymnastic competitions, including apparatus dimensions, was agreed and specified within the Code of Points[4] (rule-book) in terms of which competitions were to be organized and judged (Prestidge 1988). Tracing the histories of the four pieces of apparatus used in women's artistic gymnastics demonstrates the influence that entrepreneurs who design and supply apparatus, and innovative gymnasts and coaches, have had on developments within the sport.

Beam

Mention has already been made of the influence of Olga Korbut on the image and popularity of the sport. She can also be recognized as the gymnast who initiated a change of direction in women's gymnastics as she was the first gymnast to perform a backward somersault on the beam. Prior to this, traditional beam work had consisted almost exclusively of dance steps, balances and poses. Korbut sparked intense discussion about the nature of women's gymnastics and the safety of participants. In relation to the backward somersault on the beam, the WTC proclaimed that:

> In view of the fact that this element is not peculiar to the beam the WTC have decided to prohibit it. In this way it is hoped to avoid danger for the gymnast . . . This decision is taken with a great majority.
>
> (FIG Bulletin 2 1973: 45)

A similar discussion took place concerning a balance Korbut performed on her upper chest with her legs arched back over her head and toes touching the beam in front of her face. This required extreme hyper-flexibility of the spine and could be a source of danger to the hundreds of thousands of her young admirers who might attempt to emulate her. At a later meeting, the WTC stated that: 'the back salto should not be considered a beam exercise and that this skill and the skills involving excessive back bend be referred to the medical commission' (ibid.).

The debate continued between judges, medical personnel, coaches and gymnasts. As the 1974 world championship approached it was necessary for a definitive decision to be made if changes to the rules were to operate. Finally, a compromise decision was made concerning the backward somersault, which allowed the skill to be performed in competition provided the federation of the performing gymnast accepted responsibility, and no doubt liability, for the danger involved. By way of deterrent, the judges would be required to penalize gymnasts who paused before or after performing the skill (FIG Bulletin 2 1974: 52). Skills with excessive back arch were never mentioned again.

The final decision, with no outright banning of acrobatic skills, opened the way for gymnasts and coaches to transfer traditional floor skills to the beam. Today the beam can resemble a tumbling track with gymnasts performing the most daring acrobatic skills, much as they do acrobatics in a floor routine. All of this happens on a beam just 10 centimetres wide, 5 metres long and 120 centimetres high. This trend was enhanced when a decision was made to cover the surface of the beam, originally just bare wood, with a suede-type material over a synthetic rubber under-lay. Changes were also made to the leg supports of the beam to increase stability. The resultant degree of padding and spring encouraged yet more skill experimentation. Reflecting on the rapid increase in skill complexity on the beam in the 1970s, Gander of the FIG WTC stated: 'The gymnasts are now performing such elements on the beam that a few years ago, could not be predicted, even by experts' (Gajdos 1997: 282). Inherent in such skills is an increased degree of danger to participants.

Asymmetric bars

Early in the twentieth century women participated in parallel bars and rings work (now both exclusively men's events). When women first competed on asymmetric bars these were not anchored, stable, flexible and resilient as they are today, but were simply formed by raising one and lowering the other bar of a set of men's parallel bars. The only adaptation for stability was made by bolting supporting struts between the tops of the uprights of the higher bar and the heavy metal base. Static and strength skills were predominant. By the 1952 Olympics in Helsinki, the Soviets had introduced swinging elements and the current sport-form was born. The introduction of more dynamic swinging routines required changes in apparatus construction. The use of anchoring wires, in the interests of safety and progress, was permissible, though not mandatory, from 1953. Asymmetric tension bars were declared the official FIG apparatus from the 1967 European championships, allowing for the safe variations in widths and heights evident today (Gajdos 1997).

Since 1972 there have been a number of changes that have enabled bar skills and routine work to develop. In addition to the added safety of anchoring tension wires, the change from wooden to fibre-glass bars in the late 1970s offered a new resilience for more complex flighted skills and rebound, twisting elements. Much scientific progress was made on landing mats to secure more absorption of landing forces on surfaces that would minimize rotational ankle and knee injuries. The heights of both bars were raised to enable thicker, safer landing 'pads' to be used. Paradoxically this increased security led to more daring free flight and somersaulting skills and riskier dismounts being performed by innovative gymnasts. The oval bars (the cross sectional shape of the men's parallel bars from which the women's asymmetric bars evolved) were replaced with round bars of reduced diameter, thus enabling the gymnast to swing full circles around the bar more safely with less risk of accidental tangential release. The regulation maximum distance allowable between the two bars was increased in 1983 to enable taller gymnasts to perform the new skills (FIG Bulletin 120 1984: 90). An unintended outcome was also to advantage the smaller gymnast who could utilize more bio-mechanically efficient techniques to increase the dynamics and power of swinging and flighted somersaulting elements that characterize bar routines today. The result has been the increased 'borrowing' of skills previously performed only by men on the horizontal bar. The Women's Technical Committee of the FIG noted the first signs of men's bar work becoming fashionable for women in the early 1980s (FIG Bulletin 121 1984: 78). Examples could be seen in the increasing appearance of elements like the giant swing (full circling of the high bar in an extended body position), and the Tkatchev (a backwards free flighted skill over the high bar). In the case of the asymmetric bars then, the evolution of the apparatus has been the outcome of a complex mix of the increasing regulation of the sport to create a safer environment while, concomitantly, the dynamics of competitive pressures led athletes and coaches to innovate and thus develop routines which are increasingly exciting but also increasingly dangerous.

Vault

Prior to the 1970s vaulting apparatus and skills were conservative by today's standards. The progress of vaulting skills since has paralleled continued improvement in materials technology for apparatus surfaces that have improved both rebound potential and impact resilience/absorption. A range of springboards utilizing more flexible woods and combinations of wood and/or metal spring constructions have been introduced. Vaulting skills progressed, for example, to make the second flight phase, from leaving the horse until landing, more dynamic and acrobatic. The considerable forces involved, coupled with the increase in training repetitions to perfect these new, complex, rotational vaults led to an increase in wrist injuries. Consequently attention was paid to the padding of the surface of the vaulting horses and sprung-tops were developed with more rounded edges to reduce the effects of repetition impacts.

Both gymnasts and spectators welcomed such changes, the gymnasts exploring the possibilities of new skills and the spectators appreciating different vaults. Variety was aided by producing vaults which combined somersaults and twists during the second flight phase using the rotation generated by the gymnast when moving from feet on the board to hands on the horse. To allow a backward rotation of the body from hand contact with the horse, the gymnast had to make a half turn of the body in the first flight stage from board to horse. However, the scope for variety was soon exhausted and gymnasts effectively limited the variety of vaults further by performing only those awarded the highest tariff. In an attempt to inject some interest for spectators, the FIG ruled that in international competitions there would be a limit on the number of vaults of any one type that a team may use.

The search for innovation continued and in the 1980s a new type of vault skill was produced, the Yurchenko, named after the gymnast who first performed the vault in major competition, Natalia Yurchenko. This initiated another stage in the development of vaulting complexity and variety. The vault uses a 'round-off'[5] at the end of the approach run, allowing the gymnast to land on the board with her back to the vaulting table. This facilitated a much more efficient conversion of momentum generated in the run up into backward rotation, and a more powerful projection from the top of the table into the second flight phase. The ensuing increase in flight time and available energy gave scope for even more complexity in second flight manoeuvres. In terms of technical developments in the sport, Natalia Yurchenko's legacy is exceptional, yet she is not remembered, outside the sport, in the same way as Olga Korbut. This would itself make an interesting problem for further analysis but it highlights the fact that the social context in which Korbut performed is perhaps just as significant as the innovations she introduced to the sport.

While it had become commonplace to transfer skills traditionally performed on one apparatus to another, there was a price to pay for moving the round-off skill from the safer boundaries of the floor. Accidents increased because there was only a minute margin for error in ensuring the connections between floor, springboard and horse were accurate. To help counteract this, the FIG rules demanded that a foam rubber safety 'collar' be used around the board when round-off entry vaults were being performed. This increasing level of safety probably encouraged more athletes to attempt this high scoring manoeuvre. In the interests of further promoting safety, however, any such vaults performed without the foam rubber collar have, since 2000, received no score.

Through all of these advances the dimensions of the top of the horse or 'target area' remained unchanged until the introduction of the revolutionary 'Pegases'[6] vaulting table in 2001. But as skill complexity on to and from the top of the horse increased, so too did the risks gymnasts were prepared to take. Following increasingly serious accidents the FIG finally commissioned the development of new vaulting apparatus in the early 1990s. In 1996, the first prototype was unveiled by the company Janssen & Fritsen which had employed Dieter Hofmann,[7] among others, as a consultant. The strong rebound properties of the prototype, which heightened and lengthened the second flight, met opposition from 'the experts' and work continued until its launch at the 2001 world championships, which was treated with the razzmatazz usually reserved for a new luxury car. It was, we were told: 'the centre of attention of over 10,000 spectators and experts. It had been effectively positioned in the spotlights of the VIP area and thus optically heralded the successful synthesis of functionality and design . . . a true revolution' (Janssen & Fritsen 2001: 14). In terms of safety there were widened surfaces, a padded front to protect from injuries and an inclined support surface to allow for excellent orientation. The introduction of this new apparatus will almost certainly lead to further developments in techniques.

Some of the problems of this radical change of apparatus were soon recognized. In order to ensure equity, all gymnasts hoping to compete in the 2001 world championships had to have training access to the new vaulting table. Janssen & Fritsen donated one Pegases table to each of the 72 countries that had gymnasts competing in the 1999 world championships, while the FIG donated 30 to gymnastic federations. The production demands for the company were great, but so were the potential rewards. The global repercussions of this radical revolution in apparatus design will reach the smallest gymnasiums in the most remote parts of the world. The process of change is unlikely to end here. As Dr Michel Leglise, The FIG Vice-President and President of the Medical and Scientific Commission put it:

> The Medical Commission is generally interested in every kind of innovation that may improve the gymnasts' safety. The new vaulting table seems to mark considerable progress in this direction. Nevertheless it will be necessary to pursue further biomechanical studies in order to improve utilisation techniques, particularly in women's vaulting.
>
> (Janssen & Fritsen 2001: 16)

The cascading effect of decisions by the FIG to sanction a radical change in apparatus regulations affects every association and club in the world. It is no surprise, then, that entrepreneurial apparatus producers compete with each other to produce the best performing version of the new apparatus for the global market. The interdependent relationship of entrepreneurial manufacturers, innovative coaches and top-level gymnasts has been, and remains, central to the globalizing developments in the sport (see Maguire 1999, esp. Ch. 6).

Floor

Developments in 'floor' gymnastics have similarly involved increasing levels of complexity in skill, technique and mastery. The dimensions of the floor space, 12 metres square, have not changed, but technological advances have enormously improved the rebound properties of the 'floor' itself. Coaches and gymnasts have maximized this rebound potential to develop many new, adventurous skills. Twisting double somersaults, which 25 years ago were considered advanced movements in trampolining, are now being performed in floor sequences. Such advances, however, bring new risks. Ankle injuries are common. Other serious accidents have resulted from the greater forces generated and the diminishing degree of error possible in the more complex skills, which often involve the gymnast performing multiple rotations around two axes of the body simultaneously. After becoming World Champion in 1978, the Soviet gymnast Elena Moukhina was paralysed following a spinal injury sustained while attempting a particularly difficult and risky skill at the end of a floor routine. Ironically the skill itself would not have been possible without the advances in material technology used in the design of floor areas.

Before discussing the development of training aids it is worth summarizing the developments charted so far. Across the four pieces of apparatus used in women's artistic gymnastics, developments have been made with the intended outcomes of increasing excitement and reducing the dangers inherent in the sport. Sometimes these goals are mutually exclusive, often one unintended outcome of an attempt to make the sport safer has been to promote increasingly risky manoeuvres among the innovating elite. There are obvious parallels here with Sheard's work on boxing (see Chapter 2 in this collection) in which he argues that, while civilizing processes have been associated with the introduction of boxing gloves in an attempt to reduce levels of violence in the sport, one unintended consequence of this development has been to increase the probability of boxers inflicting serious harm (e.g. brain damage) on their opponent.

Training aids

In addition to the activities of entrepreneurial apparatus manufacturers, innovative coaches and gymnasts, the production of training aids has also accelerated the increase in skill complexity in the sport over the last 30 years. These training aids have included equipment that has minimized training risks in the learning of highly complex skills and the physical demands made on the body during the performance of the high number of repetitions necessary in the practice stages. For example, travelling support harnesses, tumbling strips of sprung wood and modified trampoline beds have helped coaches to ensure sound progressive learning stages and spatial orientation prior to skill performance on the proper apparatus. The greatest aid to progress, however, has been the virtually universal use of the foam rubber-filled pit, which is simply a hole in the floor filled with foam rubber pieces to provide a soft landing area, at floor level, from any piece of apparatus appropriately positioned. A major part of the success of the former Eastern bloc gymnasts was related to advances in the use of such training aids. This is not to suggest that the risk of injury has been eradicated in training, but it has been minimized and the fear factor of early skill-learning phases has been diminished. Yutaki Shirashi of the FIG scientific commission made explicit the link between the pit and accelerated skill complexity:

> By global use of this pit, fears in the early training period have been substantially reduced . . . in short I think it may be said that there is an extremely close relation with the pit and the high degree of difficulty of the techniques subsequent to the 1970s.
>
> (FIG Medical Symposium 1999: 96)

The reduced risks in training are, of course, rarely seen by the public at large. Consequently, the perception of the need for greater safety in the sport may not be based on an accurate overview of the sport as a whole, but may be disproportionately influenced by a few highly visible and serious injuries that occur in competition.

During the 1970s coaches' knowledge in relation to such training aids broadened considerably. For example, leading British coaches, such as John Atkinson, travelled to Russia to see the system which had produced the best gymnasts in the world for most of the twentieth century. Atkinson instigated the initiatives that facilitated the flow of information back to Britain, and allowed British gymnasts and coaches to experience at first hand the Soviet methods. The late 1970s were a time of unprecedented opportunities. For example, one project enabled the best young male and female British gymnasts and their coaches to spend a month living and training at a Russian gymnastics school. Sponsorship was found through the *Daily Mirror* newspaper and winners of the annual national competitions held between 1975 and 1985 spent a month in Russia. In 1977 Barry Benn (co-author) and his young gymnast Andrew Sweeney were among the first recipients of this award. The experience was captured and broadcast on a BBC documentary called *The Summer of '77*. Although depressed by the gap between Russian and British training opportunities and stages of development, these early pioneers returned to England with heightened aspirations and convinced that training facilities could be improved. The pits used in Russian gymnasiums were going to be essential to the progress of Britain's gymnasts. In the early 1980s, gymnastic clubs that had dedicated facilities began to install pits. Now no artistic gymnasium is built without one.

Over the last 30 years, a process of technicization has been occurring in which there has been an interdependent relationship between increases in materials technology and the resultant acceleration of technical skill proficiency. Each piece of apparatus has been regularly developed and refined by apparatus manufacturers both leading and responding to innovative skill developments. The more widespread introduction of pits and technically sophisticated training aids has helped to close the gap between East and West, raising standards and expectations world-wide. The resultant expansion in the range and complexity of skills has led to increasingly demanding training regimes for selected young people who are prepared to dedicate their early lives to the sport.

Professionalization of coaching

In Britain, the level at which a coach is able to work is recognized by British Gymnastics[8] through the coaching qualification system. Levels of qualifications indicate the knowledge and ability that coaches have in relation to the syllabus. Tracing the development of coaching syllabi provides evidence of the increasing demands made on coaches and shows how these have paralleled the technicization of the sport.

Indicative of the Eastern European impact on the globalization of gymnastics (see later), the 'Olga phenomenon' heralded an unprecedented upsurge in the popularity of the sport, particularly among girls. Clubs proliferated, as did the scale of floor and vault incentive awards provided by the then BAGA (British Amateur Gymnastics Association) (Prestidge 1988: 77). As the number of gymnasts and clubs increased so did the need for coaches and competitions. Increasingly coaches were required not just to teach children simple gymnastic skills on the floor and vaulting box, but to prepare gymnasts for competition in the four apparatus disciplines of women's artistic gymnastics, a much more demanding task. Award schemes were extended throughout the 1980s and 1990s to embrace bar and bench work,[9] and many other gymnastic disciplines. The desire to increase prestige through international success, which is an aspect of what Dunning (1986) has called the 'increasing seriousness' of sport in modern societies, was undoubtedly influential in this development.

The upsurge in demand for the sport influenced the coach training system. During the last three decades in Britain, the content of coaching syllabi in gymnastics has undergone many changes in the requirements for attaining each level of award. Expectations have spiralled in complexity and breadth in every four-yearly cycle of revision. Updating each coaching cycle involved the raising of standards of expertise and knowledge. There was increasing attention paid to the applied sports sciences of physiology and biomechanics in the early 1970s, and later to psychology and sociology. Rising expectations were reflected in the range of theoretical domains incorporated in textbooks, such as those commissioned by the BAGA in the 1980s and 1990s, exemplified by the *BAGA Women's Gymnastics Manual* (1990) by Colin Still, then National Coach for women.

The need to retain coaches qualified on the previous cycle, while making sufficient advances in each syllabus to reflect the speed of change within the sport, has created tensions that are difficult to resolve. In the late 1980s and 1990s some coaches attended 'refresher days' to update their knowledge, but that was rarely adequate as skills deemed difficult on one cycle came to be seen as simple in the next and were replaced with more complex ones. The sport changed faster than some coaches were able, or prepared, to move. Coaches were encouraged to re-appraise their desires and philosophy and decide whether they wanted to move towards the higher level of performance demanded by advances in the sport. Those who decided to move forward had to devote more time to gaining the theoretical and practical knowledge levels required at the cost of increasing their commitment to the sport. A gap was developing between the voluntary coaches who could commit one or two evenings a week to the local club and the coaches who wanted to stay at the elite end of the sport. The elite level coaches had to make gymnastics their profession and full-time commitment, in local authority or private clubs, because the demands were becoming increasingly onerous. Producing gymnasts able to compete at national and international level required increasing numbers of hours in the gym, for at least six days a week most of the year, demanding enormous family sacrifice for both coaches and gymnasts (Sports Council 1992).

Child protection imperatives have also become increasingly important on the coach education agenda. The sport requires strength, flexibility, spatial awareness, courage, aesthetic and artistic abilities but also early dedication and single-mindedness. As strength:weight ratios favour people with smaller, lighter physiques and the time-span for basic preparatory conditioning and progression from simple to complex skill learning is long, the sport needs to be started at an early age. Increasing sensitivity to the exploitation of young children and the risk/safety axis of tension in skill acquisition has ensured that criticism and caution have paralleled innovation and advancement in the sport's development. The dangers of potential child abuse in the sport have been recognized at least since 1971 when the FIG President wrote:

> Medical reports have given a warning and pointed out the dangers of abusive training without the necessary control . . . Rational and progressive preparation of children is necessary but . . . this must be done using people who are aware of their responsibilities to give training. Nobody should be so irresponsible as to think only of producing 'competitive animals' hastily trained, frequently damaged and incapable of continued progress after a certain level has been reached.
>
> (FIG Bulletin 4 1971: 20)

Heightened awareness in society of child abuse through high-profile cases in sport, alongside a growing 'blame and claim' compensation culture in the West, has led to the inclusion of these issues in coach education, and coaches are advised to consider the potential risks involved in every training decision they make. The age limits for participation at FIG and BG levels have been raised to answer critics' accusations of 'child exploitation' and age-specific championships have been established, but concerns continue and are fuelled by revelations, for example those about gymnastics in the USA by Joan Ryan (1996). Such revelations may not be the result of an actual increase in the incidence of abuse of children in the sport but, as Elias's work would indicate, the growing prominence of such issues may be a consequence of attitudinal changes and increasing sensitivity.

Although few people openly criticized the adoption of training regimes, even in England in the 1990s, that led to girls as young as eight years of age spending in excess of 30 hours training per week, many in the sport were concerned about this trend. The current Director of Coach/Judge Education for British Gymnastics, Lloyd Readhead, has contributed much to the protection of coaches and young children, for example, in producing BG's *Health, Safety and Welfare Policy* (2001). This includes protection guidelines for 'children and vulnerable adults', and recommendations on appropriate hours of training. Thus, while coaching has professionalized as a consequence of broader international pressures for success in the globalized sporting arena, these developments have occurred in conjunction with an increased concern over the dangers faced by, and the demands placed on, youngsters.

Globalization of knowledge and control

Implicit in much of what we have said so far has been the recognition of the influential part played by globalizing trends in the rapid development of gymnastics knowledge and demands on coaches post-Korbut. Television transmitted the great achievements of the Soviets, Romanians, Chinese and East Germans across the world and parents, coaches and gymnasts in the West could only look on in amazement. In the early 1970s, there was a great bank of gymnastics knowledge in the countries of the Eastern bloc. Mention has already been made of the first tentative contacts between the gymnastic communities of East and West, but the knowledge gleaned greatly expanded following 'glasnost' and, particularly, 'perestroika'[10] in the 1980s. Eastern bloc coaches were able to travel to other countries and offer their coaching services and knowledge. At the same time many of the specialist training centres opened their doors to visiting gymnasts and coaches from the West who were prepared to use their economic power to access the knowledge power of their Eastern counterparts. Many of the coaches who had produced world champions in the sport became economic migrants and gymnastics knowledge began to be shared globally. This was not a simple or untroubled process, however, as coaching regimes develop within wider cultures and the political value of winning in some former Eastern bloc countries was used to justify practices of training for talented children that were deemed abusive and exploitative in the West. Such tensions have been an integral part of the globalization of gymnastics knowledge.

FIG committees are responsible for developing policies and practices intended to control the global development of the sport. For many years compulsory routines at world championships and Olympic Games have been a decisive influence, shaping the work of coaches and gymnasts and skill development in line with the opinions of experts who designed successive 'compulsory routines' for the FIG.

These consisted of prescribed sequences on floor, bars and beam and a set vault that all competitors had to perform prior to the more diverse 'voluntary routines'. Such a steering force was particularly valuable in nations where attempts to emulate the world's best gymnasts without sufficient knowledge of sound, safe preparation, led to inevitable problems. Considered selection of certain skills for compulsory routines necessitated sharing knowledge about underlying techniques and safe teaching methodologies. But tension grew as leading nations came to regard the compulsory routines as a limiting factor on the development of gymnastics. In 1978, Romania proposed the abolition of compulsory routines on grounds that would be repeated, with minor variations, in the following two decades. Romania argued that abolition of the compulsory routines would 'contribute to the progress of gymnastics and make the process of preparation easier . . . The sport would become more spectacular' (FIG Bulletin 3 1978: 81). Italy joined the argument in 1979 (FIG Bulletin 3 1979: 93), Algeria in 1986 (FIG Bulletin 103 1986: 108), and the debate continued into the 1990s. Each time the FIG WTC voted on the decision, there was a large majority to retain the compulsory routines. However, at a meeting in 1993, the WTC's vote to retain the compulsory routines was overridden by recommendations from the FIG Executive Committee for their abandonment. A number of interrelated processes, including the growth of the sport, the media/sponsorship demands and the dependence on the sport for media coverage, had together created sufficient pressure for change.

The growth of the sport, the length of competitions and the effects on gymnasts, coaches, judges and national federations contributed to the decision to abolish compulsory routines. At the world championships held in Indianapolis in 1991, the participation of 28 teams and 22 individual gymnasts meant that 189 women (and 212 men) from 37 countries took part. The President of the FIG, Yuri Titov, in his post-championship report, stated that:

> a nine day championship with four days preparation is definitely too long. For media and public to follow the competition is virtually impossible, it is becoming too expensive for participating federations and it is very difficult for gymnasts to maintain good physical and psychological form.
>
> (FIG Bulletin 154 1992: 38)

As a judge who participated in this championship one of the co-authors (Barry Benn) supports the President's sentiments. Gymnastics competitions needed to become more attractive 'packages' for both media and public and more congenial for participants. The Executive Committee of the FIG established a working group to study the 'Gymnastics–television relationship' (FIG Bulletin 160 1994: 64), and this ultimately recommended that compulsory routines be dropped. In the FIG General Assembly of 1994, Romania demanded a secret ballot on the subject. Eleven federations voted to keep compulsory routines but 41 voted for their abolition. They were abolished at the end of the cycle in 1997. While many were advantaged by this move, some nations in the early stages of developing competitive gymnastics were disadvantaged.

Such moves were largely based on the perceived need to maintain media and public interest and support for a sport that was heavily dependent on TV contracts and funding distributed by the International Olympic Committee (IOC). Several experiments with 'audience friendly' competition formats were carried out. In the Presidential Report to the 1996 FIG Congress, the President again noted that:

> It is evident that the FIG should continue searching for ways of making competitions meet the requirements of TV and spectators. Ignorance of these requirements might lead to the isolation of our competitions and loss of popularity, both of which mean a loss of foundation for future development.
>
> (FIG Bulletin 168 1996: 126)

The first world championship without compulsory routines took place in Lausanne, Switzerland, in 1997. Audiences and television coverage both increased. The Presidential Report for that year confirmed that the event was covered by TV in 55 countries compared with 37 in 1995. There were 220 TV connections (202 in 1995) with an estimated 191 million spectators worldwide (172 in 1995) (FIG Bulletin 172 1998: 126). Competition formats are broadening; for example gymnasts can now 'specialize' on particular pieces of apparatus. In order to explore further this potential, the FIG held a high level, international media symposium in November 2001 entitled *Harnessing the Power of Marketing and Media for Gymnastics*. In his closing summary, the President, Professor Bruno Grandi, while discussing the creation and exploitation of 'stars', mentioned the significance of the 'star qualities' of Olga Korbut, her back somersault on the beam, and the importance of her particular contribution to the popularity of the sport (FIG Media Symposium 2001: 115).

An unanticipated consequence of abolishing the development function of compulsory routines, however, has been an increase in the risks that gymnasts in the less advanced nations are forced to take. It became clear that, in order to help less advantaged gymnasts and coaches to reach gymnastic maturity, a sound, safe programme of training that addressed concerns around the intensive training of children was required. Perhaps one of the consequences of this has been the establishment of a global coach education system by the FIG. Called the 'Gymnastics Academies Programme', it is designed to support 'existing training programmes for coaches within the federations and to furnish the concept as a whole to developing countries' (BG, *The Gymnast* 2002: 18). The FIG launched the first Academy in Kuala Lumpur in February 2002, and the system was developed between 1999 and 2002 with support from the IOC, Olympic Solidarity and the National Olympic Committees (ibid.). The mission and aims of the global coaching enterprise are an ambitious but important statement which serves to stress the centrality of child protection in the sport's development. They are:

> To provide a prioritized, customized and standardized coach education system for the development of competitive Gymnastics worldwide based upon

principles of sport science, health, current training, best practice and the nature of the developing child.

(FIG 2002)

The project is of particular interest in the globalization debate, as is the fact that Adrian Stan has led the work on the Gymnastics Academies Programme at the FIG's headquarters in Switzerland, since January 2002. He is a Romanian who became National Coach in his country for men's and women's artistic gymnastics in the 1980s and early 1990s. From 1993 until 2002, Stan was British National Technical Director for women's artistic gymnastics. He helped to lift the position of the women's team from seventeenth in 1991, when they failed to qualify for the 1992 Barcelona Olympics, to ninth in the world championships 2001, and qualification for the Sydney 2000 Games. Stan's work provides one example of the means by which gymnastics knowledge is being globalized, and also illustrates the West's dependency on the East in this regard.

Conclusion

We have sought in this chapter to locate some of the developments in gymnastics in the post-Korbut era – particularly with regard to apparatus and coaching – within a framework informed by figurational sociology. Broadly speaking, the gymnastics figuration is made up of a range of interdependent groups (athletes, coaches, administrators, national governing body representatives, television and the media). The impact of the pace of change within women's artistic gymnastics has influenced everyone involved with the sport. Changes in the period since the 'Korbut phenomenon' have been analysed here in relation to the technical achievements of gymnasts and the actions of innovating coaches and the ways in which these processes have both facilitated and constrained the actions of other groups within the figuration. All these aspects of the sport are likely to continue to develop. Currently, FIG officials are in the process of restructuring competition formats for commercial reasons, which will affect everyone involved. As Norbert Bueche (2001: 31), Secretary General of FIG has recently noted, the FIG 'competition format is soon to undergo serious modernization in order to better adapt to TV programming rules and regulations as well as to the public's ever-changing tastes and behaviour'. But different groups have at their disposal various power resources. In contrast, say, to a Marxist interpretation which would prioritize the influence of economic factors on the sport, the case study presented here shows the multipolar nature of power (Dunning 1999: 191–2). The presence of unintended as well as intended outcomes of intentional (often gymnastic administrators') actions further illustrates Elias's notion that power is never possessed wholly and exclusively by one individual or group, to the exclusion of others (Elias 1978).

These figurational dynamics have resulted in a curious mixture of not always complementary processes. Pressures for international success have driven the search for innovative, and often more risky manoeuvres. Many pieces of equipment have been modified, in line with safety concerns, only to enable and encourage athletes to perform more exciting and spectacular movements with even greater associated risks. As the sport has been modified in line with the desires of television executives, so the gap between the established and the developing nations has grown. The knowledge power of the coaches from the former Eastern bloc is increasingly being exchanged for the economic resources of the West, leading to a 'commingling of cultures'. A key conflict in this respect is over what types of child labour conditions are, and are not, acceptable in the pursuit of sporting success (see Donnelly 1997 for an analysis of the concept of 'child labour' in a sporting context).

The effects on the gymnasts themselves have not been discussed in detail but warrant a mention in the hope that other studies will follow. In Britain and increasingly on the global scene, the sport now has two distinctive but complementary faces. There is the elite end of women's artistic gymnastics, which demands an all-consuming commitment from the few children with the potential and desire to succeed, together with the family support, funding, training and educational opportunities that might enable them to realize their potential. There are sophisticated talent identification systems, supported by sports scientists, psychologists, lifestyle managers, choreographers, international coaches and medical back-up. There is also a more sensitive approach to children in the sport, as evidenced in the global coaching initiative. The skill complexity and training demands at the elite end of gymnastics have led to the burgeoning of a popular 'second level' of gymnastics with simplified competition requirements and festivals that demand less rigorous training regimes while maintaining competitive opportunities. Many children, who could have been lost to the sport, have found enjoyment and enrichment through this avenue. There have been problems for some parents and coaches in adapting to what they perceive as a 'second class' sport, and although the TV media are certainly not interested in this level, it has provided a useful compromise for a sport that technological developments have accelerated out of the reach of most young people. What does appear certain is that those at the elite end will continue to strive towards more daring, accomplished, challenging, high-risk performances which are at the cutting edge of a sport driven by the desire to gain complete mastery of the body and of the outer limits of human movement.

Notes

1   The FIG currently has 125 affiliated countries, over 30 million members and oversees seven gymnastic disciplines, women's artistic gymnastics being one.
2   Figures supplied by FIG, Lausanne, Switzerland – 'Events Participation Statistics, Artistic Gymnastics Championships'. (Only the top 12 teams at the previous world championships qualify for the Olympic Games. Countries are allowed to enter a small number of individual competitors.)
3   Many FIG Bulletins are available at the British Gymnastics reference library, Lilleshall National Sports Centre, Shropshire, England and the Olympic Museum, Lausanne, Switzerland.
4   Most previous copies of the Codes of Points are available in the British Gymnastics library at Lilleshall National Sports Centre, Lilleshall, Shropshire, England.
5   The 'round-off' is a skill that looks a little like a cartwheel and is commonly seen at the beginning of an acrobatic tumbling run. It allows the gymnast to change from travelling forwards to travelling backwards with little or no loss of speed.

6 Launched as the 'Pegases' vaulting table – intended to incorporate notions of the mythological Pegagus winged horse and futuristic vision (Janssen & Fritsen 2001).
7 An East German men's coach who had first declared the growing risk of the traditional horse ten years earlier (Janssen & Fritsen 2001).
8 In April 1996 the British Amateur Gymnastics Association (BAGA) became British Gymnastics (BG). The name change reflected the move from an 'amateur' to a 'professional' ethos in the sport.
9 In their preparatory stages many skills used on the beam can be learned on a bench and while few schools have beams most do have benches.
10 Glasnost – a Russian term literally meaning 'openness', which refers to the Soviet policy of promoting public debate on subjects previously considered too sensitive to discuss. Perestroika – Russian term meaning 'restructuring', which is a description of the changes following the breakdown of communism.

References

Atkinson, J. (2001) 'Gymnastics Performance and Potential – Report by the Performance Director of British Gymnastics', *British Gymnastics Annual Report*, 30 September 2001, pp. 8–9.

British Gymnastics (2001) *Health, Safety & Welfare Policy for Coaches and Clubs*, Lilleshall: British Gymnastics.

—— (2002) *The Gymnast – The Official Magazine of British Gymnastics and Trampolining* (March/April), Lilleshall: British Gymnastics.

Bueche, N. (2001) *World of Gymnastics*, 33 (June), Moutier, Switzerland: Federation Internationale de Gymnastique, p. 31.

Donnelly, P. (1997) 'Child Labour, Sport Labour: Applying Child Labour Laws to Sport', *International Review for the Sociology of Sport*, 32(4), 398–406.

Dunning, E. (1986) 'The Dynamics of Modern Sport: Notes on Achievement-striving and the Social Significance of Sport, in N. Elias and E. Dunning, *Quest for Excitement: Sport and Leisure in the Civilizing Process*, Oxford: Basil Blackwell, pp. 205–23.

—— (1999) *Sport Matters: Sociological Studies of Sport, Violence and Civilization*, London: Routledge.

Dunning, E. and Sheard, K. (1979) *Barbarians, Gentlemen and Players*, Oxford: Martin Robertson.

—— (2000) *The Civilizing Process, Sociogenetic and Psychogenetic Investigations*, Oxford: Basil Blackwell.

Elias, N. (1978) *What is Sociology?* London: Hutchinson.

Elias, N. and Dunning, E. (1986) *Quest for Excitement: Sport and Leisure in the Civilizing Process*, Oxford: Basil Blackwell.

FIG (2002) *FIG Academy Programme and Age Group Development Plan*, Moutier: Federation Internationale de Gymnastique.

FIG Bulletin (1971) No 4, Moutier: Federation Internationale de Gymnastique.

—— (1973) No. 2, Moutier: Federation Internationale de Gymnastique.

—— (1974) No. 2, Moutier: Federation Internationale de Gymnastique.

—— (1978) No. 3, Moutier: Federation Internationale de Gymnastique.

—— (1979) No. 3, Moutier: Federation Internationale de Gymnastique.

—— (1984) No. 120, Moutier: Federation Internationale de Gymnastique.

—— (1984) No. 121, Moutier: Federation Internationale de Gymnastique.

—— (1986) No. 103, Moutier: Federation Internationale de Gymnastique.

—— (1992) No. 154, Moutier: Federation Internationale de Gymnastique.

—— (1994) No. 160, Moutier: Federation Internationale de Gymnastique.

—— (1996) No. 168, Moutier: Federation Internationale de Gymnastique.

—— (1998) No. 172, Moutier: Federation Internationale de Gymnastique.

FIG Media Symposium (2001) *Harnessing the Power of Marketing and Media for Gymnastics*, Moutier: FIG.

FIG Medical Symposium (1999) *Medico Technical Symposium*,Tianjin, China, 15–16 October 1999, Moutier, Switzerland: Federation Internationale de Gymnastique.

Gajdos, A. (1997) *Artistic Gymnastics: A History of Development and Olympic Competition*, Leicestershire: Loughborough University.

Grandi, B. (2000) *World of Gymnastics*, 31 (October), Moutier, Switzerland: Federation Internationale de Gymnastique, p. 5.

Guttmann, A (1978) 'From Ritual to Record', in *From Ritual to Record: The Nature of Modern Sport*, New York: Columbia University Press.

Janssen & Fritsen (2001) 'Vaulting into the Future with Pegases', *World of Gymnastics*, 33 (June), Moutier, Switzerland: Federation Internationale de Gymnastique, pp. 14–17.

Lyberg, W. (1999) *The Athletes of the Summer Olympic Games 1896–1996 – Gymnastics*, Lausanne: International Olympic Committee.

Maguire, J. (1999) *Global Sport: Identities, Societies, Civilizations*, Cambridge: Polity Press.

Moran, L. (1978) 'The Life and Times of Olga Korbut', *International Gymnast Magazine*, April.

Prestidge, J. (1988) *The History of British Gymnastics*, Slough: British Amateur Gymnastics Association.

Ryan, J. (1996) *Little Girls in Pretty Boxes*, Aylesbury: BPC Paperbacks.

Sports Council (1992) *Training of Young Athletes Study: TOYA and Lifestyles*, London: Sports Council.

Still, C. (1990) *BAGA Women's Gymnastics Manual*, Huddersfield: Springfield Books Ltd.

Wright, G. (1980) *Olympic Greats – A Record of Achievement and Endeavour*, London: Macdonald and Jane's.

12 Conclusion

Figurational sociology and the development of modern sport

Eric Dunning, Dominic Malcolm and Ivan Waddington

Our central objective in this Conclusion is to identify some of the key underlying themes in this collection of essays and to indicate how these themes are central to the concerns of figurational or process-sociologists.

Perhaps the first point that merits comment is the title of the book itself. In one key respect, the contents differ from what one might normally expect in a book entitled *Sport Histories*. In this regard it is significant that, although the chapters focus on the historical development of particular sports, none of the authors would regard themselves as historians in terms of their disciplinary allegiance. Rather, all the authors would describe themselves as sociologists or, to be more precise, as figurational or process-sociologists.

That figurational sociologists should have produced a collection of essays of this kind is not surprising, because what some writers have called historical sociology (Abrams 1982) has always been central to the Eliasian approach. As we pointed out in the Introduction to this volume, Elias wrote extensively on the relationship between sociology and history, and the study of long-term processes of development – by 'long-term' Elias meant processes over at least three generations – was central to his work. This is most clearly evident in Elias's *magnum opus*, *The Civilizing Process*, which van Krieken (2001: 353) has described as an 'analysis of the historical development of emotions and psychological life . . . in relation to the connections . . . with larger scale processes such as state formation, urbanisation and economic development'. It is clear from the chapters here that a concern with long-term processes remains central to many sociologists of sport who have been influenced by Elias.

It would, of course, be wrong to suggest that figurational or process-sociology is unique in this respect, for interest in long-term processes was central to the work of many of the classical 'founding fathers' of sociology. It is also the case that many scholars today who work within this classical tradition have continued to make the analysis of long-term processes a central aspect of their work. This is perhaps most clearly the case in relation to Marxist scholars, many of whom have made important contributions in this regard. In this context one might mention the work of Marxist historians such as Christopher Hill (1968, 1969), E.P. Thompson (1968) and Eric Hobsbawm (1969) who have made path-breaking contributions to the understanding of English history.

There is also a significant group of Marxist and neo-Marxist scholars working within the sociology of sport though, perhaps surprisingly, their contributions to the understanding of the long-term development of sport have been considerably more limited than have the Marxist and neo-Marxist contributions to the understanding of many other areas of social life. Among the most prominent early statements of a Marxist approach to the sociology of sport were the works of Bero Rigauer (1969, 1981) and Jean-Marie Brohm (1978). These early theoretical statements have been widely criticized, not only by non-Marxists but also by modern neo-Marxist writers. The charge of economic determinism stands at the forefront in this regard. As the hegemony theorist John Hargreaves has put it, such authors have produced 'an account of sports in which they are seen as ineluctably functioning to reproduce the types of labour power required by capital, and to indoctrinate the masses with the dominant ideology of capitalist society' (Hargreaves 1986: 3). While it is true that works such as those of Brohm and Rigauer do indeed contain relatively unsophisticated elements of economic determinism, it is also the case that they tell us almost nothing about the *development* of modern sport forms through time, for both works are written at a very high level of generality, with little systematic empirical reference to the development (or indeed to the current organization) of sport in modern societies.

If these more traditional forms of Marxism are now widely regarded as inadequate, what do modern forms of neo-Marxism, in particular that based on the hegemony theory of Italian Marxist Antonio Gramsci (1971), have to tell us about the development of modern sport? An examination of the work of two leading hegemony theorists, John Hargreaves in the UK and Richard Gruneau in North America, will prove instructive in this regard.

In his *Sport, Power and Culture*, John Hargreaves (1986) sets out the guiding principles of hegemony theory. He notes that a focus on power is a central aspect of hegemony theory and that power is relational. He writes:

> When we use the term power, we are referring not to an entity, the mere possession of which enables an individual or collective agent to dominate another, but to a relationship between agents, the outcome of which is determined by agents' access to relevant resources and their use of appropriate strategies in specific conditions of struggle with other agents. Power is thus conceived here as not the exclusive possession of a single agent (the capitalist class, the political elite, men etc.); nor is it situated in, or generated at, any single location or level of the social formation (the economy, patriarchy, or whatever).
>
> (Hargreaves 1986: 3)

Hargreaves goes on to say that power 'is inherent in the structure of social relations' and that power relations 'are rarely total in scope, or totally one way in their effects' (Hargreaves 1986: 4–5). He later elaborates on the characteristics of power relations:

Power relations take different forms: the compliance of subordinate groups may be obtained through the use of physical violence, or in the knowledge that [physical violence] is likely to be used against them; or by other types of coercion, such as economic sanctions or the threat of these; through the assertion of authority, or the prestige enjoyed by agents; and through agents' persuasive powers; or through some combination of all these means. Power may be exercised with or without the resistance of power subjects, and with or without their knowledge. Also, it can be exercised effectively simply by an agent deciding to withhold action rather than by taking positive measures to coerce, demand or persuade others.

(Hargreaves 1986: 5)

Few process-sociologists would find much with which to disagree in this approach to power. Indeed, much of what Hargreaves says echoes Elias's own writings on power. In this regard, we might note Elias's comment that power 'is not an amulet possessed by one person and not by another; it is a structural characteristic of human relationships – of *all* human relationships' (Elias 1978a: 74). We might also note his insistence on the polymorphous nature of sources of power and his concept of unequal and unstable power balances or power ratios. He also insisted that, however unequal a relationship may be, no party to a relationship is ever completely powerless, with such marginal exceptions as an unloved newborn baby, perhaps particularly in a society in which infanticide is practised. It is necessary, however, to add that, notwithstanding Hargreaves's explicit recognition in the foregoing quotation of the several different forms and sources of power, there remains a suspicion, as Dunning has noted elsewhere, that hegemony theorists nevertheless retain a residual attachment to a form of economic determinism (Dunning 1999: 112–14). Although Hargreaves and other hegemony theorists would certainly deny it, this attachment nevertheless breaks through occasionally in their work. For example, in describing the development of the rules of sporting contests as one possible source of the relative autonomy of sport, Hargreaves notes that:

The rules which structure sporting contests . . . unlike those that structure competition and conflict in the *real world*, deliberately set out to equalise conditions of participation, that is, they are intended to be neutral, so that no one party to the contest has an advantage over the other(s).

(Hargreaves 1986: 11; emphasis added)

The implication that the rules of sporting contests are not part of the 'real world' – the 'real world' presumably consisting of the worlds of employment, economic competition and political conflict – involves a strange contrast that is reminiscent of Marx's famous distinction between base and superstructure. The relations of production, for Marx, constituted the economic structure of society, what Marx called 'the real foundation' on which rises a legal and ideological superstructure. Hargreaves's reference to the rules of sport as not being part of the 'real world' seems to be an echo of Marx's economic determinism. That is, Hargreaves appears to consign the rules of sport to superstructural status, seeing them as mere epiphenomena which have to be distinguished from 'the real foundation' of modern capitalist societies in which people compete within the marketplace, not on equal terms, as in the 'unreal' world of sport, but on terms that are often very unequal. By contrast, as the chapters in this volume by the Benns (Chapter 11), Curry and Dunning (Chapter 3), Malcolm (Chapter 5) and Sheard (Chapter 2) amply demonstrate, an understanding of the development of the rules of sporting contests is central to an adequate understanding of the development of modern sport. Sport is not, that is to say, a 'realm of freedom' made illusory, as hegemony theorists claim, by capitalism but a complex and increasingly important part of modern social life. Its rules are crucial to its structure and dynamics.

But let us leave aside these questions of whether or not hegemony theorists have effectively managed to move away, as they claim to have done, from the economic determinism characteristic of older forms of Marxism. Our primary question here relates not to such issues but, rather, to the question of the degree to which hegemony theorists have made a significant contribution to our understanding of the development of sport in the same way that other Marxist writers, in other sub-disciplines, have made a significant contribution to our understanding of other aspects of British or North American social development. What then, for Hargreaves, are the key questions to be addressed in relation to the development of sport?

It is here, perhaps, that both the advantages and the disadvantages of the Marxist legacy on which hegemony theorists draw are most apparent. Hargreaves is quite explicit about the central objectives of his analysis of modern sport: 'Our central thesis is that sport was significantly implicated in the process whereby the growing economic and political power of the bourgeoisie in nineteenth-century Britain was eventually transformed into that class's hegemony in the later part of the century' (Hargreaves 1986: 6–7). This central theme is reiterated elsewhere:

> When considering subordinate groups' involvement in sports, one of our major themes would be the ways in which they manage to evade and subvert controls, the respects in which the sport-power relation enables them to resist pressure from dominant groups and to make tangible gains for themselves, as well as the ways in which it reproduces their subordination.
>
> We will be making this point with particular reference to the question of how class relations enter the picture, in order to assess the role of sport as a factor in the composition and recomposition of class relations in Britain.
>
> (Hargreaves 1986: 6)

On the very first pages of his book, Hargreaves makes it crystal clear that the concern of hegemony theorists is focused almost exclusively on questions concerning the dynamics of class relations:

> We are, therefore, not so much concerned with giving a comprehensive account of sport as such, nor with analysing all respects in which sports are

related to other aspects of society, but with understanding the way in which sports as cultural formations may, in certain respects, be connected to the power apparatus. We do not, indeed we cannot, attempt to match the technical expertise of the variety of sports specialists, or the enthusiast's knowledge of the rule and law of sports. Nor is it necessary to do so for our purposes. We wish to probe issues concerned with the way power is structured that lie at the intersection of political theory and the sociology of culture. In particular, we are concerned with the relation between sports and working-class culture, and the extent to which sport has played a role in accommodating the British working class to the social order.

(Hargreaves 1986: 1–2)

Again we find here a failure to understand that a concern with the 'rule and law of sports' is not simply a matter for the sports enthusiast but that it is also central to understanding the development of modern sports. More generally, however, one finds in the work of Hargreaves an almost exclusive focus on the dynamics of class relationships, which is replicated in the work of other leading hegemony theorists. For example in *Class, Sports, and Social Development*, Richard Gruneau (1983) emphasizes that his analysis 'is *not* meant to be a detailed social history of Canadian sport' (italics in original) but that it focuses on two issues: 'the "problematic" of the institutional structuring of games and sports in Canada' and 'the ways in which the enabling and constraining features of sport at different stages in its development have been connected to class relations and the various processes governing their reproduction and transformation' (Gruneau 1983: 92). He goes on to argue that

two factors are essential to an understanding of the basic character of Canada as a social formation: (1) the role of social class as a key factor in conflicts over various resources in Canadian society; and (2) the idea that class structures and patterns of social development are greatly influenced by the relations of domination and dependency that occurred between a metropole (or center) and a hinterland (or periphery).

(Gruneau 1983: 93–4)

Of course few scholars – and certainly not process-sociologists – would deny that class-based and other forms of domination are important for an understanding both of social life in general and of the development of sport in particular. As we noted previously, the concept of unstable power balances or power ratios is a central concept within process-sociology and there are many similarities between Elias's concept of power and the concept of power used by hegemony theorists. However, and notwithstanding the genuine contribution that hegemony theorists have made to the understanding of modern sports – Dunning has described Gruneau's book as making a 'major contribution both to the sociology of sport and to Marxist sociology' – it is our view that their almost exclusive focus on the dynamics of class relationships nevertheless places major restrictions on their ability adequately to understand the development of modern sport. For example, as White (Chapter 4) and Dunning and Curry (Chapter 3) make clear in this volume, and as Dunning and Sheard (1979) have also made clear elsewhere, it is impossible to understand the development of two major world sports – association football (soccer) and rugby – without a detailed analysis of relationships within and between the English public schools in the second half of the eighteenth century and the first half of the nineteenth. Of course, it is true that the changing situation of the English public schools during that period cannot be understood in isolation from a number of broader social processes (one of which involved changing patterns of class relations) associated with the development of Britain as an urban-industrial nation-state. Dunning and Curry, and earlier Dunning and Sheard, appropriately locate their analyses of changes in the public schools within this broader pattern of overall social development. However, it is important to emphasize that the primary focus of their analysis is not simply on changes in the class structure *per se* – though they recognize that these form an essential context for understanding developments within the public schools – but on the changing patterns of relationships within schools between boys and boys, and boys and masters, and between schools in terms of the dynamics of status competition that formed a vital part of the public schools generally conceived as a social field. It is not, we think, overstating our case to suggest that a recognition of the importance of understanding the changing relationships within and between the public schools and their significance for the development of modern sport is not something to which a hegemony theory approach would be likely to direct the researcher. In the cases of soccer and rugby, however, it is impossible to develop an adequate analysis of the early development of these sports without such a focus.

The limits of a hegemony theory approach are also highlighted by other chapters in this volume. For example, Ken Sheard's analysis of the relationship between violence, violence control and civilizing processes in relation to the development of boxing (Chapter 2) again illustrates the importance of moving beyond the dynamics of class relations. Of course, as Elias recognized and as other process-sociologists have recognized as well (Dunning *et al.* 1988) civilizing processes are themselves interrelated with a number of other social processes one of which – but only one of which – concerns the development of class relations. Nevertheless it is clear that the relationship between civilizing processes, violence and the control of violence within sport cannot be understood simply in terms of the dynamics of class relations; indeed, an exclusive focus on class relations would generate an understanding of violence and violence control within sport which would be, at best, inadequate. Put more simply, it is difficult to see how the use of hegemony theory would lead researchers to address the kind of processes that are central to Sheard's chapter and, indeed, to other chapters in this volume – most notably those of Kiku (Chapter 10), Malcolm (Chapter 5), Smith (Chapter 9) and White (Chapter 4) – in which the analysis of civilizing processes is a central concern.

The same could be said about a number of other chapters here. For example, Chapter 11 by Tansin and Barry Benn focuses on technical developments in the apparatus used in women's gymnastics and the way in which these developments –

originally designed largely as a response to concerns about the safety of gymnasts – facilitated the development of more exciting and spectacular, but also more dangerous, routines on the part of gymnasts. Of course it is clear that the development of technologies in sport is related to the commercial interests of companies that manufacture and promote sports technologies – and we are happy to acknowledge that neo-Marxist writers have made important contributions to our understanding of commercialization processes in sport (Beamish 1982; Sewart 1987). However, it is equally clear that one cannot understand all the *unintended* consequences of the introduction of new technologies into women's gymnastics if one concentrates simply on the links between technology and commerce.

The almost exclusive focus of hegemony theorists on the dynamics of class relations is, in our view, similarly limiting when one is seeking to understand the *international* development of modern sport. It is telling that both Kiku (Chapter 10) and Bloyce (Chapter 6) focus not just on the changing balances of class power within, respectively, Japan and the United States, but also on changing international balances of power. An explanation of the sportization of baseball which ignored the broader context of Anglo-American relations would, clearly, be a very partial explanation. Similarly, one cannot adequately explain the development of baseball in Japan without reference to America's twentieth-century status as a world power and Japanese perceptions of modernity, inferiority and superiority. In addition to this, Malcolm's work (Chapter 5) highlights how, while a focus on English class relations may be relatively adequate in explaining sporting developments in mid-nineteenth century England, as the twentieth century progressed, the networks of interdependency – the figurations involved – expanded to such an extent that the explanatory potential of a narrow natiocentric frame of reference became increasingly limited.

There is one further respect in which a contrast can be drawn between the contributions of process-sociologists and Marxists/hegemony theorists to the understanding of the development of modern sport. The contributions of process-sociologists in this field are numerous and well known. These include the early work of Dunning (1961) and the more recent work of Curry (2001, 2002, 2003) on the development of football; the work of Dunning and Sheard (1979) and, more recently, the work of White (2000) and Sheard (1997a) on rugby; the work of Brookes (1974, 1978) and more recently of Malcolm (2002) on cricket; and the work of Sheard on boxing (1992, 1997b) and, most recently, on the sportization of birdwatching (1999). In addition, the chapters contained in the present volume extend figurational analysis to a number of other sports: tennis, baseball, motor racing, gymnastics, clay pigeon shooting and Japanese martial arts, a striking testimony to the continuing interest of process-sociologists in long-term social processes. To what extent could it be said that Marxist/hegemony theorists have made similar contributions to our understanding of the long-term development of sport?

As we noted previously, the early traditional Marxist statements in the sociology of sport by Rigauer (1969, 1981) and Brohm (1978), and to these we might add Bourdieu (1978), were not only written at a high level of generality but they also focused on developing a theoretical statement about the nature of sport in contemporary societies. Put more briefly, and notwithstanding their Marxist character, they lacked a properly developmental or historical perspective. Some leading hegemony theorists, however, do claim to offer a developmental perspective on modern sport. Prominent among them are the two authors whose work we have discussed, namely John Hargeaves and Richard Gruneau. However, the work of both authors is seriously flawed in this respect.

Hargreaves's book is subtitled 'A social and historical analysis of popular sports in Britain'. However, it involves little in the way of what would be regarded as traditional historical scholarship and is based almost exclusively on secondary sources. In this respect, it does not reflect the kind of detailed historical work that characterizes the work of the process-sociologists cited earlier. Many years ago, C. Wright Mills (1959: 160) pointed out in his discussion of the relationship between sociology and history that historical study not only 'encourages a widening of one's view to embrace epochal pivotal events in the development of social structures' but that it also invites what he called 'grubbing for detail'; one finds little evidence of such 'grubbing for detail' in Hargreaves's book. Other hegemony theorists have been prepared openly to acknowledge their unwillingness, or their inability, to dirty their hands with historical research. For example Ian Taylor's first paper on football hooliganism (1971), which drew on a very speculative history both of football clubs and football hooliganism, was honestly and accurately subtitled 'a speculative sociology of football hooliganism'. Much the same could be said of the work of John Clarke on football hooliganism (1978). The work of Taylor and Clarke is not only speculative – in the sense of not being firmly grounded empirically – but, as Dunning *et al.* (1998) suggested, it also reflects a romanticized view of the past, particularly of the past of the working class. Moreover, despite – or perhaps because of – the brief nod they offer in the direction of the history of the game, the explanations Taylor and Clarke offered were, in effect, present-centred forms of explanation (Dunning *et al.* 1988: 30). In these respects, they stand in marked contrast with the detailed and original historical research on football hooliganism carried out by what has become known as the 'Leicester School' (Dunning *et al.* 1988; Murphy *et al.* 1991).

As is the case with process-sociology, the intellectual origins of hegemony theory lie in a perspective which emphasized, perhaps above all else, the importance of understanding long-term processes of development. The absence of systematic, detailed, empirically grounded analysis of long-term processes of the development of sport within the work of hegemony theorists is accordingly particularly disappointing.

This is especially so given Gruneau's emphasis on the continuing need to address the problems that were central to the work of early classical sociologists. Gruneau identified in this connection the central concern of the classical authors as revolving around 'a deep concern about concrete historical paths of social development' and he was critical of American functionalists, and in particular of Talcott Parsons, for his 'devaluation of the focus on historical process and development' (Gruneau 1983: 6). Gruneau argued that the popularity of functionalism, particularly in the United States, led to a withdrawal from what he called 'a "classical" style of inquiry' and he went on to argue, correctly in our view, for the need 'to situate the study of sport in the mainstream of the sociological enterprise and to formulate new research initiatives based on a sensitivity to the best features of sociology's classical tradition' (Gruneau 1983: 2–3). However, if one examines the work of hegemony theorists closely and searches for detailed historical analysis of the development of either particular sports or sport in general, then one looks in vain. In effect, and not withstanding Gruneau's comments, it would seem that the hegemony theorists of sport have themselves eschewed the study of one of the basic problems in the work of classical scholars; namely, this concern with long-term processes. In this regard, the work of most hegemony theorists on sport has – despite the occasional nod in the direction of speculative history – been characterized by what Elias (1987a) called a 'retreat into the present'.

In the light of the preceding arguments, we think it is fair to suggest that, while figurational or process-sociologists may not be uniquely concerned with long-term processes, it is the case that, more than any other identifiable theoretical framework within the sociology of sport, figurational sociology has facilitated a more consistent and thoroughgoing developmental approach. In this respect, *Sport Histories* may be regarded as *distinctively figurational*. But what else, in addition to their consistently developmental approach, marks out the chapters in this book as distinctively figurational?

We have already referred to the fact that, in Chapter 11, Tansin and Barry Benn argue that an unintended consequence of technical developments in the apparatus used in women's gymnastics – developments designed largely as a response to concerns about the safety of gymnasts – was to facilitate the development of new gymnastic routines which were actually *more* dangerous. The identification of such unintended consequences in the development of modern sports is a recurring theme in this book. For example, Sheard (Chapter 2) argues that specific changes in the rules of boxing, supposedly designed to reduce participants' injuries, have had the unintended consequence of increasing the likelihood of boxers suffering brain damage. Twitchen (Chapter 8) argues that, paradoxically and in a quite unintended way, British hostility towards motor racing played a crucial part in saving the sport from extinction in its early years after the 'calamitous loss of life' in the 1903 Paris–Madrid race, while White (Chapter 4) argues that the growing inability of the Rugby Football Union to preserve the traditional amateur form of the game as it had developed in England was an unintended consequence of the internationalization of rugby union. It is important to emphasize that, for Elias and the writers included here, these unintentional consequences are not merely accidents, the product of humans who, with hindsight, might have done things differently. Rather, the identification of such unintended consequences is a logical outcome of Elias's conceptualization of social processes. In order to explain this point more fully, it will be helpful if we briefly revisit some key aspects of Elias's approach.

As we have argued elsewhere (Murphy *et al.* 2000), Elias's concept of 'figuration' is designed as a way of helping to move towards a resolution of the age-old problem within sociology that has variously been described as the relationship between the

individual and society, free will and determinism, personality and social structure
or, in its currently popular formulation, the agency/structure debate. In this regard,
Elias's approach recognizes that human action is, to a greater or lesser degree,
consciously directed towards achieving certain goals and that all human action
necessarily involves both cognition and emotion. In this sense his concept takes
fully into account the fact that humans are thinking and feeling animals, and that,
especially in modern, highly individualized societies, we each have our own more
or less highly individualized patterns of intentions, preferences and desires. At the
same time, however, Elias also emphasized that the outcomes of complex social
processes cannot be explained simply in terms of the intentions of individuals.
Indeed, it is important to recognize that the *normal* result of complex social
processes involving the interweaving of the more-or-less goal-directed actions of
large numbers of people includes outcomes that no one has designed and no one
has chosen. The study of the complex interweaving of planned and unplanned
social processes was central to Elias's approach.

It might be objected that Elias's concept of what he called 'blind' or 'unplanned
social processes' (Elias 1987b: 99) involves nothing more than what has long been
recognized by social scientists under other names. It is true that the idea of the
unintended or unanticipated consequences of social action has a long history and
that it may be found in the work of some classical sociologists and philosophers,
while in economics it may be found – though in a specific and very limited way –
in Adam Smith's concept of the 'guiding hand' and in the work of more modern
free market advocates such as Hayek (1945).[1] Within sociology, the idea of
unanticipated consequences is probably most closely associated with the work of
Robert Merton (1936, 1949). However, as Mennell (1989) has pointed out, there
are some important differences between the concept of unanticipated consequences
as developed by Merton, and Elias's concept of blind social processes. Mennell
points out that Merton focuses, in particular, on what may be regarded as an oddity
of social life, namely the 'self-fulfilling' prophesy, with passing mention of the
converse 'self-contradicting' prophesy. Such situations may have a certain
fascination but they are, suggests Mennell, fundamentally a trivial diversion
because they are simply an unusual and rather special case of something that is not
only much more common, but also of considerably greater theoretical significance.
Mennell (1989: 258) expresses what he sees as the major difference between
Merton and Elias thus:

> Much more clearly than Merton, Norbert Elias recognizes that people's
> knowledge of the figurations in which they are caught up is virtually always
> imperfect, incomplete and inaccurate. The strategies of action which they
> base on this inadequate knowledge therefore more often than not have
> consequences which they do not foresee. So unanticipated consequences are
> not a curious footnote to sociology but nearly universal in social life. For
> Merton, the self-fulfilling prophecy is like a boomerang: the consequences of
> men's [sic] actions rebound upon their initiators. For Elias, the analogy is much
> less exotic and much more commonplace: like the effect of a stone dropped

into a pool, the consequences of people's actions ripple outwards through society until they are lost from sight. Their effects are felt, not at random but according to the structure of the figuration in which they are enmeshed, by people who may well be quite unknown to each other and unaware of their mutual interdependence.

There is another, and perhaps more fundamental, difference between Elias's work and that of Merton. Whereas Merton's discussion of unintended consequences was largely individualistic, Elias's focus was on pluralities of people, for Elias was concerned not with single acts but with aggregates of intentional acts. The largely individualistic character of Merton's position was explicitly recognized by Merton himself in his early classic article which, he acknowledged, dealt mainly 'with isolated purposive acts rather than with their integration into a coherent system of action' (1936: 895). Although Merton's later (1949) discussion is perhaps less individualistic, it remains the case that Elias's approach focuses more systematically, not on isolated individual acts, but on the complex interweaving of the actions of many people, not all of whom will even be known to each other. The essays in this volume provide a number of examples of such processes specifically in relation to sport.

As we noted earlier, the question of 'blind social processes' or unintended consequences is closely related to another key issue in sociological theory, namely the question of what is usually called the relationship between the individual and society, or agency and structure. In a society such as ours, which is characterized by a relatively high level of individualism, there is often a tendency to think about social processes in individualistic terms; that is, to account for social processes in terms of one or two individuals whose actions are held to have been decisive for subsequent developments. Not surprisingly, such 'explanations' – we use the inverted commas deliberately, for such 'explanations' really explain very little if, indeed, they explain anything at all – are by no means uncommon in historical writing about the development of sport; the most famous example, at least in Britain, is probably that relating to William Webb Ellis who, it is often held, 'invented' the modern sport of rugby with a single deviant act, namely disregarding the rules of the game and picking up and running with the ball (Macrory 1991).

Such 'explanations' are based on what Elias called a *Homo clausus* model of human beings; that is, the view of individuals as self-contained and separate from other people. The concept of figurations was developed to convey the idea that sociology is concerned not with *Homo clausus*, but with *Homines aperti*, with people open to others and bonded together in dynamic constellations. As Elias put it:

> The image of man [sic] as a 'closed personality' is . . . replaced by the image of man as an 'open personality' who possesses a greater or lesser degree of relative (but never absolute and total) autonomy *vis-à-vis* other people and who is, in fact, fundamentally oriented toward and dependent on other people throughout his life. The network of interdependencies among human beings is what binds them together. Such interdependencies are the nexus of . . . the

figuration, a structure of mutually oriented and dependent people. Since people are more or less dependent on each other first by nature and then through social learning, through education, socialization, and socially generated reciprocal needs, they exist, one might venture to say, only as pluralities, only in figurations.

(Elias 1978b: 261)

Given this approach, it is hardly surprising that figurational sociologists have little sympathy with the individualistic, *Homo clausus* explanations – also called 'great man' theories – which are sometimes offered for the development of modern sports. For figurational sociologists, the development of any modern sport is, as the chapters in this volume demonstrate, a *social* process, and a process of some complexity which cannot be meaningfully reduced to the actions of a single individual. In this context, it might be noted that it was, of course, Dunning and Sheard (1979) who were the first to 'de-bunk' the Webb Ellis myth. Comparable to the Webb Ellis myth is the claim that baseball was 'invented' by a single individual, Abner Doubleday. As Bloyce notes in Chapter 6, on the development of baseball, a number of historians have pointed out that this 'explanation' is nothing more than an individualistic 'origin myth' and Bloyce himself seeks to explain the sport's development in terms of the broader context of nationalism, commercialism and changing interdependency ties.

It is important to emphasize that Elias did not argue that social processes can be understood without reference to the actions of concrete human individuals. Indeed, he acknowledged the role – albeit a limited role – that individual people sometimes play in processes of development. Thus he argued that, while the belief 'in the unlimited power of individual people over the course of history is wishful thinking', it is similarly unrealistic to believe 'that all people are of equal importance for the course of history' (Elias 1991: 54). Elias's position is perhaps best exemplified here in Chapter 2 by Ken Sheard, who effectively questions the centrality of the role that historians have often attributed to a single individual, James Figg, in the development of boxing. While recognizing Figg's particular talents as a tutor, publicist and entrepreneur, Sheard emphasizes the importance of the network of relationships in which Figg was involved – and most notably his relationships with significant and powerful people. He also locates the early development of boxing within the context of broader processes such as commercialization.

We should perhaps make one final point about the role of individuals within the development of particular sports. At first glance, it might seem that Chapter 11 by Tansin and Barry Benn does precisely what we have argued a good process-sociological analysis should *not* do; that is, to focus on the role of one individual, in this case the Soviet gymnast, Olga Korbut. However, a closer examination will show that the focus of the Benns' chapter is not actually on Olga Korbut – for example we are told very little about the famous gymnast herself in their chapter – but on what they call the 'Olga Korbut phenomenon'. In other words, the focus is not on a single gymnast but, rather, on the way in which the gymnastic routines she performed and played a part in developing – almost certainly under the very strict control of her Soviet coaches – came, as a result of media exposure, to symbolize a new approach to the sport. In this regard, the biography of Olga Korbut is very different from a sociology of the 'Olga Korbut phenomenon'. Indeed, given the very tight control that the Soviets exercised over their international athletes, it would be very ironic if Olga Korbut were to become the focus of a 'great woman' theory of gymnastics, with all that such theories imply about levels of socially produced individualism!

Finally, and perhaps unsurprisingly, one further theme emerging from this collection is the relationship between civilizing processes and the development of sport. It is perhaps worth noting in this connection that Stokvis (1992) has criticized figurational sociologists for, as he sees it, viewing modern sport as representative of a 'specific stage in the process of civilization'. He argues that this approach 'is too limited' and that it 'leads sociological research on sports too often to matters of violence and its control' to the neglect of other aspects of the development of sport such as the formal organization and standardization of sport, its diffusion in national societies and throughout the world and professionalization and commercialization (1992: 121). This debate has already been taken forward and it is not our intention to provide a detailed discussion of the responses of Dunning (1992), Murphy *et al.* (2000) and Malcolm (2002) here. However, it is perhaps worth noting that, within the collection of essays presented here there seem to be four broad types of approach, characterized by a different emphasis on the explanatory role of civilizing processes. Chapters 3, 9 and 10, by Dunning and Curry, Smith, and Kiku, respectively, make explicit links between the development of the sports that are the focus of their own work and the compatibility of this evidence with broader theories of civilizing processes. Others, for example Bloyce (Chapter 6) and Cooper (Chapter 7), by contrast, make little or no mention of civilizing processes in their work. A third group, more particularly Tansin and Barry Benn (Chapter 11) and Alex Twitchen (Chapter 8), address sports in which the control of direct interpersonal or face-to-face violence has not been central, but which have developed with significant reference to issues of safety and the generation of pleasurable forms of excitement. Finally, Chapters 5, 2 and 4 by Malcolm, Sheard and White respectively, focus on the co-existence of civilizing and de-civilizing processes, demonstrating how these often occur concurrently, perhaps affecting different groups in contrasting ways.

This diversity may initially surprise those with a prior knowledge of the sociology of sport for, as Stokvis's (1992) critique suggests, there is a widely held perception that figurational sociologists of sport are preoccupied with issues of violence and its control. Despite an increase in the number and range of figurationally informed, non-violence-orientated studies, in recent years,[2] it remains the case that a substantial proportion of the work produced by figurational sociologists of sport has focused on sports in which forms of controlled violence are socially tolerated and/or which attract violence-prone spectators. That is because, along with material production, violence and violence-control figure centrally among what one might call the 'deep structures' involved in the sociogenesis and psychogenesis of 'civilizing processes' in Elias's non-evaluative, technical usage of that concept

(Elias and Dunning 1986; Dunning 1999; Elias 2000). Further to this, the significance of sport in modern societies is partly connected with a 'quest for excitement'; the 'controlled decontrolling of emotional controls' which players and spectators can experience (Elias and Dunning 1986; Dunning 1999). These, of course, are partly connected with violence-control but they also form pre-conditions for the monetarization, commercialization, professionalization and global spread of sports, all of them issues which, *pace* Stokvis and others, have been treated by figurational sociologists of sport since the beginning (Elias 1971).

Notes

1 Free market economists argue that the most rational form of economic organization is that which comes about as the unintended outcome of the actions of large numbers of people pursuing their own individual interests. We have no space to develop a detailed critique of this position here, but we would note that, if this were the case, planning would be very simple and unproblematic and would have extremely predictable outcomes, for we would simply have to decentralize all economic decision making down to the individual level and await the inevitably successful outcome. Those in government must wish that economic planning were indeed so easy!

2 See, for example, the work on globalization (e.g. Maguire 1994), on drugs, health, pain and injury (Waddington 1995, 2000; Roderick 1998; Roderick *et al.* 2000; Malcolm *et al.* 2001) on race (Malcolm 1997, 2001), commercialization (Malcolm 2000; Malcolm *et al.* 2000) and gender (Maguire and Mansfield 1998; Colwell 1999; Smith 2000). *Pace* Stokvis, it is also the case that Dunning and Sheard's *Barbarians, Gentlemen and Players* (1979) was centrally concerned with commercialization and professionalization and not just with violence and violence control.

References

Abrams, P. (1982) *Historical Sociology*, Wells, Somerset: Open Books.

Beamish, R. (1982) 'Sport and the Logic of Capitalism', in H. Cantelon and R. Gruneau (eds) *Sport, Culture, and the Modern State*, Toronto: University of Toronto Press, pp. 142–97.

Bourdieu, P. (1978) 'Sport and Social Class', *Social Science Information*, 17(6), 819–40.

Brohm, J.M. (1978) *Sport – a Prison of Measured Time*, London: Ink Links.

Brookes, C. (1974) 'Cricket as a Vocation', unpublished PhD thesis, University of Leicester.

—— (1978) *English Cricket: The Game and its Players through the Ages*, London: Weidenfeld and Nicolson.

Clarke, J. (1978) 'Football and Working Class Fans: Tradition and Change, in R. Ingham (ed.), *Football Hooliganism: The Wider Context*, London: Inter-Action Imprint

Colwell, S. (1999) 'Feminisms and Figurational Sociology: Contributions to Under-standings of Sports, Physical Education and Sex/Gender', *European Physical Education Review*, 5(3), 219–40.

Curry, G. (2001) 'Football: A Study in Diffusion', unpublished PhD thesis, University of Leicester.

—— (2002) 'The Trinity Connection: An Analysis of the Role of Members of Cambridge University in the Development of Football in the Mid-nineteenth Century', *The Sports Historian*, 22(2), 46–73.

—— (2003) 'Forgotten Man: The Contribution of John Dyer Cartwright to the Football Rules Debate', *Soccer and Society*, 4(1), 71–86.

Dunning, E. (1961) 'Early Stages in the Development of Football as an Organised Game', unpublished MA thesis, University of Leicester.

—— (1992) 'Figurational Sociology and the Sociology of Sport: Some Concluding Remarks', in E. Dunning and C. Rojek (eds), *Sport and Leisure in the Civilizing Process: Critique and Counter-critique*, Basingstoke: Macmillan.

—— (1999) *Sport Matters: Sociological Studies of Sport, Violence and Civilization*, London: Routledge.

Dunning, E. and Sheard, K. (1979) *Barbarians, Gentlemen and Players*, Oxford: Martin Robertson.

Dunning, E., Murphy, P. and Williams, J. (1988) *The Roots of Football Hooliganism: An Historical and Sociological Study*, London: Routledge & Kegan Paul.

Elias, N. (1971) 'The Genesis of Sport as a Sociological Problem', in E. Dunning (ed.), *The Sociology of Sport*, London: Frank Cass.

—— (1978a) *What is Sociology?*, London: Hutchinson.

—— (1978b) *The Civilizing Process*, Oxford: Basil Blackwell.

—— (1987a) 'The Retreat of Sociologists into the Present', *Theory, Culture and Society*, 4(2–3), 223–47.

—— (1987b) *Involvement and Detachment*, Oxford: Basil Blackwell.

—— (1991) *The Society of Individuals*, Oxford: Basil Blackwell.

—— (2000) *The Civilizing Process, Sociogenetic and Psychogenetic Invesigations*, Oxford: Basil Blackwell.

Elias, N. and Dunning, E. (1986) *Quest for Excitement*, Oxford: Basil Blackwell.

Gramsci, A. (1971) *Selections from the Prison Notebooks* (ed. and trans. by Quintin Hoare and Geoffrey Nowell Smith), London: Lawrence and Wishart.

Gruneau, R. (1983) *Class, Sports, and Social Development*, Amherst, MA: University of Massachusetts Press.

Hargreaves, J. (1986) *Sport, Power and Culture*, Oxford: Polity.

Hayek, F.A. (1945) 'The Use of Knowledge in Society', *American Economic Review*, 35(4), 519–30.

Hill, C. (1968) *Puritanism and Revolution*, London: Panther.

—— (1969) *Reformation to Industrial Revolution*, Harmondsworth: Pelican Books.

Hobsbawm, E. (1969) *Industry and Empire*, Harmondsworth: Pelican Books.

Maguire, J (1994) 'Sport, Identity Politics and Globalization: Diminishing Contrasts and Increasing Varieties', *Sociology of Sport Journal*, 11(4), 398–427.

Maguire, J. and Mansfield, L. (1998) '"No-Body's Perfect": Women, Aerobics, and the Body Beautiful', *Sociology of Sport Journal*, 15, 109–37.

Malcolm, D. (1997) 'Stacking in Cricket: A Figurational Sociological Reappraisal of Centrality', *Sociology of Sport Journal*, 14(3), 263–82.

—— (2000) 'Football Business and Football Communities in the Twenty-first Century', *Soccer and Society*, 1(3), 102–13.

—— (2001) '"It's not Cricket": Colonial Legacies and Contemporary Inequalities', *Journal of Historical Sociology*, 14(3), 253–75.

—— (2002) 'Cricket and Civilizing Processes: A Response to Stokvis', *International Review for the Sociology of Sport*, 37(1), 37–57.

Malcolm, D., Sheard, K. and White, A. (2000) 'The Changing Structure and Culture of English Rugby Union Football', *Culture, Sport, Society*, 3(3), 63–87.

—— (2001) 'The Management of Injuries in Elite Rugby Union: The Effects of Commercialization and Globalization', in *Sociology of Sport and New Global Order: Bridging Perspectives and Crossing Boundaries*. Proceedings of the 1st World Congress of Sociology of Sport, Yonsei University, Seoul, South Korea.

Macrory, J. (1991) *Running with the Ball*, London: Collins Willow.

Mennell, S. (1989) *Norbert Elias: An Introduction*, Oxford: Basil Blackwell.

Merton, R.K. (1936) 'The Unanticipated Consequences of Purposive Social Action', *American Sociological Review*, 1(6), 894–904.

—— (1949) *Social Theory and Social Structure*, Glencoe: Free Press.

Mills, C. Wright (1959) *The Sociological Imagination*, New York: Grove Press.

Murphy, P., Williams, J. and Dunning, E. (1991) *Football on Trial*, London: Routledge.

Murphy, P., Sheard, K. and Waddington, I. (2000) 'Figurational Sociology and its Application to Sport', in E. Dunning and J. Coakley, (eds), *Handbook of Sports Studies*, London: Sage.

Rigauer, B. (1969) *Sport und Arbeit*, Frankfurt: Suhrkamp.

—— (1981) *Sport and Work*, New York: Columbia University Press.

Roderick, M. (1998) 'The Sociology of Risk, Pain and Injury: A Comment on the Work of Howard L. Nixon II', *Sociology of Sport Journal*, 15, 64–79.

Roderick, M., Waddington, I. and Parker, G. (2000) 'Playing Hurt: Managing Injuries in English Professional Football', *International Review for the Sociology of Sport*, 35(2), 165–80.

Sewart, J. (1987) 'The Commodification of Sport', *International Review for the Sociology of Sport*, 22(3), 171–90.

Sheard, K. (1992) 'Boxing in the Civilizing Process', unpublished PhD thesis, Anglia Polytechnic University, Cambridge.

—— (1997a) '"Breakers Ahead!" Professionalisation and Rugby Union Football: Lessons from Rugby League', *The International Journal of the History of Sport*, 14(1), 116–37.

—— (1997b) 'Aspects of Boxing in the Western "Civilizing Process"', *International Review for the Sociology of Sport*, 32(1), 31–57.

—— (1999) 'A Twitch in Time Saves Nine: Birdwatching, Sport, and Civilizing Processses', *Sociology of Sport Journal*, 16(3), 181–205.

Smith, S. (2000) 'British Non-elite Road Running and Masculinity: A Case of "Running Repairs"?', *Men and Masculinities*, 3(2) 187–208.

Stokvis, R. (1992), 'Sports and Civilization: Is Violence the Central Problem?', in E. Dunning and C. Rojek (eds), *Sport and Leisure in the Civilizing Process: Critique and Counter-Critique*. Basingstoke: Macmillan.

Taylor, I. (1971) '"Football Mad": A Speculative Sociology of Soccer Hooliganism', in E. Dunning (ed.), *The Sociology of Sport*, London: Frank Cass.

Thompson, E.P. (1968) *The Making of the English Working Class*, Harmondsworth: Pelican Books.

van Krieken, R. (2001) 'Elias and Process Sociology', in G. Ritzer and B. Smart (eds), *Handbook of Social Theory*, London: Sage.

Waddington, I. (1995) 'The Development of Sports Medicine', *Sociology of Sport Journal*, 13(2), 176–96.

—— (2000) *Sport, Health and Drugs: A Critical Sociological Perspective*, London: Spon.

White, A. (2000) 'The "Civilising" of Gloucester Rugby Football Club. A Historical Sociology of the Development and Management of an Elite, English Rugby Union Football Club, 1873–1914', unpublished PhD thesis, University of Leicester.

Index